GEORGE THE FOURTH

ROYAL DUKES

by Roger Fulford

With 8 illustrations.

Cloth, 15s. net. *Fourth Impression.*

"An excellent book, exciting, wise and ironic. . . Mr. Fulford gives us a series of sober and most intelligent psychological studies of these men. They live in his pages—the foolish but amiable Frederick Duke of York, the simple and touching William IV, the Duke of Kent, martinet, the detested (but not entirely unpleasing) Duke of Cumberland, Augustus of Sussex and Adolphus Frederick of Cambridge."—HUGH WALPOLE in the *Book Society News.*

"An accurate picture of the men as they were on the background of their time . . . a delightful book . . . at once sparkling and sensible."—ROBERT BERNAYS in *John o' London's Weekly.*

"Mr. Fulford explores a by-path of history with zest and a ready wit."—*The Times.*

"A most satisfying book this, intelligent, impartial and flavoured with an unusual dryness of wit."—*The Bystander.*

GERALD DUCKWORTH & CO., LTD.
3 Henrietta Street, London, W.C.2

GEORGE IV

WEARING A COAT
OF HIS OWN DESIGN

GEORGE THE FOURTH

by

ROGER FULFORD

GERALD DUCKWORTH & CO. LTD.
3 HENRIETTA STREET, LONDON, W.C.2

First published in 1935
Revised and Enlarged Edition, 1949

Printed in Great Britain by
The Camelot Press Ltd., London and Southampton

CONTENTS

BOOK I

BOOK II

BOOK III

CONTENTS

Book I

Book II

Book III

INTRODUCTION

To add to the biographies of George IV needs, I think, a word of explanation or, as some might be inclined to put it, a plea in extenuation. There has been, as a glance at the list of authorities at the end of this book shows, a great variety of books about him during the last hundred years. To have followed some of my predecessors and written, what might be called, "a wine, woman and song" life, enlivened by a little gentle raking in the muck-heap of his relations with his wife, would have been at once boring to the writer and unprofitable to the reader. It has been done over and over again. I have tried, by an examination of the memoirs, lives and diaries of his contemporaries, to present an intelligible picture of one who was certainly not "an Angel," as his sister called him, but equally certainly not a fantastic monster as he is too commonly regarded to-day.

I have deliberately not sought unpublished manuscripts, partly because his papers at Windsor are to be published within the next year or two, and partly because I found that there was so much printed material which had apparently never been used in previous biographies that it was not necessary. I have refrained from the modern biographical habit of calling him by his Christian name—a habit which, in biography as in real life, seems sometimes to conceal only a nodding acquaintance with the person so referred to. To his contemporaries, his friends, and even his intimates, he was the Prince or the King; there seemed, therefore, no adequate reason why he should suddenly become George to me.

It is not, of course, possible to thank all those who in one way and another have helped and encouraged me to write this book. I should, however, like to express my gratitude to His Majesty the King for permission to reproduce three of the pictures at Windsor Castle; to their Royal Highnesses the Duke and Duchess of York for the privilege of visiting the Royal Lodge; to the Manager of *The Times* newspaper for permission to use extracts from the paper; to Mr. Thomas Balston for reading the proofs; to Sir Nelson Rycroft for sending me information about Kempshott House; to Mr. H. Roberts for helping me with the details of the Pavilion; to Mr. John Summerson for much wise advice;

to the librarians at the Reform Club, and the officials at the London Library, for most valuable and ungrudging help; and to Messrs. Leman, Chapman & Harrison for permission to look through Queen Caroline's private papers. For all this I wish to record my deep sense of gratitude.

ROGER FULFORD.

May 1935.

8

INTRODUCTION TO SECOND EDITION

I have thought it best to leave the Introduction which I wrote in 1935, when this book was first published, substantially unchanged. I included some references to the Silver Jubilee of King George V, which was still brightening the scene when the book was published in the summer of that year. These now seem somewhat out of date and are, in consequence, omitted.

Since 1935 there has been one important addition to our knowledge about George IV, and that is the splendid edition of his letters and papers from the Royal Archives, edited by Professor Aspinall and published by the Cambridge University Press in 1938. By the gracious permission of H.M. the King and with the consent of Professor Aspinall and the Cambridge University Press, I have drawn freely on this material, which covers the time when George IV was Regent and King. All students of the Regency era and all interested in the life, character and political outlook of King George IV will be deeply grateful to Professor Aspinall for his masterly work on these papers, which should go far to correct some popular fallacies. I remember that in 1935 I was sent an abusive letter, and even rebuked by a reviewer, for being too favourable to the character of George IV. So hard do old prejudices die. I think I can now claim that Professor Aspinall's researches confirm that the King was not only far less raffish, but was far more talented, than is generally supposed. If any readers think this an unduly partial judgment, I would refer them to the Duke of Wellington. His considered verdict on the King will be found on pp. 138-9 of this book.

R. F.

August 1948.

9

Book I

PRINCE OF WALES

I

On August 12th, 1762, the day on which George IV was born, Horace Walpole was writing to the British envoy at Florence, and, after announcing the birth of a Prince of Wales, added, "The prospect of your old neighbour at Rome does not improve." The "old neighbour" was James Francis Edward Stuart, only son of James II and the central figure in the warming-pan story, known in England as "the Old Pretender," but still an object of interest to Englishmen, and still, to a handful of Jacobites, King James III, rightful King of Great Britain. In the early part of his life of exile, his long, melancholy face flitted imploringly from Catholic Court to Catholic Court, till it finally came to rest in a state of almost permanent prayer at Rome. The poet Gray, who saw him here, said that when he prayed, which was often, and when he smiled, which was seldom, he had the look of an idiot. It seems almost ridiculous that this gawky, devout personage should, sixteen years after the obliteration of Jacobite hopes at Culloden, still have had any prospects at all.

Yet even in the seventeen-sixties there were people in England whose hearts beat stronger at the remembrance of their rightful King. Jacobitism had survived not so much on account of political grievances as on account of personal grievances against the first two Hanoverian Kings. Their inability to master English, but their facility in acquiring a vivid vocabulary of bad language, their rages (George I scheming to deport George II to America and George II destroying George I's will), their lumping German mistresses, and their total lack of sensibility were all a permanent advertisement for the Stuart cause. Certainly no family has ever made the monarchy so comical for so long as the earlier Hanoverians. George II, in addition, had the unkingly gift of making himself ridiculous on any solemn occasion, and for this reason was dubbed by a fellow sovereign "the comedian": but even a comedian might have been able to forget his calling at the deathbed of his wife. Not so King George II, who was heard babbling to his dying wife of the mistresses he was going to keep after she was no more.

It would consequently be expecting too much of the laws of nature to suppose that the children of George II could be anything but odd. The most normal of them was his eldest son Frederick, Prince of Wales, which may explain why his fond father called him "the greatest ass and the greatest liar and the greatest *canaille* and the greatest beast in the whole world." His only other son who survived was William, Duke of Cumberland, more familiarly known as "Billy the Butcher." He weighed nearly twenty stone, was blind in one eye, and suffered from a suppurating wound in the leg. Although he was in fact a man of some æsthetic appreciation, as was evidenced by his development of Windsor Park and his encouragement of the manufacture of Chelsea china, he was regarded by the public as a monster of brutality. Apart from three married daughters, George II's family was completed by the Princess Caroline and the Princess Amelia. The Princess Caroline devoted herself to charity, and was never seen in public. The Princess Amelia, who had been engaged to Frederick the Great, was fond of strong language and unlimited loo. She scandalised Georgian society by going to church in a riding habit, with a dog tucked under her arm, and it was doubtless these singular ways that endeared her to her father. She was known to be his favourite child, though the only recorded expression of his affection was that he used sometimes to nod at her.

Was it surprising that people who came into contact with this Court, and heard all the tittle-tattle about it, should have sometimes thought wistfully of the exiled family in Rome? In George II's reign there were still people living who could remember the Court of Charles II, and many must have heard from their parents of those gay and brilliant days, when the King attracted to Whitehall much that was licentious, but all that was brightest and most intelligent in English life. The Pretender, from his gloomy exile in Rome, to many still seemed to whisper the last enchantment of that glorious age.

But on October 25th, 1760, George II, dogged to the last by his unfortunate genuis for the ridiculous, fell down dead on leaving the water-closet. His eldest son, Frederick, had died

nine years before, and his grandson, a young man about whom
not much was known, but whom Horace Walpole was quick to
describe as "genteel," took the centre of the stage, as George III,
and the eccentric members of his family fell into the background.
The new King saved the English monarchy. Had he inherited his
grandfather's ruffianly qualities, and been content, like him, to
allow the corrupt Whig oligarchy to govern and to plunder
England, he must have been driven from the throne in the
disturbances following the French Revolution. Very carefully,
very shrewdly, and by an adroit use of political methods, he broke
the power of the Whigs who, since 1688, had dominated England.
Naturally, to the Whigs, whose views have coloured every page of
English history, this was, in the language of schoolboys, a Bad
Thing, but less partial observers will think that it was not a Good
Thing that men like Lord Holland should be able to stuff their
pockets with a million pounds of Government money, or that
the best offices should always be controlled by a rather dull ducal
triumvirate of Bedford, Portland, and Devonshire.

The monarchy was saved by George III's political conduct,
and it was strengthened by his personal conduct. He was one of
the phenomena of heredity: his grandfather, father, uncle,
brothers and sons were all notorious for their private lives, yet
his reputation, in the midst of these murky surroundings, was
untouched. He was moral, domesticated, and insular—three
qualities which stamped the middle classes who were to emerge
during his reign, and whose thoughts were prevented from stray-
ing into revolutionary channels by seeing on the throne someone
whom they could respect and understand. For the first time since
1688 an Englishman sat on the throne of England: for the first
time since 1649 the Defender of the Faith was a man who
practised its principles.

Because when he died he was old, blind, and mad, people tend
to forget that he came to the throne as a young man of twenty-
two with marked abilities and great personal attractions. He was
described by one of his wife's ladies-in-waiting as fair and fresh-
coloured, with fine teeth, blue eyes, and light auburn hair which
grew "very handsomely to his Face. He had extremely good
solid sense and more knowledge than most Princes, he was
perfectly good natured, a most dutiful Son, a fond Husband, an
affectionate Brother and a firm friend."

The year after he came to the throne he married Princess Charlotte of Mecklenburg-Strelitz, who was seventeen, and who, in spite of her youth, shared his simple tastes and love of domesticity. She had beautiful colouring and hair, but a wide mouth and spreading nostrils destroyed any claims she may have had to beauty. Indeed, someone who had always known her said, rather unkindly, when she was an older woman, "I do think that the bloom of her ugliness is going off." But whatever her defects of appearance, they were amply redeemed by her gifts of character. She was shrewd and sensible, agreeable and talented, with all the little indoor accomplishments which distinguish a good housekeeper from a bad; she remained devoted and loyal to her husband in circumstances of exceptional difficulty, and gave to English society a moral tone which it badly needed.

The year after his marriage the King bought Buckingham House for the Queen, which was a pleasant red-brick building facing St. James's Park and standing in its own grounds. Here the Royal Family could lead a far more retired life than was possible at St. James's Palace. The barrack-like palace on the river (Somerset House), which had formerly belonged to the queens of England, was given up, and for a country retreat the King and Queen went down to Kew or Windsor. This lack of display, or, as it was described at the time, "living quite alone with only menial servants," was something quite new in English Court life, and was strongly disapproved of by the upper classes. Although the King was fond of seeing people, and although both he and the Queen were fond of dancing, they entertained hardly at all, and gave only the minimum of Court balls and official entertainments. They preferred to devote themselves to the welfare of their enormous family of fifteen strong, healthy, and intelligent children.

It is curious to contrast the domestic life of the King and Queen of England—the King being roused at five by an alarum, and lighting his own fire, drinking just a cup of tea for breakfast, and seldom taking wine—with that of the elderly sovereign across the Channel, Louis XV. His Court betrayed all that elegant licentiousness and glittering fatuity which the ignorant and shallow-minded have ever acclaimed as being the very essence of the eighteenth century. It has long been the custom for those who have fashioned this gilded, sparkling caricature of eighteenth-century life to explain, if not to excuse, George IV's character by the fact of the dull respectability of his childhood. The argument proceeds on the assumption that the sudden emergence from the gloom of home life into the brilliant world of witty gentlemen, gaming-tables, gay little actresses and flowing wine seems brilliantly alluring if the home has been particularly dull. It is only possible to say that those few lucky people brought up in homes where drunkenness, gambling, and abandoned women reign supreme seem to find these things just as alluring when they reach manhood as their less fortunate friends, who have been accustomed to sober, prudent, virtuous parents. Can we seriously believe that George IV's character would have been materially different if he had been brought up in the brilliant surroundings of Versailles by an immoral father like Louis XV and a step-mother like the Du Barry?

He showed, from the first, signs of vigour and individuality, and the mob who followed him as a small baby when he took the air in Hyde Park, called out, "God bless him, he is a lusty, jolly, young dog truly." When, at the age of four, he was inoculated for smallpox, he was asked whether he did not find it dull having to stay in bed, but he gravely replied, "Not at all, I lie and make reflections." His earliest recollection was of his great uncle, the Duke of Cumberland ("the Butcher"), who was dressed in a snuff-coloured suit, playing with him in the gardens of Bucking-ham House. In after life, the Prince used to say, "He took me in his arms and placed me on his knee, where he held me for a long time. The enormity of his bulk excited my wonder." As a small boy he was thought to be good-tempered but timid, and it was possibly to correct this last failing that the King presented him, on his fifth birthday, with twenty-one brass guns, of 1-lb. calibre, on travelling carriages—a somewhat formidable toy. When the Prince was ten, he and his brother, Prince Frederick, were given apartments of their own in Buckingham House, and followed a regular time-table of instruction from seven till three, when they dined. After dinner they had their fencing master, and, whatever the weather they had to go out for a walk in the grounds in the morning.

As the Prince passed from boyhood to youth, his handsome appearance, his facility in conversation, his agreeable manners, his humour, and even his mimicry of the guttural accent of his great-aunt Amelia, impressed people and prejudiced them in his favour. But from the very first the King saw much in his son's character of which he strongly disapproved. He wrote to Lord Holderness, the Prince's tutor, when the Prince was twelve, of the boy's "evading application . . . duplicity . . . bad habit . . . of not speaking the truth"; and he ends with a sentence which epitomises the difference between George III and his eldest son: "Truth is the constant attachment of an honest heart, and is more estimable than any of the advantages to be acquired by birth or education." That laudable sentiment reveals George III's character in all its healthy simplicity, but in the character of his brilliant son there was little that was healthy; nothing that was simple.

II

"May I presume to ask a favour of my dearest friend, and that whatever present she makes me of her hair the setting of it may be quite plain, for it will always be dearer to me than life itself,—that on the back of it there may be the day of your birth, without your dear name, and the Year of that event ever so dear to me, with a Motto of your own, and on the front of it the following motto . . . *Toujours Aimée*. Allow me also if it is not hurting too much your delicacy to give you a plain Bracelet. . . . The Mottos on that shall be the front one in hair, what you please; on the back, the day of the Month on which I was born and the year, and *Gravé à Jamais dans mon cœur*."

This letter was written by George IV, in 1779, when he was not quite seventeen, to Mary Hamilton, who had a place at Court about his sisters. It was, so far as we know, the first of those many occasions when his heart was given with many flourishes of *billets-doux*, exchanges of hair, mottoes and trinkets, protestations of undying affection, and hints of a ceremony at the altar. Although Mary Hamilton was six years older than he, he was gaily envisaging the possibility of marrying her.

The chief interest of this romance lies in the light it throws on his appearance and character when he was just grown up. He wrote a description of his appearance, in the third person, to Mary Hamilton, which may have been rather conceited even for a youthful lover of seventeen, but which was unquestionably accurate. ["He] is now approaching the bloom of youth, he is rather above the common size, his limbs well-proportioned, and upon the whole well made, tho' rather too great a penchant to grow fat, the features of his Countenance are strong and manly, tho' they carry with them too much of an air of hauteur, his forehead well shaped, his eyes tho' none of the best, and tho' grey are yet passable, tolerable good eyebrows and eyelashes, *un petit nez retroussé cependant assez aimé*, a good mouth tho' rather large, with fine teeth, a tolerable good chin, but the whole of the countenance is too round. I forgot to add very uggly ears. . . ."

And then he goes on to describe his character. "His sentiments and thoughts are open and generous, above doing anything that is mean, (too susceptible, even to believing people his friends, and placing too much confidence in them . . .) grateful and friendly to excess where he finds *a real friend* . . . rather too familiar to his inferiors but will not suffer himself to be browbeaten or treated with haughtiness by his superiors. Now for his vices, or rather let us call them weaknesses—too subject to give loose or vent to his passions of every kind, too subject to be in a passion . . . he is rather too fond of Wine and Women."

This is a very fair appraisement of his character, but to get a complete picture it is necessary to add to it slightly. He was gifted with an extraordinary charm of manner which, throughout his life, was to fascinate members of both sexes, but he had also a curious feminine vanity and caprice which developed strongly as he grew older. And for one who was, on his own showing, very easily influenced by his friends, he was a deplorable judge of character. How bad a judge, he was to show before the jeweller can have had time to engrave that trite little *"Toujours Aimée"* on the setting of Mary Hamilton's hair. Because that winter of 1779 he was writing to her to say that he had fallen violently in love with Perdita Robinson, and he ended up his letter to Miss Hamilton, *"Adieu, Adieu, Adieu,* TOUJOURS CHÈRE. Oh! Mrs. Robinson."

He first saw Mrs. Robinson when she was playing the part of Perdita in *A Winter's Tale.* She was four years older than he, extraordinarily lovely, very unconventional, and excessively sentimental. Her small carriage, with a device of a basket painted on the door which from a distance might have been taken for a coronet, was frequently seen in the Park: it was preceded by outriders, consisting always of her lovers and sometimes of her husband. In the carriage sat the Robinson, dressed as the notion seized her, perhaps in the latest fashion, perhaps as a provincial miss, and often as an Amazon. When the Prince saw her at the theatre, he bowed to her, and she subsequently said, "I felt the compliment and blushed my gratitude." He then sent her his miniature, with one of those fatal French mottoes, "*Je ne change qu'en mourant.*"

All through 1780 he was writing violent love-letters to her, making preposterous promises of what he would pay her when he was given his establishment, and almost certainly offering her marriage. When his passion had died down, it became essential to get the letters back, and George III had to find the enormous sum of £5,000 for this purpose. He called it a "shameful scrape," characteristically adding, "I never was personally engaged in such a transaction which perhaps makes me feel this the stronger."

Mrs. Robinson was bitterly disappointed, but it seems difficult to suppose that she can have ever expected any other ending to the affair, unless, perhaps, that her final payment would have been more than £5,000. She wrote sadly to a friend how she had sacrificed to the Prince "the brilliant hours of youth and the conscious delights of correct conduct," but it is only fair to say that ever since her marriage in 1774 correct conduct was a delight of which she was consistently unconscious. It was many years later that she published a poem, which contained the verses which have always been thought to apply to the Prince:

> *Ah within my bosom beating*
> *Varying passions wildly reign;*
> *Love with proud Resentment meeting,*
> *Throbs by turn of joy and pain.*

> *Joy that far from foes I wander,*
> *Where their taunts can reach no more;*
> *Pain that woman's heart grows fonder*
> *When her dream of bliss is o'er.*

Yet, in spite of all these misunderstandings, it was Mrs. Robinson who, at the end of her life, wrote that memorable description of the Prince as he appeared at the age of twenty.

"The graces of his person, the irresistible sweetness of his smile, the tenderness of his melodious and manly voice, will be remembered by me till every vision of this changing scene shall be forgotten."

Mrs. Robinson did not exaggerate. Everyone who has written of him as a young man has testified to the splendour of his appearance. No one can seriously question his personal charm when Thackeray said, "I suppose that he was very graceful," and when Byron evolved the well-known lines:

> . . . the Prince of Princes at the time
> With fascination in his very bow.

It is sometimes difficult, when reading all the descriptions of the Prince's personal gifts, to avoid thinking of him as a courtly dancing-master, a sort of glorified Mr. Turveydrop. This is quite wrong. He had a natural good taste, a variety of interests, and just that zest for life which fitted him to lead and adorn English Society at its most brilliant period.

"They who did not live before 1789 knew not the sweetness of life." This remark of Talleyrand's referred to France before the Revolution, but it applied equally to social England before the long years of war with revolutionary France made life an altogether sterner, more solemn business. To use the phrase "never was society so brilliant" is always a cliché, and generally a writer's device for heightening the effect of the "maelstrom" which he is shortly going to describe, but it is certainly true that England at the close of the eighteenth century was justified in feeling really proud of its society. The great hostesses of the day —the Duchess of Devonshire, Lady Bessborough, Lady Melbourne, and Mrs. Crewe—opened their doors to all that was wittiest, most intelligent, and most original among the nobility, politicians, artists, and writers. Ponderous commercial men, reactionary members of Parliament, glittering Jewesses, and pretentious vulgarians had no part in this world: they led their happy useful little lives in the precincts of Holborn and the City. Society then was an aristocracy: an aristocracy of birth, tempered by intelligence.

From this brilliant world King George III and Queen Charlotte completely cut themselves off. They were never popular with the upper classes, whom they regarded as frivolous and wicked.

Their idea of social life was a visit to a friend's house, with a good deal of chatter and a fine display of Royal curiosity—for example, an evening at Mrs. Delany's, with "tea, coffee, ices, and fruite," the Queen sitting on the sofa, the King politely putting a screen in front of Mrs. Delany so that the fire should not hurt her eyes, the Princess Augusta playing on the harpsichord, the Prince of Wales singing or looking over Mrs. Delany's nine volumes of embroidered flowers. It was doubtless very beautiful and very domestic, but was it any life for a full-blooded Hanoverian of eighteen? Was it surprising that the Prince should begin to look forward to the time when, in his own words, he would "dash into the wide world"?

In 1780, therefore, when the Prince was eighteen, and of age for purposes of kingship, the question of a separate establishment for him became urgent. It was essential that a youth of his reckless, impatient temperament, and with his determination to predominate in the world, should have been allowed the maximum of money and liberty, in the same way that a mettlesome horse should be given its head to work off quickly its excess of spirits. But George III, having himself been tied to his mother's apron-strings, was determined to tie his son no less securely by the purse-strings. He wrote to Lord North, with a slick generalisation, that "it is ever better that Persons should feel their situations will by degrees improve, and particularly Young persons." This showed no understanding of his son's character. Accordingly the Prince was given a small allowance and horses of his own, but his governor and sub-governor were to remain, and he was still to live under his father's roof at Buckingham House. His father called it "an honourable establishment." It would be a mistake to blame the King for what was unquestionably a niggardly arrangement. He had to consider the claims of an enormous family and the unpopularity of approaching Parliament for money. Although the Prince inherited from his father most of his gifts of artistic appreciation, George III was cast in a far less generous mould. There was no sympathy between the two men: their characters were mutually antagonistic. The Prince no doubt had a grievance against his father, and it was during the three years of this "honourable establishment" that he was at his wildest, undoubtedly not discouraged by feeling how much his amours and extravagances were annoying the King.

The Prince at once came under the influence of one of the most unsatisfactory members of his family—George III's younger brother, Henry Frederick, Duke of Cumberland. He was described as being "a little man and gay, a great Whig and hating the clergy." His gaiety, stimulated perhaps by a dislike for things ecclesiastical, had involved him in a disagreeable lawsuit with Lord Grosvenor, in which the Earl had been awarded £10,000 on account of the Duke's liaison with his wife. The Duke was also the father of someone who styled herself the Princess Olive of Cumberland, and who, with her descendants, was to make a number of appearances in nineteenth-century history, sometimes claiming the crown, alleging a previous marriage of George III as making all his descendants by Queen Charlotte illegitimate; but more often content with a claim to legitimate relationship with the Royal Family. In 1771 the Duke married the widow of a Mr. Andrew Horton, thus infuriating the King, who, the following year, introduced the Royal Marriage Act, which virtually forbade a descendant of George II to marry a commoner without the sovereign's consent. Although the Duchess of Cumberland was beautiful and witty, she was unfortunately rather coarse-minded, and it was said that her conversation was so broad that it was really advisable to wash out one's ears after listening to her. The Duke and Duchess lived in Pall Mall, and at night the Duke might be observed presiding at his faro bank, dealing standing up, and calling out in princely language, "Don't punt more than 10 guineas and no tick." It was, therefore, hardly surprising that George III felt this elegant Duke and Duchess to be scarcely qualified to launch a youth of eighteen into polite society.

And it was during this period, while he was still living at Buckingham House, that the Prince formed, from his father's point of view, an even more disastrous friendship, which was to influence him always, and to affect profoundly the fortunes of the Whig Party. The Duke of Cumberland introduced him to Charles James Fox.

Those who have written about Fox have been generally well steeped in Whig prejudices, and have referred to his friendship for the Prince as politically necessary, but in terms which suggest they would rather he had been in communication with the Devil. In fact Fox had deep affection for the Prince, great admiration for his gifts, and real anxiety that he should develop into a genuine Whig. On the other side, it was only natural that someone of the Prince's expansive nature should have been attracted by "the sweet and lofty character" of the most lovable figure in English political life. The following note, written by the Prince, shows his almost boyish regard for the great man:

"DEAR CHARLES,

I am waiting for you at your own house; pray come directly if you can, as I wish very much to speak to you. I will not detain you three minutes.

Yours most truly,

GEORGE P.

If you have not got your own carriage, you had better take somebody else's."

It is probable that George III never forgave his son for being friends with Fox; it is certain that this friendship embittered him against Fox for a generation. At the beginning of 1783, Fox became Foreign Secretary in the Duke of Portland's Government, and it was observed that, when he went to kiss hands with the King, George III put back his ears like a horse which is bent on throwing its rider.

In August 1783 the Prince would be twenty-one, and it would be impossible to delay giving him a definite establishment and a house of his own. The arrangements for this were one of the main causes of disagreement between the King and his Whig Ministers. In June 1783 the Duke of Portland proposed to the King that the Prince should be granted £100,000 a year. This would have meant asking Parliament for an annual grant of £88,000, as the remainder would have been derived from the Duchy of Cornwall. The Duke also proposed that the King should personally pay the Prince's debts to tradesmen, which then amounted to £29,000. It was proposed that there should be no increase in the Prince's income when he married, though his wife would naturally have been granted a dowry.

When, in the middle of June, the Duke of Portland wrote to the King, outlining these proposals, the King was simply aghast. He was heard to say, "I wish I were 80 or 90 or dead," but these dismal desires did not prevent him from pouring out his indignation on the heads of his unhappy Ministers. He began his

22

letter to the Duke of Portland, "It is impossible for me to find words expressive enough of my utter indignation and astonishment," and ended it with the blistering comment, ". . . when the Duke of Portland came into Office I had at least hoped he would have thought himself obliged to have my interest and that of the Public at heart, and not have neglected both to gratify the passions of an ill advised young man." But the King's anger did not prevent him from summoning to his aid his own natural astuteness. He made an adroit counter-proposal to the effect that he would personally give the Prince an annual allowance of £50,000, which, with the revenue of the Duchy of Cornwall, would have amounted to a total income of about £62,000, and that the Ministers would simply ask Parliament for a lump sum of £50,000 to pay off the Prince's debts and to fit up a house for him. This proposal put the Government in an exceedingly difficult position. As Whigs they were the champions of retrenchment, and yet, in the King's words, "when they think it will answer their own wicked purposes . . . [they] are ready to be most barefacedly lavish." With the King and certainly two members of the Cabinet opposed to them, Fox and Portland could never have carried the proposed grant for £100,000 through Parliament. But they had pledged themselves to the Prince.

Fox recklessly offered to stand by his pledge to the Prince. The Prince, although he complained vigorously of his father's treatment, agreed that the matter should be left to the Cabinet to decide, without regard to any pledges which might previously have been made to him. He wrote to Fox:

> "Queen's House,
> June 18th, 1783.
>
> DEAR CHARLES,
>
> After what has already passed, I did not require this additional proof of your friendship and attachment: and you will see by the letter I have this instant written to the Duke of Portland, how ready I am to take your advice, and that I leave it entirely to the Cabinet.
>
> Yours most sincerely,
> GEORGE P."

No fair-minded person could disagree with Fox's comment, "The Prince has behaved in the handsomest manner." In consequence, the King's proposal was accepted, and the Prince found himself in possession of £62,000 a year and a house.

It was decided that Carlton House should be fitted up for him. Carlton House stood where Waterloo Place now is, and covered the sites of the Athenæum and United Services Clubs and part of what is now Carlton House Terrace. It was built for Lord Carlton in 1709, and, although it was small and not particularly impressive, there was ample compensation in the magnificent gardens, which reached down to the Mall, and extended westwards as far as the wall of Marlborough House. They had been laid out by William Kent, between 1732 and 1735, for Frederick, Prince of Wales, who bought Carlton House from Lord Carlton's nephew, and were partly copied from Pope's garden at Twickenham. They were one of the early attempts at landscape gardening, and at breaking with the old tradition of "verdant sculpture" which had been ridiculed by Pope's remark, "Adam and Eve in yew, Adam a little shattered by the fall of the tree of knowledge in the great storm, Eve and the serpent very flourishing." But although the gardens were a constant source of admiration, no good description of them seems to have survived. We only know that there were some fine elms, a cascade, a temple paved with Italian marble and decorated with painting and sculpture, and that statues, including one of King Alfred and one of the Black Prince, were scattered throughout the grounds.

Inside, the house was very old-fashioned, as it had not been lived in since the death of George III's mother in 1772; consequently there was great scope for improvement and alteration. The Prince actually moved in to Carlton House between June and August 1783, and immediately employed Henry Holland on the task of making it more habitable. Holland added a Corinthian portico, which now forms the front of the National Gallery, and he cut off the front of Carlton House from the gaze of passers-by in Pall Mall by a screen of Ionic pillars, which were the subject of a rather inane contemporary jingle:

> *Dear little columns all in a row,*
> *What do you do there?—We really don't know.*

With his extravagant taste, and with a house that was asking for a small fortune to be spent on it, the Prince never showed any sign of living within the income his father thought sufficient.

As this question of his allowance and his debts was a permanent grievance with the Prince, a perennial subject of public discussion, and eventually drove him to his fatal marriage, it is essential that it should be viewed in proper proportion. So many people who have written on the subject have been blinded by the Great God Gold which—in breach of the first and second commandments— the nineteenth century fashioned and worshipped. The people who created this yellow monster were sufficiently clever to persuade the world that to disobey it was just as wicked as to disobey the commandments of the Christian religion. Mortgages, policies, bonds, "little bits of paper" (as our grandfathers described promissory notes), and all the paraphernalia of the usurer were regarded as sacred and holy, but the man who resorted to such things to supplement his income was looked upon as something between a thief and an adulterer. These bourgeois views did not prevail—least of all among the upper classes—in eighteenth-century England. It is, therefore, of primary importance to treat the Prince's debts as a practical problem and not a moral one.

The first question is whether the Prince's income of £62,000 was adequate. This question is not dismissed by the banal and obvious comment that £62,000 is the equivalent of more than £100,000 to-day—an annual sum which should be sufficient for any young man of twenty-one. The point is that, for someone of the Prince's reckless tastes and extravagant ideas of comfort, it clearly was not adequate. But there is a more important question than this, and that is whether it was just.

At the beginning of the seventeenth century the income of the Prince of Wales was £60,000, and James II, as Duke of York and heir presumptive to the throne, received £100,000: by 1783 the cost of living had doubled since the previous century. George II, as Prince of Wales, had received £100,000, and when, in his niggardly fashion, he only allowed his son Frederick, Prince of Wales, £50,000, the Prince appealed to Parliament against his father's action, and only lost by narrow majorities in both the House of Commons and the House of Lords. In the same way George II allowed his grandson, afterwards George III, £50,000. The precedent for a small allowance seems therefore to have no greater authority than George II's dislike of his eldest son.

It only remains to explain why George III took so strong a line on this question. He made it prefectly clear that the moment the

25

Prince made a marriage of which he approved he would provide him with the full allowance of £100,000. In other words, like most foolish fathers, he was determined to have some say in the choice of his daughter-in-law. It was a determination that was to have the most disastrous results on the Prince's happiness all his life.

The King, having had his own way in the matter of money, might at least have shown some friendliness to his son, but he wrote a savage letter to a member of the Prince's household, which was to be shown to the Prince, in which he referred to his son's neglect of every religious duty, his want of common civility to the Queen, and his total disobedience to every injunction given him, and added, "I must hope . . . that a continuation of Levity may not shorten his Days and make him too late repent at not having followed the advice of an affectionate but distressed Parent." The Prince replied, with possibly more attention to pomp than truth, "Indiscretions I may have been guilty of, but of none with a criminal intent. A real sense of my Duty to— added to a most affectionate regard—for their Majesties with a sincere inclination to show it upon all occasions, has, and I hope ever will be the constant Rule of my Conduct."

George III's condemnation of his son's character during these years (1780–1783) has found emphatic support from the pens of subsequent writers. We can imagine the relish with which writers of a later period, in their drab clothes and elastic-sided boots, surrounded by their plush draperies and massive hideous furniture, racked their vocabularies in search of adjectives to condemn this Prince, of whose junketings they genuinely disapproved, but of whose brilliance and gaiety they must have been secretly envious. And even a recent writer[1] on the period can say, "He wallowed in vice. It was done elegantly in beautiful clothes, amidst luxury and in a scented atmosphere." It seems improbable that this writer's description of the Prince was any more accurate than his description of the atmosphere in the eighteenth century.

The Prince at this period was no doubt thoughtless, selfish, and reckless, enjoying masked parties, gambling, drinking, and furious riding and behaving, in short, like the great majority of his contemporaries. It is unfortunate that those who are so foolish as

[1] His Honour Sir Edward Parry.

to attach importance to the wildness of youth should not have acquired the wisdom of Horace Walpole, who wrote of the Prince, "As I too am always partial to youth—having not at least the spleen of age—I make the greatest allowance for inexperience and novel passions."

No particular scandal attached itself to the Prince's name during this period, and after parting from Mrs. Robinson he was supposed to have fallen in love with Lady Melbourne, who was a woman of charm and ability, somewhat older than he, who used to dance with him as an observer said, "something in the cow style; but he was in ecstasies with it." He disliked pomp, and gave out that he wished to be invited to private suppers without any form. He frequently had young men to dine with him at Buckingham House, "and they go in their frocks and are received without the least ceremony." After the ridiculous nightmare of the earlier Georges, and with a King like George III, who shunned society, the popularity of the Prince in London society was unbounded. As the King saw his son sinking deeper and deeper into this life, of which he profoundly disapproved, he regarded him as more than half way to hell. This, coupled with his horror of Fox, created a permanent barrier between father and son.

Bad as the relations of father and son were, they were exacerbated by the political events of the latter half of 1783, and the beginning of 1784. On September 3rd, 1783, the King, in the course of a letter to Fox on the treaty with the American colonists, used the curious phrase, "In States, as in men, where dislike has once arose I never expect to see cordiality." He instanced the truth of this otherwise false generalisation by suddenly demanding the resignation of Fox and North on December 18th. The following day Pitt, at the age of twenty-four, kissed hands as First Lord of the Treasury, and the Whigs, who had practically governed England since the death of Queen Anne, were to lord it no more for half a century. The new session of Parliament had opened on November 11th, and on the same day the Prince took his seat in the House of Lords. He was dressed in black velvet, richly embroidered with gold and pink spangles, and lined with pink satin; his shoes had pink heels, his hair was dressed much out at the sides, and very full frizzed with two very small curls at the bottom. As soon as the ceremony was over he hurried to the

House of Commons to listen to Fox's speech. For the next few months Pitt's Ministry, ardently supported by the King, gained increasing support in the House of Commons, luring into its ranks many ostensible Whigs, whose principles proved no match against the smiles and blandishments of the dispensers of patronage. In March 1784 the King granted Pitt a dissolution, and the General Election which followed was one of the most bitter ever fought in this country, the Whigs naturally setting out in full cry against their former colleagues who were now supporting the Government.

Fox, who sat for Westminster, was opposed by one of "the Whig rats." It was a vitally important election in the age of rotten boroughs, because Westminster was one of the very few popular constituencies, in which practically every householder had a vote. To fight the cause of the people, supported by all that was most daring and intelligent in English life, must be the dream of every intelligent political candidate. What could be more effective than the Duchess of Devonshire, setting out on her canvass at 8 o'clock in the morning, and calling out to the voters, "A plumper for the people's friend, our friend, everybody's friend." The Prince was absolutely open in his support of Fox, and he rode through the streets of Westminster wearing Fox's colours. It is surprising—and rather disagreeable—to have to record that the "Whig rat" should have secured any votes at all, but in fact he did astonishingly well, and Fox was only elected by a majority of 236.

As soon as the result was known, a great procession set out from Westminster for Devonshire House in Piccadilly. "The Man of the People" was drawn in a triumphal chair, decorated with laurels, and attended by squadrons of gentlemen on horseback in blue and buff uniforms. Floating in the breeze, in front of the state carriages of the Duchesses of Portland and Devonshire, was a banner bearing the words, "Sacred to Female Patriotism." The members of the procession uncovered as they passed Carlton House, and they were welcomed in the courtyard of Devonshire House by the Prince himself. He stood on the low wall surrounding the house, looking into Berkeley Street, with the Duchess of Devonshire on one hand and the Duchess of Portland on the other, cheering the "Sons of Freedom" as they left.

On May 19th, he gave a fête in the garden of Carlton House, starting with breakfast and ending at six in the evening, to celebrate Fox's triumph over the Court candidate. It was on the same day that the King drove along the Mall, in state, to open the new Parliament. Only a low wall divided the gardens of Carlton House from the Mall, and the King must have seen the nine marquees, heard the strains of the four bands, and the shouts of revelry in what was called "a revival of old English hospitality." That night the Prince entertained Mr. Fox and a few select friends to dinner, after which they all went on to Mrs. Crewe's party, where the famous toast was given, "Buff and Blue and Mrs. Crewe," to which the hostess replied, "Buff and Blue and all of you." That year the Prince of Wales's birthday was not observed by his parents. It was scarcely surprising. But there was something even worse in store for the King and Queen.

III

Since the affair with Mrs. Robinson rumour had linked the names of several women with the Prince, though there had been nothing particularly scandalous nor specific. It was probably just after the Westminster election, though the exact date is uncertain, that he first met Mrs. Fitzherbert. Very soon all his affection was completely centred on her. The vulgar estimate of him as a lustful rake is disproved by his falling in love with a woman of the character and qualities of Mrs. Fitzherbert. Women of her type —beautiful, amusing, intelligent, devout, and modest—neither attract debauchees nor consort with them.

Mrs. Fitzherbert had all that quiet assurance and conscious respectability which are the very proper attributes of the old Roman Catholic families. She was born a Smythe of Acton Burnell, married first a Weld of Lulworth, who only lived a year after marriage, and then a Fitzherbert of Swynnerton. The very names seem to inspire a slight contempt for the new nobility of Henry VIII's reign, and to conjure up visions of recusancy laws, priests' hiding-places, and illicit whiffs of incense. Indeed Mrs. Fitzherbert's second husband might well be regarded as a victim of the No Popery Riots, led by Lord George Gordon, because it was an injudicious bath, following his efforts to quell the rioters, that hastened his end.

After the death of her second husband, Mrs. Fitzherbert lived quietly abroad, and it was not until 1784 that she appeared again in London society. She had a house in Park Street, and at the same time she rented Marble Hill at Richmond, a perfect specimen of early eighteenth-century architecture and a triumph of dilettantism, the house having been designed by Lord Burlington, the gardens laid out by Pope, and the cellar stocked by Swift. All that summer, as Fox has testified, the Prince was in a frenzy of love, and frequently visited Mrs. Fitzherbert at Marble Hill, so that wits were heard to repeat the jingle:

> *I'd crowns resign*
> *To call thee mine,*
> *Sweet lass of Richmond Hill.*

Indeed it seemed more than probable that nothing less than the abandonment of his right to the crown would have enabled the Prince to call Mrs. Fitzherbert his. Her religion, which was a bar to an irregular connexion, equally made marriage impossible. If the Prince married a Roman Catholic, he forfeited his right to the crown under the Act of Settlement which enacted that those marrying papists were *de facto* excluded from the throne. There is no doubt that Mrs. Fitzherbert was in love with the Prince, a fact which appears to have been overlooked by her devoted executors, cousins, and Roman Catholic biographers, who regard any manifestation of normal passion as out of place in one to whom they have contrived to attribute the insipid qualities of a cloistered deaconess. In fact Mrs. Fitzherbert was selfish, cunning and swayed by a vile temper. On one occasion she threw her slipper at her illustrious paramour. Considering her very grave faults of character, all glossed over by her Popish adorers, the Prince is deserving of some admiration for the constancy of his devotion to this lady.

The accredited story is that after months of violent pursuit which culminated in the Prince stabbing himself and thereby tricking Mrs. Fitzherbert into Carlton House, where he gave her a ring, she fled from his importunities to France. Mrs. Fitzherbert's biographers attribute this flight abroad to priestly influence and an endeavour to escape an immoral connexion. It seems far more probable that her going abroad was not a flight, but a ruse, and that she was to be joined abroad by her lover, where they could have some kind of religious ceremony, or where they could live at peace from the scandal and clatter of tongues in England. In the middle of August 1784 the Prince suddenly wrote to his father announcing his intention of going to live abroad for a time. It is true that he gave as his reason the desire to economise, but the vigour of the King's reply suggests that his real object in going was to join Mrs. Fitzherbert, and was well known to the King. After saying that he had shown the letter to the Queen, George III wrote:

"His [the Prince's] character would be for ever blasted in this country and in Europe. . . . He will in every sense be ruined and lose the affection and protection of him who yet remains

His very affectionate Father."[1]

(As father and son had hardly met, except on formal occasions, for a twelvemonth, "the affection and protection" were not particularly obvious.) It seems most likely that when they were thus baulked of their intention of going abroad, the Prince became urgent that they should take every risk and go through some ceremony of marriage. It has to be remembered that for the true Hanoverian there was something almost magically attractive in an illegal marriage. The Prince's uncles had both indulged in it, his brothers were to show their weakness for it, and he himself had offered marriage to Miss Hamilton and Mrs. Robinson.

Mrs. Fitzherbert left England in November 1784 to escape the Prince's proposals of marriage, not because she was reluctant to marry him, but for fear of the effect of marriage on the Prince's position, and of the risks in which the clergy and witnesses would involve themselves.[2] During the year that she was abroad, she was in constant communication with the Prince, and when she returned, apparently feeling that any further resistance was useless, in December 1785, they were married at her house in Park Street, on December 15th, by the Reverend Robert Burt, her brother and uncles acting as witnesses.

But however secretly the marriage was performed, it was impossible in that golden age of gossip to keep it quiet, and in

[1] This correspondence is in the Public Record Office.
[2] Under the Royal Marriage Act, the clergy or witnesses at a marriage contravening the Act were guilty of felony.

the same month an observer wrote to the Duke of Rutland, "I never saw his Royal Highness so sedate and rational. The world will have it, that he is meditating that which is not very rational though it may be very sedate." At the beginning of 1786 a pious Roman Catholic, concealing a love of gossip in anxiety for the true faith, wrote, "Mrs. Fitzherbert has, I believe, been married to the Prince. . . . God knows how it will turn out—it may be to the Glory of our Belief, or it may be to the great dismay and destruction of it." The fact of the Prince's marriage was widely believed at the time, and indeed ever since, until it was finally proved by the publication, at the beginning of this century, of the relevant documents, which had been stored at Coutts' Bank and are now at Windsor Castle.

There can be no doubt that it was not only an act of pure folly on the Prince's part, but very dangerous as well. The arguments against the marriage had been clearly set before him by Fox, in December 1785, as soon as he knew that Mrs. Fitzherbert was returning. He wrote to the Prince on December 10th, stressing the danger to his rights to the crown of marrying a Roman Catholic, particularly with "the King not feeling for you as a father ought," and with the nation full of its old prejudices against the Catholics. He then went on to say that it could not be a legal marriage, and that there would always be an uncertainty as to whether he was married or not, which would give rise to peculiar difficulties in the event of there being children. After apologising for writing with such freedom, he added, "If I were Mrs. Fitzherbert's father or brother, I would advise her not by any means to agree to it, and to prefer any other species of connexion with you to one leading to so much misery and mischief."

The Prince replied at once:

"MY DEAR CHARLES,—Your letter of last night afforded me more satisfaction than I can find words to express, as it is an additional proof to me (which I assure you I did not want) of your having that true regard and affection for me which it is not only the wish but the ambition of my life to merit. Make yourself easy, my dear friend. Believe me, the world will soon be convinced that there not only [is not] but never was any ground for these reports, which of late have been so malevolently circulated. I have not seen you since the apostasy of

Eden. . . . Believe me at all times, my dear Charles, most
affectionately yours,
GEORGE P.

Carlton House,
   Sunday Morning 2 o'clock December 11 1785."

Refreshing as it must ever be to find the heir to the throne
dealing in such vigorous language with those who, like the first
Lord Auckland (Eden), desert the cause of progress for more
profitable but less reputable paths, it is difficult to describe the
Prince's letter except as a masterpiece of deceptive literature.
We may hope that as he wrote Sunday morning, so boldly and so
unnecessarily, he was seized by a qualm of conscience as he
remembered that not only was he fully intending to marry Mrs.
Fitzherbert, but that the arrangements were actually in train.
It was a deception that might well have destroyed Fox's friendship for the Prince, and was, in fact, to have serious results
later on.

But rightly as the Prince should be condemned for his folly
in marrying Mrs. Fitzherbert, and for his underhand deception
of Fox over this, it is essential to view the marriage in its proper
light. Under the Royal Marriage Act, the Prince, being under
twenty-five, could not marry without the permission of the King.
As that permission was not given, the marriage was not legal, and
had no more effect in law than a bigamous marriage.

Mrs. Fitzherbert's champions are rightly jealous of her honour,
but to rake up citations from the Council of Trent, and indeed
all the profundities and obscurities of Roman Catholic dogma,
does not alter the fact that the marriage was illegal by the law of
England, whatever may have been its precise significance at the
Vatican. To say of Mrs. Fitzherbert, as Mr. Wilkins does after
publishing the proofs of the marriage,[1] "the honour and virtue
of this much misunderstood woman are now established beyond
doubt, and her memory cleared from every shadow of stain," is
as lyrical in language as it is foolish in sentiment. The proper
interpretation to put on the marriage is that it was a solemn
undertaking before God by the Prince that if he had been a private
citizen he would have married Mrs. Fitzherbert, and that, whatever might happen to him thereafter, he would regard himself as
married to her. There is no shadow of doubt that Lord Holland

[1] *Mrs. Fitzherbert and George IV.*

was correct when he repeated the words of an intimate friend of Mrs. Fitzherbert's, "It was at the Prince's own earnest and repeated solicitations, not at Mrs. Fitzherbert's request, that any ceremony was resorted to. She knew it to be invalid in law; she thought it nonsense and told the Prince so."

IV

There was never the slightest likelihood of them living happily ever afterwards. Apart from the difficulties of the Prince's rank, it was putting too great a strain on the words in the Marriage Service about help and comfort in adversity for the bridegroom to bring to the bride, admittedly a handsome income, but several hundred thousand pounds' worth of debts as well. It should not be imagined that this vast debt, which had been amassed in two or three years, was caused entirely by reckless personal extravagance; a large part of it was the result of the repairs and embellishments at Carlton House, and at the Pavilion which the Prince was building for himself at Brighton. Of course it is true that much of the work at Carlton House might be regarded as unnecessarily extravagant. George III, with a father's tiresome frugality, had written of "only painting it and putting handsome furniture where necessary." But it was hardly likely that the furniture and stuffy domestic decorations of his grandmother would have satisfied the Prince.

As has been said, Henry Holland was employed in altering the structure of the house, and Gaubert, who had been a cook, was responsible for the decorations. The work on Carlton House was never ending, and the chief improvement effected in the years immediately after the Prince got in was in the arrangement of the ground floor or basement. On the north, facing Pall Mall, there were only two stories, but on the south side, facing the Mall, the ground dropped very rapidly and it was found possible to contrive another floor on that side which from the north was regarded as a basement but from the south might be called the ground floor as its windows opened into the gardens: the rooms on the south side were consequently very low. In addition to these alterations, more splendid quarters for the servants were also added. New kitchens, wine-cellars, and larders were built, and a pastry scullery, a silver scullery, a coffee-room pantry, a footmen's hall, a maids' kitchen, and a confectionary. A bow-windowed bedroom was added for the Prince, with a dressing-closet and "hot bathe" room opening out of it. On the first floor were three spacious rooms overlooking the gardens, the state apartment, used for audiences, a small music-room, and one of the most attractive features of the house a Chinese drawing-room, which was decorated in yellow silk, and was filled with Chinese furniture and china.

Horace Walpole, whose judgment is final on such matters, saw it in 1785, and wrote, "There is an august simplicity that astonished me. You can not call it magnificent; it is the taste and propriety that strike. . . . In all the fairy tales you have been, you never was in so pretty a scene. . . . How sick one shall be after this chaste palace, of Mr. Adam's gingerbread and sippets of em-broidery!"; and he said it would be the most perfect palace in Europe. He added the apt and spiteful comment that all the tin-mines in Cornwall would not pay for a quarter of it.

It was only too true. Although in April 1785 the Prince had been in receipt of his allowance for less than two years, he owed at least £160,000. The King showed no sign of relieving him from this embarrassment. In an interview that he had with Sir James Harris, afterwards Lord Malmesbury, the Prince said, "He [the King] hates me: he always did from seven years old." The Prince showed Harris the correspondence which he had had with the King in the autumn of 1784 on this debt question. Harris described the Prince's letters as "full of respect and deference," but the King's as "harsh and severe. . . . They were void of every expression of parental kindness or affection." Harris added that after hearing them read and reading them himself, he was com-pelled to subscribe to the Prince's opinion. But although, as has been said, the Prince wanted to go abroad and live in economical retirement with Mrs. Fitzherbert, and actually said to Harris, "I am ruined if I stay in England; I disgrace myself as a man," no steps to deal with the debt were taken, and when he "married" Mrs. Fitzherbert he must have owed between two and three hundred thousand pounds, with no prospect other than his father's death of paying them off.

Throughout the early part of 1786 attempts were made to patch things up between the Prince and his father, but, as the King refused to help unless the Prince married and ceased to be a party man, these attempts broke down. Consequently in the summer of 1786 the Prince decided to retrench on his own account. On July 9th he wrote to his father of the pressing importunities of many indigent and deserving creditors, and of the risk of "legal insults, as humiliating to me as I am persuaded that they would be offensive to your Majesty." He then announced his intention of reducing every expense, "even those to which my birth and rank entitle me." Within a few days Carlton House was shut up, the servants dismissed, the carriages and horses sold, and the Prince and Mrs. Fitzherbert jogged down to Brighton in a hired chaise.

The scandal and gossip that resulted were tremendous, but through it all sympathy was generally with the Prince. It was felt that the King had been harsh, and the Prince's exaggerated, flamboyant economy made a good impression. This lasted for some six months, and, as the King showed no signs of relenting, the Prince, acting on the advice of his Whig friends, decided, at the beginning of 1787, to appeal himself to Parliament.

Accordingly, on April 27th, Alderman Newnham—a City merchant—announced in the House of Commons that he would move that an humble address be presented to His Majesty praying him to take into his Royal consideration the present embarrassed state of affairs of the Prince of Wales. The House of Commons at that time was predominantly Tory. When Pitt rose to speak—

> Mild and more mild he sees each placid row
> Of Country Gentlemen with rapture glow;
> He sees convulsed with sympathetic throbs
> Apprentice Peers and Deputy Nabobs,
> Nor Rum Contractors think his speech too long
> While words like treacle trickle from his tongue.

It was hardly to be expected that such a sycophantic body would desert the King (from whom all honours flowed) for his rebellious son (from whom one day, perhaps, honours might flow). Pre-eminent in the class of apprentice peers was Mr. Rolle, one of the members for Devonshire. Though he was always careful to speak of himself as an independent country gentleman, and to assure the House of Commons that he had nothing to expect from the King, he eagerly accepted a proffered barony in 1797. In the House of Lords he distinguished himself by going up to a Whig Lord Chancellor, when he was sitting on the Woolsack, and saying, "My Lord, I should like you to know that I have the greatest contempt for you both inside this House and out." It was he who, like some ancient ghost, fell on attempting to kiss Queen Victoria's hand at her coronation. Mr. Rolle was therefore well qualified by virtue of his rude determination to raise a question from which more delicate minds might have shrunk, and he called on the country gentlemen in Parliament "to attend to a question which might affect both Church and State." This was an allusion to the Prince's marriage to a Roman Catholic. Fox then, in vigorous language, denied the marriage, and described it as a "miserable calumny . . . a malicious falsehood . . . a tale only fit to impose on the lowest order of persons in the streets." On being further pressed by Mr. Rolle, he said it "not only could have never happened legally, but never did happen in any way whatsoever," and he added that he had spoken from direct authority.

It was obviously most improper to have this kind of discussion going on in Parliament, and the Cabinet, after sitting all day with constant communications with Buckingham House, sent a message to the Prince that if he would withdraw his motion everything would be settled to his satisfaction. The motion was accordingly withdrawn, but the King then turned round and said that he would only come to the Prince's aid if he was furnished with a complete list of debts, and if the Prince would undertake to run into debt no more.

The list of debts was furnished to the King as follows:

Bonds and debts	£13,000
Purchase of houses	4,000
Expenses of Carlton House	53,000
Tradesmen's bills	90,000
	£160,000

Parliament was asked to pay that sum, to provide another £60,000 for the completion of Carlton House, and the King undertook to pay his son an extra £10,000 a year. The Prince was once again received at Court, but even at their first interview the King could not refrain from the disagreeable remark that he had lost his character, but that he might retrieve it if he would not live with such scoundrels.

It is therefore not unfair to say that for £160,000 down, and £10,000 a year, the Prince sacrificed the reputation of Mrs. Fitzherbert. Gillray celebrated this by a caricature of Mrs. Fitzherbert grasping a crucifix and sitting forlorn on a rock: the Prince, Fox, and other leading Whigs, sail away in a boat called *Honour*, while the Prince says, "I never saw her in my life," and Fox cries, "No, never in his life damme."

The usual story of what happened is that Fox, acting on the Prince's denial that he was going to marry Mrs. Fitzherbert in the letter of December 11th, 1785,[1] made his recklessly untrue statement in reply to Mr. Rolle. The following morning the Prince was supposed to have seen Mrs. Fitzherbert, and to have said, "Only conceive, Maria, what Fox did yesterday. He went down to the House and denied that you and I were man and wife." Mrs. Fitzherbert could hardly be expected to take it in such a jaunty manner, and it is certainly true that she was furious with Fox, and said, "He has rolled me in the kennel like a street-walker." The story then goes on that the Prince asked Grey to say something in the House of Commons modifying Fox's statement and paying tribute to Mrs. Fitzherbert. Grey refused, and the Prince then asked Sheridan, who made his well-known speech about "one [i.e. Mrs. Fitzherbert] on whose conduct truth could fix no just reproach, and whose character claimed, and was entitled to, the truest and most general respect."

Many years later when the Prince was King, he dictated to Mr. Croker his version of this episode. He refers throughout to "my supposed marriage," and "the absurd story of my supposed marriage." He said that when Fox mentioned it to him, he contradicted it with "pooh, nonsense, ridiculous." In the heat of debate Fox used some expressions which Mrs. Fitzherbert regarded as slighting: Sheridan happened to call on her, and was so distressed on her account that he quite spontaneously made his eulogy of her in the House of Commons. He also said that he never saw Grey at that time. As an old man, Grey left on record that he not only was asked by the Prince to modify what Fox had said, but that the Prince admitted to him that some ceremony had taken place.

It may well be imagined that in this conflict of testimony which involved the honour of the fountain-heads of Whiggery,

---

[1] See page 32.

Fox and Grey, their many biographers, and the noble compilers of the *Memorials of Fox*[1] and the *Memoirs of the Whig Party*[2] (the very titles exuding an odour of sanctity), have not been idle in the defence of their gods. How readily scornful phrases flowed from their pens as they held up to permanent odium the hapless young man of twenty-five who had deceived their heroes and who was deserving of neither mercy nor respect. How good and virtuous they sound as they lament that habits of enjoyment should have led these great men to confound the fortunes of their party with an abandoned dissolute rake. But, if the reader will keep a firm hold of certain facts, this torrent of indignant morality need not necessarily overwhelm him. These writers say that Fox was so furious with the Prince that he never spoke to him for a year afterwards. How, then, do they explain that a month afterwards the Prince was writing to Fox in exactly the old affectionate terms? If Fox was so furious with the Prince's duplicity, how was it that he allowed a further denial to be made in his name in the House of Commons in 1789, even adding that he was satisfied that what he asserted on a former occasion was strictly true? How is it possible to reconcile the fact that Grey twice denied the marriage in the House of Commons, in 1789, with his statement, in old age, that the Prince told him in 1787 that a ceremony had taken place? Such things can only be explained by Whig writers by the simple— if not wholly creditable—method of ignoring them.

It is probable that in the future further documents may come to light which may help to explain this most baffling incident. At the present it only seems safe to say that Fox, Sheridan, Grey, and, of course, the Prince were well aware that a ceremony had taken place, but that they, like Mrs. Fitzherbert, attached no particular importance nor value to it. They can be hardly blamed for thinking that the interests of the State and of the Whig Party were of greater importance than their avowal of a ceremony in a London drawing-room which would have agitated the public mind, destroyed the position of the Prince, and ruined his political advisers.

V

Although during the years after he settled into Carlton House the Prince appeared before the public in an unpopular light,

[1] Earl Russell.　　　[2] Lord Holland.

notably in the debates on his debts and in the Regency squabbles
in 1789, he was not yet really unpopular, and, as he was always
particularly sensitive to public opinion, these years when he was
at his gayest and was almost adored by London society were
unquestionably the happiest of his life.

With one aspect of the Prince's early years countless writers
have familiarised the public. We all know how he followed
Dr. Johnson's advice—

> *Wild as wind and light as feather,*
> *Bid the sons of thrift farewell.*

His principal friends were Sir John Lade, the famous Whip;
Lady Lade, a vulgar but amusing woman; the Duke of Orleans
(*Philippe Égalité*), who introduced to France, just before the
Revolution, many of the Prince's fashions, and who won a little
distinction as a pioneer balloonist, but whose death on the
guillotine was not generally lamented; Beau Brummell; George
Hanger, afterwards Lord Coleraine; the Barrymore brothers, who
were successively Earls of Barrymore, and who were known as
Hellgate, Newgate, and Cripplegate; and a particularly foul-
mouthed Barrymore sister, who was known as Billingsgate. At
Brighton and London they behaved like a band of merry under-
gratuates, playing tricks on old ladies, giving shooting-parties in
the middle of the town, betting, and drinking.

One of his favourite pursuits at this time was racing, and before
the reduction of his establishment, in 1786, he had twenty-five
animals in training at Newmarket, and when he took to racing
again, in 1788, he won 190 races between that year and 1791.

It is often loosely said that the Prince was ordered off the turf.
He was the owner of a well-known horse called Escape. On
October 20th, 1791, at Newmarket, Escape, who was ridden by
Sam Chifney, was badly beaten, the odds being 2–1 against the
Prince's horse. On the following day, when the odds had risen
to 5–1 against Escape, the horse won easily, beating some of the
horses which had defeated it on the previous day. The Prince
and Chifney were both supposed to have made large sums of
money on the second day, although this was subsequently denied.
After the race, Sir Charles Bunbury, one of the stewards of the
meeting, said to the Prince, "If you suffer Chifney to ride your
horses, no gentleman will start against you." The Prince replied

that if it was clear that Chifney had done wrong he would cease to employ him. An enquiry by the stewards followed, and Chifney was examined, but nothing was clearly proved against him. The Prince refused to race again at Newmarket, and allowed Chifney £200 a year, to show that he had not lost confidence in him. Chifney subsequently wrote an account of the incident under the flamboyant title of "Genius Genuine," in which he attributes his success on the second day to following the Prince's advice to make play with Escape instead of, as the trainer had advised on the previous day, holding him in at the beginning. There was never any question of the Prince's having acted dishonestly, except in the imagination of contemporary gossips, and the facts go far to exonerate Chifney from all blame. The result was that the Prince gave up racing until the last years of his life, when his colours were seen again at Ascot and Epsom.

The same year that he moved into Carlton House saw his first visit to Brighton, where he went in the summer, to visit his uncle, the Duke of Cumberland, who had taken a house there. He arrived on a Sunday, and, notwithstanding the day, the populace had done their best to give him a cordial welcome, in which a round of cannon fire was to play a prominent part. The proceedings were slightly marred by an indiscretion in loading one of the guns, which blew a gunner on to the beach, mortally wounding him. However, the sparkling air of Brighton, its sea which, according to medical opinion, contained a greater percentage of salt than any other watering-place in England owing to its remoteness from a river mouth, the splendid views of the Downs, not then obliterated by the monotonous gifts of Victorian and Edwardian architects, and its general air of friendly informality, all charmed the Prince.

In 1784 he rented a house for the summer in Brighton, on the site of which he built the Pavilion. This was originally designed by Henry Holland, and was habitable in 1787. The middle of the building was one circular, lofty room, with Corinthian pillars in a semi-circle outside. There were two wings built on to this, the ground floor of one wing being the dining-room, and the ground floor of the other the drawing-room. Above the dining-room and drawing-room were bedrooms. Its classical proportions were good, but inside it was not particularly well designed, the dining-room, owing to its nearness to the kitchen, being almost insufferably hot, which gave rise to Sheridan's well-known jest, "It is quite right that we should be prepared in this world for that which we know will be our lot in another."

At about the same time Robert Adam designed a house for Mrs. Fitzherbert in the grounds of the Pavilion. This house was pulled down after a few years to make room for the house which still stands and is known as Mrs. Fitzherbert's. Adam's house was a fine piece of architecture, though it is rather suggestive of the company the widow was keeping when we read that she had an ale cellar, a small beer cellar, a wine in casks cellar, and a wine in bottles cellar. But in spite of these provisions for indulgence, Mrs. Fitzherbert's influence over the Prince was wholly admirable. Though their connexion may have been irregular, their life at Brighton was one of almost blameless domesticity.

Fox and Sheridan were frequent visitors at the Pavilion, and we read of the Prince and Mrs. Fitzherbert going down to the beach to welcome a boat-load of aristocrats who had escaped from France. Every summer leaders of English social life found their way to Brighton to take their part, under the Prince and Mrs. Fitzherbert, in a world that was gay, cheerful, and amusing, but not seriously deserving the moralist's condemnation.

> *'Tis at Brighton, the mirror of watering places,*
> *Assemble their Honors, their Lordships and Graces,*
> *Nay, England's first Prince—and the famous Dame Fitz.*
> *And old friends meet new friends of fashion and wits.*

VI

In the autumn of 1788 the Prince's life of elegant enjoyment was rudely interrupted. Ever since the King had returned from Cheltenham in August, where he had gone to drink the waters, his health had given rise to anxiety. In October, Court functions had to be postponed, and he was too unwell to travel from Kew to Windsor. People spoke of "a flurry of spirits" brought on by remaining the whole day in wet stockings, an act of imprudence which it was thought had driven the disorder from the legs to the bowels. Mr. Grenville, afterwards Prime Minister in the Government of All the Talents, with a simple faith in the motive power of medicine, wrote that "the physicians' medicines repelled it from the bowels to the brain. The physicians are now endeavouring by warm baths to bring it down to the legs again." But not even the charms of warm water persuaded the malady to take up its residence in the Royal legs.

Towards the end of October, the King was able to return to Windsor, and, meeting Miss Burney in one of the corridors, spoke to her of his health with tremendous rapidity of speech, and told her that he hardly slept one minute all night. To Lady Effingham he said, "My dear Effy, you see me, all at once, an old man." His favourite son, the Duke of York, came to Windsor to see him, and he was pleased at this mark of anxiety, and constantly repeated, "So good is Frederick." The good Frederick was so alarmed by what he saw that he sent an express for the Prince to come up from Brighton. The Prince arrived at Windsor on November 5th. The Queen appeared distressed at his coming, and that evening, at dinner, the King suddenly broke out, and catching the Prince by the collar thrust him violently against the wall. The Prince was reduced to tears, and his sisters rubbed his temples with Hungary water. This incident is often quoted as an example of the Prince's cowardice, but would his belligerent critics suggest that he should have knocked his father down?

For the two succeeding nights the Prince and the Duke of York sat up all night, fully dressed and wearing their stars, with the physicians and gentlemen of the household in a room adjoining that in which the King was. For sixteen hours the King never stopped talking, till his voice was faint through hoarseness. On the second night he suddenly got up and came into the anteroom, and was amazed to see the concourse of men. One of the doctors tried to persuade him to go back to bed, but he penned him in a corner, and said, "You are nothing but an old woman." It was after this that the doctors, the Royal Family, and all who had seen the King, were convinced that he was dying. At this period of his father's illness, the Prince behaved considerately and with decency. Not that this was particularly to his credit, because the pathos of the Queen's situation might have roused a flicker of sympathy in even the most soulless sot. It was "the good Frederick" who said to his mother, when she objected to his rummaging through the King's private papers, "Madam, I believe that you are nearly as deranged as the King." But Fanny Burney is careful to emphasise the thoughtful and respectful way in

43

which the Prince behaved to his mother. When the King's delirium was at its height, the Prince went to see his father, and the attendants thought he had not been recognised, but the King said afterwards, "Yes, I knew him very well, and he cried to see me so ill."

But though during these early days of the King's illness cordiality and sympathy reigned among the Royal Family, discord and turbulence reigned supreme in the world of politics. For four years Pitt had gone from strength to strength, inspired by the favour of his sovereign and the confidence of the great majority of his fellow countrymen. Judiciously distributing places and peerages, he was fast depleting the solid ranks of the Whigs. In those four years, what furtive changes of coat there had been, what stealthy scuttling of rats! As the centenary of the Glorious Revolution came round, Whig prospects had never looked blacker. On November 5th, 1788, Coke of Norfolk gave a banquet to celebrate the centenary. He and his guests sang the words of the famous post-prandial song specially composed for the occasion:

> The trumpet of Liberty sounds through the world,
>   And the Universe starts at the sound;
> Her standard Philosophy's hand has unfurled,
>   And the nations are thronging around.
>
>   Fall, tyrants! fall! fall! fall!
>   These are the days of liberty!
>   Fall, tyrants, fall!
>
> Shall Britons the chorus of Liberty hear
>   With a cold and insensible mind?
> No—the triumphs of freedom each Briton shall hear,
>   And contend for the rights of mankind.

But so firmly was Pitt entrenched in power that the Whigs must have felt it more than probable that Britons would for ever listen to their blandishments with "a cold and insensible mind." They cannot possibly have told that, even as they sang, the King from whom Pitt derived his strength was not expected to live. But, as the seriousness of his condition was gradually realised, the activity in Whig circles knew no bounds. Messengers sped across Europe to summon Fox from his holiday, lists of Cabinets were drawn up, old enemies were reconciled, and some of Pitt's most recent converts from Whiggery began to look uncomfortable. Even Lord Chancellor Thurlow—an ex-Whig—offered his advice to the Prince. Pitt himself thought that nothing could save his Government, and he made arrangements to return to Lincoln's Inn to resume his practice at the Bar.

But then, by one of those odd floutings of even the best medical opinion, the King suddenly improved. On November 12th he was out of danger, and on November 29th he was moved from Windsor to Kew. The only misfortune was that, although he had physically recovered, he remained completely mad. In the middle of December it was necessary to put him in a strait waistcoat, and he said, in a lucid interval, "It settles the matter completely, and I am now sure of never appearing in the world again; for you know a man that has been in a strait waistcoat can never wear a crown again."

That he should never wear the crown again was certainly the hope, if not the intention, of his eldest son and the Whigs. The sudden dashing of all their hopes through the King not dying left them bitter and reckless. Fox had returned, and he and the Whigs took the view that, as there was a void in the Royal authority, because the King was incapable, and had been for weeks, of transacting any public business, it was automatically filled by the heir to the throne. Pitt, on the other hand who knew that the moment the Prince was invested with Royal power he would dismiss the Government and send for the Whigs, saw his opportunity, and introduced a Regency Bill, which was strictly to limit the Regent's power.

Fox's view that a void in the Royal power caused by death was indistinguishable from a void caused by madness was natural and constitutionally sound. Pitt's view that the Prince should become Regent with limited powers of sovereignty may have been justified by circumstances, but it was artificial and unconstitutional as there was no means of obtaining the Royal consent to the Regency Bill, nor even of affixing the King's signature to it. The only constitutional authority for Pitt's view was a very shadowy and unsatisfactory precedent of what happened during Henry VI's reign, and, when Pitt quoted this in the House of Commons, Fox airily dismissed it by saying "he had endeavoured to entangle the understanding of gentlemen in the intricacies of metaphysics." Pitt had that agreeable arrogance of the true Tory who really feels that it is a national disaster if a Tory administration is not in office: it is certainly difficult to disagree with Sheridan, who said of Pitt's conduct at this time that "he was governed by party considerations and by the impulse of his own personal ambition."

The debates on the Regency Bill, which lasted throughout December 1788 and January 1789, were as vigorous and bitter as any that have taken place at Westminster. Every schoolboy is brought up to believe that Burke's speeches, which are now models of literature and oratory, were delivered to a bored and drowsy House. That may have been true of some of his speeches, but there was no dozing when he spoke on the Regency Bill. He stung the Tories to fury by speaking of Pitt as "one of the Prince's competitors," and his allusion to the King startled his friends and horrified his opponents. He said: "His illness was caused by no act of theirs, but ought they at that hour of sickness and calamity to clothe his bed with purple? Ought they to make a mockery of him, to put a crown of thorns on his head, a reed in his hand, and dressing him in a raiment of purple to cry, 'Hail, King of the Britons!'"

These violent displays of political passion had their counterparts in society and in the Royal Family itself. Fashionable ladies were divided into camps—some wearing regency caps, which were mountains of tumbled gauze with three feathers in front, ornamented in gold with *Ich dien*, and costing 7½ guineas—others wearing what they were pleased to call constitutional coats. And in the Royal Family itself the Queen and her daughters were ranged against the Prince, the Duke of York, and the King's brothers, the Dukes of Gloucester and Cumberland. The Queen no doubt felt that the Prince and the Duke of York had deliberately encouraged the violence of the Whig opposition, and they were, in consequence, refused admittance at Kew. The Princes were excusably furious, and the Duke of York did not hesitate to refer to their exclusion in a speech in the House of Lords. Completely cut off from their father, and merely receiving a slightly fuller bulletin than was daily posted at St. James's Palace, the Princes spread the wildest stories of how the King struck, kicked, and bit anyone who came near him, of how he suddenly threw himself into a shallow pool of water when out walking at Kew, and of how he said, "Hush, hush! don't talk of stars, we must not talk of stars; you know I am *mopsimus* and don't like French mottoes."

The Prince no doubt felt that with the King out of his mind he could afford to treat the enmity of the Queen lightly. He described the restrictions on the Regent's power which Pitt proposed as those which "no dictator could possibly, I think, have been barefaced enough to bring forward." At the beginning of 1789 he sent to Pitt a formal letter of protest, drafted by Burke, and its violent passages amended by Sheridan. In after life the Prince described this as "one of the most beautiful and noble compositions that ever was penned." And while there might perhaps be two opinions as to that, there could be no doubt of the wisdom which in every sentence emphasised the Prince's grief at the calamity which had fallen on the nation through his father's illness, and at the horror the King would feel at these mutilations of Royal power when sanity returned. In those early days of 1789 the Prince and his political associates felt certain that the King's recovery was remote, and, as the Regency Bill passed through the House of Commons to the accompaniment of almost hysterical objurgations from the Whigs, they could comfort themselves that even if the Prince's power under the Bill was to be limited, at least he would have the right to dismiss Pitt and to send for Fox.

All through January and the early days of February Whig minds were absorbed in exotic dreams of patronage and high office under Government. Cabinets were drafted, redrafted, and submitted to ponderous Whig dukes, there was to be a steady stream of ecclesiastical preferment, a gentle rain of field-marshal-ships on Royal princes, and Mrs. Fitzherbert was to be a duchess. But while the Prince and the Whigs were enjoying these nebulous pleasures, the Queen and Princesses had more solid grounds for comfort. The King had suddenly improved, and on February 20th the Princess Augusta was writing to Miss Goldsworthy (one of the ladies-in-waiting):

"I have the pleasure, my dearest Goully, of telling you we had the happiness of a Visit from my dear Papa. Last night he came up stairs at 7 and staid till $\frac{1}{2}$ past 9. Thank God my dearest Goully, for this comfort. Thank God for his great mercy to us. I am so very happy that I really could hardly believe my eyes when I saw him; he was so composed, so kind, so exactly what you and all our real friends could wish. . . .

Your most affect. my dearest Goully,
AUGUSTA SOPHIA."

The King's recovery was rapid and complete, and all hope of office for the Whigs vanished. Those of Pitt's supporters who had shown signs of deserting him scuttled back again, but for the Prince and the Whigs there was no shelter whither they could scuttle to escape the contemptuous dislike of the King and his people. Naturally the Queen poured out to the King her account of the behaviour of his two eldest sons, and, although the King saw them, "taking care that the conversation should be cordial and general," the breach in their relations was widened and became the prime topic of gossip and scandal. At the beginning of March the King refused to see them, on the grounds of avoiding all business and agitation. Consequently they had no opportunity of explaining their share in recent events, although the King had discussed these with some of his Ministers. The Prince therefore sent to the Queen a letter, drafted by Fox, protesting vigorously against this exclusion of himself and the Duke of York:

". . . and thus instead of having the preference, to which we had so just a claim, and which we were induced to expect, we dare not even attempt to counteract the impressions, which our enemies, who have daily access to the King, may have given of the part we took in the late important occurrences. Your Majesty must surely be of opinion that this state of things is neither decent nor just. . . ."

(There was only one "enemy who had daily access to the King," and that was the Queen.) The Queen gave a concert at Windsor to celebrate the King's recovery, to which the Princes were not invited. When they protested, she replied, "We have asked those persons who have voted in Parliament for the King and me."

In the middle of the summer, when the breach in the Royal Family showed signs of widening, Burke drew up a tremendous manifesto, from the Prince to his father, which occupied two hours in reading and set out the propriety of the Prince's behaviour, his affectionate devotion to his father, and the unnatural behaviour of the Queen. It was very wisely decided not to send this, as it left the King no alternative but to separate himself from the Queen or to banish his sons from his presence.[1]

[1] This paper seems to have been in the possession of Sheridan, and was referred to in Moore's *Life of Sheridan*, and it has since been published, the greater part of it in Fitzgerald's *George IV*. Sheridan had, of course, no right to this document, and George IV, at the end of his life, was anxious to recover it—"particularly out of the respect I feel towards my mother's memory."

It is, of course, easy to string together an impressive roll of adjectives in condemnation of the Prince's behaviour during his father's illness. It was selfish, mischievous, disloyal, unfilial, and in many ways intolerable, but some modification of criticism must be allowed in a young man of twenty-six, living on the worst possible terms with his parents, who suddenly sees his magnificent inheritance dangling just in front of him. And, admirable character as Queen Charlotte was, surely her behaviour in putting herself at the head of the Tory Party is no less reprehensible than that of her son in remaining a Whig partisan? But it was not only the Prince's relations with his family that were affected by his behaviour; his popularity with the citizens of London (largely owing to their affection for Pitt) seriously suffered. When he drove to the Opera, shortly after the King's recovery, a mob surrounded his coach, and, forcing open the door, said, "Cry Pitt for ever." The Prince sharply answered, "Damn Pitt; Fox for ever."

In August, perhaps as some antidote to the jeers of the London mob, he journeyed up to the Whig stronghold of York. The Prince was the first Royal personage to stay regularly, and without state, with his friends in the country, which no doubt explains why he was always popular in the Provinces even when he was most unpopular with the London mob. In replying to an address of welcome from the Corporation, he said that he was glad his behaviour during the King's illness "had not been mistaken by the respectable citizens of York for an extravagant lust of power or an unbecoming haste to assume that seat, which to be called to as late as possible is the constant and warmest wish of my heart." But perhaps even the Prince felt slightly uncomfortable when the Lord Mayor's chaplain, the Reverend John Parker, read a poem he had composed, which was surely as indifferent in composition as it was embarrassing in its religious comparisons:

> ". . . The Saviour of the world did sure inspire
> Thy heavn'nly conduct, so much like his own!
> And seldom seen so near an earthly throne!
> The wond'ring world stood gazing, with surprise,
> And Britons, on reflection idolize
> The Pious, tender, filial heart that bled
> O'er dismal woes—pour'd on his Royal Father's head."

He was the guest of Lord Fitzwilliam at Wentworth House, a few miles outside York. A great fête was given in his honour at Wentworth, and thousands of people assembled in the grounds. After dinner the Prince appeared at the portico of the house with a speaking trumpet, through which he shouted, as he raised his glass, "The King's Health," and then, "Happiness to the People." The enthusiasm of the crowd, stimulated by fifty hogsheads of ale, was tremendous.

VII

"I never will marry! My resolution is taken on that subject. I have settled it with Frederick.[1] No I never will marry." The Prince said this to Lord Malmesbury, and he also told Lord Charlemont, whom he had known since boyhood, that he did not wish to marry because he knew that he was of all men the least suited for a forced and blind connexion to which Royal personages were usually condemned. As late as June 1794 it seemed unlikely that he ever would marry, for Mrs. Fitzherbert was still "My dear Love," and he "Ever Thine G. P." And yet two months later, in August 1794, George III was triumphantly writing to Pitt that the Prince or Wales had told him that he had broken off all connexion with Mrs. Fitzherbert and that he was anxious to enter "into a more creditable line of life by marrying."

It is obvious that had the Prince been a free agent he never would have married. He was driven to the altar by two things. The first, of course, was the eternal question of debt. In 1792 he owed £400,000, £127,840 of which was attributable to improvements at Carlton House and probably nearly as much to the Pavilion. It also included what the Lord Chancellor called, "Newmarket and other extravagances more referable to profusion than essential to dignity." It has also to be remembered that, on a large part of this £400,000, he was paying a most exorbitant rate of interest. In 1789 he had actually borrowed £12,500 from Dutch bankers, to be repaid at his father's death, a fact which came to George III's notice, and which he rightly described as "mortifying to my feelings." But although the Lord Chancellor approached the King to extricate his son from debt, George III could only suggest "moderate retrenchment" or marriage. It was

[1] The Duke of York.

not so much the charms of matrimony as the more solid advantages of gold that drew the Prince towards marriage, though whether this was a more "creditable line of life" than living in reputable poverty with Mrs. Fitzherbert must be left to the moralists to decide. The majority of people will feel that the Prince's primary motive for marrying was contemptible and showed the worst side of his character. Equally it is difficult to avoid a feeling of irritation against George III for forcing his son to marry, and for displaying the obstinate, tyrannical folly of middle-aged paternalism.

The other reason for the Prince's marriage was less discreditable. The Duke of York had been married for three years and showed no signs of producing children. The Duke of Clarence was just settling down with Mrs. Jordan to produce that almost interminable family of illegitimate FitzClarences. Prince Edward was living with an elderly French lady in Canada, and there was no sign of a legitimate grandchild to George III. This necessity to provide an heir was undoubtedly an influence in persuading the Prince to marry.

Because the marriage was inspired principally by commercial considerations and was unadorned by any element of romance, it need not necessarily have been a failure. Whatever may be our feelings as to the reasons which prompted the Prince to marry, we cannot doubt that in his choice of persons he showed a foolish indifference which must damp our sympathy for the twenty-five years of misery he was to endure from the woman of his choice. It showed how hopelessly undeveloped one side of the Prince's character was. He had never had to do what was uncongenial, and when he found himself compelled to marry, he had not the slightest conception of making the best of it. He displayed instead a childish petulance which the best of us leave in the nursery and only the most insufferable carry with them through life. He had to marry: he did not care: he would take the first and most obvious frump from the serried, frumpish ranks of the German Princesses. There never seems to have been the least selection or consideration, and those writers who urge that he almost married the future Queen Louise of Prussia might perhaps have discovered that she already had had a husband for twelve months.

One name alone was ever considered. As George III wrote

"His wish is that my niece, the Princess of Brunswick may be the person." Caroline Amelia Elizabeth was the daughter of that Duke of Brunswick who was a famous soldier and led the allied troops against France in the early days of the Revolutionary War, and whose fatal manifesto about putting the rebellious citizens of Paris to the sword precipitated the capture of the Tuileries and the imprisonment of Louis XVI and Marie Antoinette. Her mother was the Princess Augusta of England, a sister of George III. Her brother, Byron's "Brunswick's Chieftain," also a gallant soldier, was killed at Quatre Bras. In 1794 the Princess was twenty-seven: she was short but good-looking with a pile of fair hair. Judging, therefore, by her family and her appearance, the Prince might well have thought that he had made a tolerable choice. Many people, with creditable if sentimental chivalry, and blinded by the pathos of her subsequent career, have preferred to dwell on these somewhat limited charms and to ignore the mental instability which they concealed. Although there was madness on both sides of her family, she could not fairly be called mad, but her mind, always limited, delighted in what was vulgar and trivial.

It was not likely that the Princess's parents, who were over-joyed at this unexpectedly brilliant alliance for their daughter (the Duchess, a typically garrulous Hanoverian, could talk of little else), would have warned their prospective son-in-law of these defects in the Princess's character. But there was one person who had ample opportunity for judging, and who should have informed the Prince. Lord Malmesbury, who, as Sir James Harris, had had a distinguished if unorthodox diplomatic career, was sent to ask for the Princess's hand. Ce rusé Harris, as Mirabeau dubbed him, displayed in this mission those tortuous methods which were at once the charm and strength of the old diplomacy. He spent several weeks in Brunswick, noting down in his diary the many curious conversations he had with the Princess, perhaps the oddest and least seemly of which was his telling her that if she encouraged anyone to make love to her she would be guilty of high treason. Lord Malmesbury's comment is specially signific-ant: "This startled her." Then the Princess did not wash and became offensive from that omission, added to which she wore coarse petticoats, coarse shifts, and thread stockings, none of which were well washed or changed often enough. And few would disagree with Lord Malmesbury that it was "nasty and indelicate" of her, when she had a tooth pulled out, to send it down to him by one of the pages. It will occur to most of his readers that, instead of giggling about it all in his diary, he ought to have informed the English Royal Family. The Prince never forgave him.

The Princess, her mother, and Lord Malmesbury set out for England at the end of December 1794, but, owing to the successes of the French in the Netherlands, they were held up and did not reach the English coast till the beginning of April. Many weeks were spent in Hanover, where the old Duchess, chattering away to the last, and telling dirty stories of George III as a boy, finally left them. Considering what the Duchess was like we can hardly be surprised that Lord Malmesbury had to speak to the Princess about the indelicacy of her language. They arrived at Greenwich on Sunday, April 5th.

There was much contemporary gossip because Lady Jersey, for whom the Prince was known to have an infatuation, was appointed as one of the Princess's ladies-in-waiting, and met her at Greenwich. She immediately criticised the Princess's clothes, which criticism scandalised Malmesbury; though if the Princess was setting out to meet the Prince in her usual dirty linen and coarse petticoats, criticism would seem to have been kindly rather than misplaced.

Queen Charlotte described Lady Jersey as little and bewitching. She certainly was most beautiful, and had that ecclesiastical background (her father was an Irish Bishop) which sets off abandoned loveliness to the best advantage. Her husband was seventeen years older than she, and they were both enthusiasts for amateur theatricals. Lady Jersey was also a skilled harpist, though by character she was perhaps ill-suited to twang this heavenly instrument. Her contemporaries used to apply Othello's words to her:

> This hand is moist, my lady. . . .
> This argues fruitfulness, and liberal heart;—
> Hot, hot, and moist: This hand of yours requires
> A sequester from liberty, fasting, and prayer,
> Much castigation, exercise devout.

It would be tempting to argue that Lady Jersey could not have been the Prince's mistress because she was forty-two, a grandmother, and had known him as a friend for fifteen years. But the caprices of Hanoverian passion make such deductions impossible. The Prince, in spite of that marriage ceremony in the drawing-room, had never remained faithful to Mrs. Fitzherbert, and it is probable that he was actually living with Lady Jersey before he broke with Mrs. Fitzherbert in the summer of 1794. At any rate, by the time of the Princess's arrival, it was common knowledge that Lady Jersey was the Prince's mistress. There could have been no greater mistake on the part of Queen Charlotte who was ultimately responsible for her prospective daughter-in-law's attendants, than allowing Lady Jersey to be appointed one of the Princess's ladies-in-waiting. The Prince no doubt encouraged the appointment, but nothing could be more cruel than allowing his mistress to eclipse his wife, than setting off his wife against the brilliant background of Lady Jersey. The Princess's little gifts of nature—those *épaules impertinentes*, that fine bust, and that magnificent hair—must have looked slightly pitiful beside the conscious attractions of Lady Jersey.

The first meeting between the Prince and his wife can hardly be called propitious. He greeted her politely enough, but turned immediately to Malmesbury and said, "Harris, I am not well; pray get me a glass of brandy." After he had left the room, the Princess turned to Malmesbury and said, "*Je le trouve très gros.*" (The Prince then weighed nearly seventeen stone in his boots.) The Prince went at once and poured out his feelings to the Queen, and later that day he was seen on horseback thundering past Mrs. Fitzherbert's house at Richmond.

That evening the Prince and Princess dined together with the Princess's ladies-in-waiting and the gentlemen of the Court: the Princess's behaviour was embarrassing at dinner, as she threw out vulgar hints about the Prince and Lady Jersey. She had heard that he greatly admired a fine head of hair, so when they were first alone she took out her comb and let her hair flow all over her shoulders. And she said herself, "You should have seen the poor man's face."

They were married in the Chapel Royal on April 8th, 1795. An observer of the ceremony wrote, "He looked like Death and full of confusion, as if he wished to hide himself from the looks of the whole world." It is surely not necessary to search for the cause of this confusion, as some writers have, in the fact that the Prince was drunk, nor, as others have, to find in it a proof of his conscience reminding him of his previous "marriage" to Mrs. Fitzherbert. The cause of his confusion was surely on his left arm. She was observed to be in "the highest spirits . . . smiling and nodding to everyone." We may well believe that he echoed the words of Henry VIII to Thomas Cromwell, on the morning of his marriage to Anne of Cleves, "My lord, if it were not to satisfy the world and my realm I would not do that which I must do this day for none earthly thing." But the wedding passed off conventionally enough, and, like some hideous mockery, the choir, accompanied by stringed instruments and a bassoon, sang:

> "For Blessed are all they that fear the Lord,
> O well is thee! O well is thee! and happy shalt thou be,"

and then burst into the chorus, "Happy, happy, happy, happy, happy shalt thou be." Church bells were pealing throughout the country, and a great crowd cheered them as they drove away. A coach-load of wedding-cake drove out from Carlton House.

The first few days of the honeymoon were spent at Windsor, the Prince and Princess afterwards going to Kempshott House near Basingstoke. They were at Brighton for the summer, and arrived at Carlton House at the beginning of the winter. On January 7th, 1796, the Princess Charlotte was born. It is very difficult to tell exactly what happened during their brief experience of married life, but it is almost certain that after the first night of marriage they never shared the same bed.

The Princess gave a most damning account of the Prince's behaviour during the few months in which they lived together. She said that at Kempshott the only woman, apart from herself, was Lady Jersey, and the men were blackguard companions of the Prince who were constantly drunk and filthy, "sleeping and snoring in boots on the sofa." She also said that the Prince made her smoke a pipe, and that he declared that the child she was expecting was not his. All this, which is quite unsupported, is a typical distortion of the Princess's mind. It may be observed that from what we know of the Prince's friends they were not "snorers in boots on sofas," but something a good deal livelier.

The Prince never recounted, so far as we know, his side of the quarrel, but we do know that he said, "I would rather see toads and vipers crawling over my victuals than sit at the same table with her." We also know that Lord Malmesbury, who was favourable to the Princess, dined with them shortly after their marriage, and described her behaviour as "very light and even improper." We can hardly fail to sympathise with a man, accustomed to the most beautiful and intelligent women in England, who suddenly finds himself tied to someone whose intellectual interest in scandal and impropriety well equipped her for a prominent place in the society of charwomen.

After the Princess Charlotte's birth, they both lived in Carlton House, though they seldom met. Such communication as was necessary was done in writing, and the Prince used to send her stiff little notes headed, "The Yellow Room, Carlton House." In March he left Carlton House for Windsor, and on April 30th, 1796, wrote to her in the following terms:

"MADAM,

. . . Our inclinations are not in our power, nor should either of us be held answerable to the other because nature has not made us suitable to each other. Tranquil and comfortable society is, however, in our power: let our intercourse therefore be restricted to that, and I will distinctly subscribe to the condition which you required through Lady Cholmondeley, that even in the event of any accident happening to my daughter (which I trust Providence in its mercy will avert) I shall not infringe the terms of the restriction by proposing, at any period, a connexion of a more particular nature. I shall now finally close this disagreeable correspondence, trusting that, as we have completely explained ourselves to each other, the rest of our lives will be passed in uninterrupted tranquillity.

I am, Madam,

With great truth, very sincerely yours,

GEORGE P.

Windsor Castle, *April* 30 1796."

To an earlier generation this letter seemed monstrously cynical and wicked, but few would now disagree that it outlined with commendable simplicity the only course which lay open to them. The Princess in her reply said:

"Du reste, je conserve toute la reconaissance possible de ce que je me trouve par votre moyen comme, Princesse de Galles, dans une situation à pouvoir me livrer sans contrainte, à une vertu chere à mon cœur, je vieux dire la bienfaisance. Ce sera pour moi un devoir d'agir de plus par un autre motif sçavoir celui de donner l'exemple de la patience, et de la resignation dans toutes sortes d'epreuves. Rendez moi la justice de me croire, que je ne cesserai jamais de faire des vœux pour votre bonheur, et d'être votre bien devouée,

CAROLINE."[1]

In the autumn of 1796 the Princess went to live at the Old Rectory, Charlton, then a delightful village with a prospect of London in the distance, and within easy reach of Blackheath and of the river at Greenwich. Two years later the King made her Ranger of Blackheath, and she then went to live in the Ranger's house there. The Princess Charlotte lived with her father, but her mother could see her frequently. There seems to have been some kind of attempted reconciliation at the end of 1797. The Princess went to stay at Carlton House, but the negotiations came to nothing when she declared to the Prince, in the presence of Lord Cholmondeley, that she would thereafter "have no further intercourse with me nor would she submit herself to any Rule or Regulation of mine."[2]

Before the Princess came to England she had expressed to Lord Malmesbury her desire to be popular, and if it had not been for this craving she might have been content to display *la bienfaisance* so *chere à mon cœur,* and to have won the respect and sympathy of all her husband's future subjects by showing *l'exemple de la patience et de la resignation.* But at the end of May 1796 she was going night after night, in ostentatious solitude, to the ballet and curtseying to the audience, who cheered themselves hoarse. Those fatal cheers seemed to drive all thought of *la bienfaisance, la patience, et la resignation* from her poor scattered brain, and in their music she was to find, for the next twenty-five years, the stimulus to thwart and ridicule the Prince and, we may hope, the consolation for the loss of her child, her position, and the affection of her husband.

Irresponsible, unattractive, and scatter-brained as the Princess was, she had the gift of attracting popular sympathy, and from her arrival in England dates the beginning of an intensive

[1] This letter has always been given in English. I give the original French in which it was written. The Princess never spoke or wrote English accurately.
[2] Letter from the Prince to George III in the Record Office.

campaign of ridicule and criticism which was directed against the Prince. Apart altogether from the circumstances of his marriage and the position of Lady Jersey, which were wonderful material for romantic scurrility, the discussion in Parliament of his debts, at a time when the country was bearing increased burdens in connexion with the war with France, drew down upon him additional unpopularity.

It was disclosed that since 1792 his debts had increased by over £200,000 to the enormous sum of £630,000, which had all been incurred in seven years. The popular belief, blindly repeated by later writers, that this load of debt was the result of a brilliant, reckless, dissipated, spendthrift life is not borne out by the facts. The greater part of the debt was attributable to the decoration and improvements at Carlton House, and though our forefathers had no doubt every justification for their growls and grumbles, it was not as though their money all disappeared in gurgling streams of wine, or stood in piles and bundles on the green baize gaming-tables, or found its way exclusively to the adornment of fly-by-nights. The greater part of the money was spent in laying the foundations of a collection of furniture and pictures which is a tribute to the almost inspired good taste of the collector and a permanent enrichment of our national life.

The Government made the following proposals: The Prince should have £125,000 a year exclusive of the revenue of the Duchy of Cornwall; £27,000 was to be paid for preparations for the marriage, £25,000 for finishing Carlton House, and a jointure of £50,000 for the Princess. It was proposed that £25,000 should be set aside each year for the liquidation of the debt. It will therefore be seen that, as a result of marrying, the Prince's actual income was increased by some £40,000. There can be no doubt that he felt aggrieved that his debts were not paid off entirely on his marriage, and that most indefatigable but most foolish of orators, the Duke of Clarence, said there was a stipulation that, if the Prince married, his debts should be paid. He added that the Prince was "in the situation of a man who, if he could not get a haunch of venison, would rather take any other haunch than go without." The folly of this speech was that the public fastened on it as a clear proof that the Prince had simply married for money, which, as has been explained, was true, but should have been kept from the public. In the House of Commons supporters of Government voiced the opinions of Cobbett, who had written of those who had to find the money for the Prince's extravagances, "that virtuous, industrious, forgiving and too generous people from whose care and toil he had, for thirty-three years derived the means of living in ease, splendour and even extravagance." Even Whigs like Grey took the opportunity of lecturing the Prince. But, as always, the sanity, the generous outlook, and the contempt for prudish prejudices of Fox stand out refreshingly in the middle of these arid, conventional views. He was critical of the Prince, but quite rightly more critical of the niggardly way in which the King had behaved since the Prince came of age. And when we remember the enormous increase in comfort and splendour which developed in England in the latter half of the eighteenth century there was surely force in his words, "It would ill become me to be very pointed in my disapprobation of imprudent expense in others; but I would say to the City, to Westminster, to the public at large, 'If you complain of increased habits of expense, begin the reformation by reforming Your-selves.' " A point which was reinforced by his saying, "I remember to have heard a lady, as weak and as frail as the frailest of her sex, say not ludicrously but seriously, 'I am conscious of my faults; but I hope I atone for them by my marked disapprobation of such faults in others.' "

It cannot, therefore, be said that the Prince's position was materially improved by marriage. He had exchanged the soothing charms of Mrs. Fitzherbert for the constant irritation of a vulgar, slightly demented Princess. He was saddled with a considerable load of debt and that ageing grandmother, Lady Jersey. Even in Brighton, where he was almost worshipped, his popularity suffered after his marriage, and it was quite impossible after he had separated from the Princess for him to live there with Lady Jersey. They accordingly spent the autumn of 1796 together at Bognor, which was just being developed by a rich City merchant called Sir R. Hotham, who was bitterly disappointed that the residents would not change the town's name to Hothampton. The Prince was delighted with Bognor, and stayed there for several weeks. Lady Jersey for some unaccountable reason—possibly the recollec-tion of that episcopal father—always referred to him as the Primate, and she wrote to a friend at the beginning of October that the Primate "is going to fly round Dorsetshire make a nest for me and my young ones and perch in London." The "nest" which the Prince selected was Crichel House in Dorset, a vast, white, classical house, where they passed the winter.

Although Lady Jersey was triumphantly writing that "the conduct of the Primate as usual is perfect," it was abundantly clear to everyone except herself that he was rapidly tiring of her. They finally parted in 1798, the Prince on his side vowing that he would never withdraw his protection from her and her family. Lady Jersey was always reluctant to take this as final, and two years later, at the Duchess of Devonshire's breakfast at Chiswick, where the Prince was a guest dressed *en polisson* in a brown suit, round hat, and brown wig, she was observed "coasting round the Prince," and it was noticed that he was annoyed and eyed her askance.

The Prince, now that his marriage had completely collapsed, was desperately anxious to be reunited to Mrs. Fitzherbert. In the winter of 1795, six months after his marriage to Princess Caroline, he had drafted a will in which he described Mrs. Fitzherbert as his lawful wife, and in which he made considerable bequests to her. In 1799 he sent her a copy of this will, and wrote in the accompanying letter, "How I have ever loved and adored you God only knows, and now I do *now* he also knows . . ." And, most significant of all, he sent her a painting of his right eye in a locket on which was engraved "*Rejoindre ou Mourir.*" Having obtained permission from the Pope, Mrs. Fitzherbert consented to return to him. At the beginning of 1800 they were seen together at the Opera in a box high up, while the Princess of Wales was present in another part of the house. Whether or no we follow the Pope's opinion in regarding Mrs. Fitzherbert as the canonical wife of the Prince, there can be no doubt, as was said at the time, that by appearance and character she was admirably suited to be his wife, while the Princess had the shallow mind and flighty temperament customarily associated with a mistress. There could equally be no doubt that Mrs. Fitzherbert was far better qualified than the Princess to make the Prince happy, and, as she herself said, the years that followed their reconciliation were the happiest of her connexion with him. But with the opening of the new century public affairs and political complications combined to disturb the Prince's tranquillity.

VIII

In the autumn of 1800 Pitt and his Cabinet colleagues were discussing, unknown to the King, the advisability of making political concessions to the Irish Catholics. The King was privately informed of what was going on, and was also privately advised that he could not, consistently with his Coronation Oath, agree to any such measure. At the beginning of 1801 the King wrote to Pitt urging that neither of them should allude to the subject again. Pitt offered his resignation. The King read the Coronation Oath to his wife and daughters, adding, "If I violate it I am no longer sovereign of this country, but it falls to the House of Savoy."[1] A few days later he went completely out of his mind. All the animosities and political intrigues of 1788 were once again set in motion, but after a few weeks the King recovered, dismissed Pitt, and accepted that monument of incompetence, Addington, as the Prime Minister. The Prince said to Lady Bessborough, one of his most intimate friends, "As Heaven's my witness I love my Father to my heart, and never think of his sufferings without tears," and Lady Bessborough assures us that as he spoke the tears ran down his cheeks. But, just as in 1788, he was refused all admission to his parents, and he was left to feel that if his father continued mad, his rights to the Regency would be usurped by Addington. Although he had every inducement to act with indiscretion during these weeks of his father's illness, his behaviour gave rise to no particular criticism.

However, when hostilities between England and France broke out again after the Peace of Amiens in 1803, he was able to give expression to his pent-up feelings in a public dispute with his father and Addington. There was in that year great public anxiety at Napoleon's threatened invasion of England. As a youth the Prince had been appointed a colonel in the Army, and later was made colonel of the 10th Light Dragoons. He always took a great interest in this regiment, was careful that smart, good-looking young officers should be commissioned in it—for example, Beau Brummell, to whom he gave a commission as an

---

[1] The House of Savoy was descended from Charles I's youngest daughter, the Duchess of Orleans. But James II's grandson, the Cardinal of York, was still alive, and had a better title than the House of Savoy.

Eton boy—and on occasions he went into camp with them. But no other Army appointment nor promotion had come his way, although one of his younger brothers was a Field Marshal and three of his younger brothers were Lieutenant-Generals. It must not be assumed that this lack of promotion was a further mark of the King's dislike for his eldest son; it was a settled point in Hanoverian family policy that the heir to the throne should not be given high military or naval rank. But when the invasion scare developed in 1803, and a scourge of nervous patriotism swept across the country leaving in its train a number of awkward squads busily drilling, the Prince was undoubtedly placed in an invidious position. He therefore applied for a military command, hoping, in his own words, that this might "excite the loyal energies of the nation."

No notice was taken of his appeal, and he accordingly wrote to Addington, in July 1803, pointing out the obloquy which must attach itself to him if he was thought by his countrymen to be indifferent to their danger. The King replied, through Addington, that no further mention should be made to him of the subject. On August 2nd the question was raised by the Prince's friends in Parliament; the strangers' gallery was cleared, but no satisfactory answer was forthcoming from Ministers. On August 6th the Prince wrote direct to the King, "I ask to be allowed to display the best energies of my character; to shed the last drop of my blood in support of your Majesty's person, crown and dignity." The King replied applauding his son's zeal and spirit, but hoping that he would hear nothing further of the subject. The Prince replied to this with a very strong letter in which he referred to his wounded mind, and said, "My next brother, the Duke of York, commands the army; the younger branches of my family are either Generals or Lieutenant-Generals; and I, who am Prince of Wales, am to remain Colonel of Dragoons. There is something so humiliating in the contrast, that those who are at a distance would either doubt the reality, or suppose that to be my fault which is only my misfortune." It is known that these letters were written for the Prince by Sir Philip Francis, who is generally believed to have been the author of the Junius letters, and they were undoubtedly sparkling and vigorous in composition. The letters which the Prince also addressed to his brother, the Commander-in-Chief, on this subject were composed by himself, and were chiefly remarkable for the way in which the most offensive sentences invariably began "my dearest brother."

There was a certain amount of popular sympathy for the Prince, and adroit references appeared in the broadsheets to the Black Prince and Crecy and Poictiers, and one of these sheets ended up with the words, "Drive the devoted armies of Bonaparte to Hell and Perdition. ICH DIEN." But George III remained adamant, and the Prince's only consolation was, as he told Fox, that "the King desired me to be on his right hand whenever he took the field." It is difficult to stifle a regret that Napoleon did not succeed in invading England to be met by this odd, but gallant, couple prancing at the head of the English levies.

Rather unwisely the Prince published the whole of the correspondence, which infuriated his father, who referred to him as "the publisher of *my* letters." For nearly a year father and son did not meet, and when the King and Queen gave a Drawing-Room the Prince gave out that he was too ill to attend, but he was observed driving ostentatiously throught the streets of London. This breach was particularly inopportune because throughout 1804 the King, through the Lord Chancellor, was engaged in a most delicate negotiation with his son. The Princess Charlotte, an attractive, high-spirited child, was then eight years old, and it was essential that her education should be taken properly in hand. Up till now she had lived at Carlton House, or Warwick House which adjoined it, with a governess, and had been allowed to go to Blackheath to see her mother. There is no doubt that the Prince was fond of his daughter, but like his generation, and indeed many succeeding generations, he was a thoroughly selfish father, who would have never dreamed of inconveniencing himself for his children. He was away at Brighton, or on visits to his friends, for a great part of the year, and the Princess was left to the melancholy seclusion of Warwick House, which was hardly affected · by even the brightest of governesses.

The King was devoted to children, and, as the Princess Charlotte was his only grandchild, he was anxious to see as much of her as possible. Her education was, of course, of enormous importance to the country, and the King proposed that she should come and live at Windsor and that he and the Queen should be responsible for her education. But, as the negotiations dragged on, it became clear that one of the King's objects was that the child should see very much more of her mother. In November the King and the Prince met for the first time since their squabble over the Prince's military command, and the following letter from the King to the Princess of Wales shows what was at the back of his mind:

"Windsor Castle,
November 13th 1804.

MY DEAREST DAUGHTER-IN-LAW AND NIECE,

Yesterday I and the rest of my family had an interview with the Prince of Wales at Kew, care was taken on all sides to avoid all subjects of altercation or explanation, consequently the conversation was neither instructive nor entertaining, but it leaves the Prince of Wales in a situation to show whether His desire to return to His family is only verbal or real, which time alone can show; I am not idle in my endeavour to make enquiries that may enable me to communicate some plan for the advantage of the dear child you and me with so much reason must interest ourselves [in], and its effecting my having the happiness of living more with you is no small incentive to my forming some ideas on the subject, but you [can] depend on their being not decided upon without your thorough and cordial concurrence for your authority as mother it is my object to support. Believe me at all times my dearest Daughter-in-law and Niece, your most affectionate Father-in-law and Uncle

GEORGE R."

As soon as the Prince realised that one of the King's objects was to allow the Princess an increased influence over the child, he threatened to break off the negotiations. The matter was not finally settled till the beginning of 1805, when it was arranged that the Princess Charlotte should live with her father when he was in London, but that she should go to her grandparents when he was away.

The Prince was hardly to be blamed for thinking that his wife would be a deplorable influence on his daughter. Ever since they had separated, in 1796, there had been disgusting stories about the Princess's behaviour, and in 1802 there had been a strong rumour that she had given birth to a child. At the end of 1805, Sir John and Lady Douglas, a somewhat vulgar knight and his wife, who had been close friends of the Princess, made a statement to the Duke of Sussex detailing the most scandalous behaviour on the part of the Princess, culminating in the birth of a child. The Duke told the Prince. It was impossible for the Prince not to take some official notice of this statement, because there was nothing to prevent the Douglasses, who were furious with the Princess, from spreading their story, which might well have prejudiced the rights of the Prince's daughter to the throne.[1] He was able to persuade the King to appoint four members of the Ministry of All the Talents, which had succeeded Pitt's Government at the beginning of 1806, to enquire into the charges. This was known as the Delicate Investigation.

The Commissioners discovered that in the autumn of 1802 she had taken into her house, and in fact, if not legally, adopted the infant child of a woman who happened to come to the door to ask the Princess's help to find work for her husband. The child's name was William Austin, and his father had gained a little precarious employment by turning the mangle for the laundress who washed the Prince or Wales's linen. Considering how, even in those days, people delighted to invent and spread scandals about the Royal Family, it was in itself a foolish and dangerous action for someone in the Princess's position. Lady Douglas swore that the Princess had constantly told her that she was pregnant and revelled in describing her symptoms.

It has always been usual to discredit Lady Douglas's evidence as being merely the imagination of a jealous mind. But it seems more than probable, from what we know of the Princess's character, that she got some kind of vicarious pleasure from feigning pregnancy or that the child was really hers, and that the bulk of Lady Douglas's evidence, which amounted to a catalogue of the number of times that the Princess had hinted, or told her outright, that she was pregnant, was not necessarily untrue. It is therefore obvious that the Prince and the members of the Government had fairly solid grounds for enquiring into the origin of this infant. There was, however, no evidence to prove to the satisfaction of the Commissioners that he was not the child of Mr. and Mrs. Austin.

It is unfortunately necessary that a life of George IV must contain some account of those vagaries which passed for romance

[1] Lady Douglas alleged that the Princess had said that she would pretend that the Prince was the father of the child.

in his wife's mind, and which, in turn, delighted, shocked, and bored English people at the beginning of the nineteenth century. Her champions at the time, and those who subsequently, masquerading as historians, espoused her cause, never hesitated to regard the Delicate Investigation as a triumph for her and even a certificate of morality. But no one in possession of all the relevant facts could fail to come to a totally different decision. For the labours of the Delicate Investigation were not confined to the parentage of William Austin. A variety of witnesses testified to the Princess's general misbehaviour. The evidence of some of these witnesses, who might be suspected of an ulterior motive, should, in fairness to the Princess, be discounted. But there are four witnesses who, in the words of the Commissioners to the King, "cannot, in our judgment, be suspected of any unfavourable bias, and whose veracity, in this respect, we have seen no ground to question." These witnesses all agreed in their accounts of her behaviour with Sir Sidney Smith, the defender of Acre, Captain, afterwards Rear-Admiral, Manby, and Mr. Lawrence, the portrait painter,[1] which, in the words of the Commissioners, necessarily gave occasion "to very unfavourable interpretations." It is not necessary to believe that the Princess's behaviour with these distinguished gentlemen was criminal; it is perhaps kinder and more accurate to believe the words of a contemporary, "The Princess is of that lively vivacity that she makes herself familiar with gentlemen." In any woman her behaviour would have given rise to scandal, but for someone in her position it was abandoned folly.

After the report of the Commissioners, the King wrote to the Princess, ". . . there have been circumstances of conduct on the part of the Princess which His Majesty never could regard but with serious concern." The words "and disapprobation" were added, but rather surprisingly struck out by the King's command. It was also clear that the King, acting on strong representations from the Prince, was going to refuse to receive the Princess at Court. The reprimand by the King and his refusal to receive her at Court were serious blunders. It was most unjust that the Princess, whatever she had done, should have been condemned and punished without being heard in her own defence: it was contrary to every principle of English law.

[1] This publicity for a time rather checked the number of Lawrence's female sitters.

The Princess was fortunate throughout this period in having the advice of one of her neighbours at Charlton, Mr. Perceval, the Tory leader. It was he who drafted her exceedingly shrewd replies to the King, threatened to publish, and actually had printed, the whole of the evidence (known as "The Book"), and made it a condition of the Tories taking office in 1807 that the King should receive the Princess. Mr. Perceval had those stolid virtues and limited capabilities which have always won the admiration of the Tory Party, and his generous heart and pinchbeck intelligence could hardly have been better shown than by his remark, after the Princess had driven him up to London from Charlton, "To the Tower or the scaffold in such a cause."

One result of the Delicate Investigation was that the Princess lost her best friend in England and her only friend in the Royal Family, the King. There can be no doubt that as the King had read out to him, because by this time he was completely blind, the report of the Commissioners and extracts from the evidence, his earlier sympathy for the Princess must have completely vanished. Indeed he told the Prince that she was "an infamous woman" and, what he most hated in the world, "a female politician," and that he would forbid the Queen and his daughters to have any intercourse with her except on official occasions. As this was told to Croker by the Prince, whose powers of invention were always liable to run away with the truth, it should be rather tentatively accepted; though the King's general attitude to the Princess is borne out by the Queen, who said "he declared that . . . The Princess could not be received as an Intimate in his Family and no nearer intercourse could he admit than outward marks of Civility." Partisans of the Princess appear to have overlooked the fact that she lost the King's protection not through his madness in 1811, as they always suggest, but through her own folly at a much earlier period. The King, in fact, said that if "it had been one attachment, and even a child, he would have screened her if he could have done it with safety to the Crown but that there seemed so much Levity and profligacy that she was not worth the screening."

As rumours of an enquiry into the Princess's behaviour began to spread, the Prince's unpopularity rapidly increased. It was inevitable for the public to take the superficial view that the Prince was seeking to persecute his wife for a breach of the marriage vow while expecting to be allowed to break it himself regularly and publicly. If they had known that he had written, as he had, to George III to say that he could not read of his wife's conduct "without having as an Individual all the Feeling of a Father, a Husband and a Man of Honour wounded," they must have felt that such high-falutin language was ludicrous from him. People at the time failed to see that it was essential for him, in view of all the gossip and chatter, to take some steps to preserve the rights to the throne of the Princess Charlotte, because, as has been said, one of the most serious aspects of the evidence was the Princess's suggestion to Lady Douglas that she would pretend that the Prince was the father of the child. Although William Austin died in a lunatic asylum, that need not necessarily have prevented him from proving a formidable, nineteenth-century Perkin Warbeck. Indeed one can imagine ingenious persons pointing to his unfortunate detention as conclusive proof that the blood of George III and the House of Brunswick ran tumultuously in his veins.

IX

The year 1807 saw the beginning of that long period of ridicule and lampooning which the Prince was to endure until his wife's death, and, by a strange coincidence, it saw the beginning of his unpopularity with the Whigs which was to last all his life and to spit out from many dusty nineteenth-century memoirs after he was dead. The Prince's politics might fairly be summed up in the phrase, "faithfulness to Fox." He could not be called a Whig, because he did not believe in any of the things for which the Whigs stood at the beginning of the nineteenth century—peace with France, Parliamentary reform, Catholic emancipation, or even emancipation of the slaves. But he would have been prepared to support any of them if Fox had sponsored them as he did in the case of the French Revolution, of which he cannot possibly have approved: Fox did approve, and so we find the Prince bravely describing Burke's *Reflections on the French Revolution* as a "farrago of nonsense." He said himself that ever since he had entered politics he had looked up to no one but Fox. When, therefore, Fox came into office as Foreign Secretary and Leader in the House of Commons in Lord Grenville's Government (known as the Ministry of All the Talents) at the beginning of 1806, the

Prince at once became a political figure of the first importance. Within a very few weeks of the formation of the Government Fox was in close consultation with the Prince on the Catholic question. The Prince explained that he was against any concessions, which was not really a very important pronouncement, but he seems to have persuaded Fox that, as the agitation of the question might bring on the King's madness and as it was useless to look for any consent from the King to a measure of Catholic relief, it would be advisable to leave the Catholic question alone during the King's lifetime. As the mention of concessions to the Roman Catholics always roused the King to a perfect frenzy, it is difficult to see what other course was open to the Ministers, as it was far better for them to concentrate on peace and other reforms rather than on one which was temporarily impossible.

But the Government had only a few months to get accustomed to the pleasures of office when the news came that Fox was dying of dropsy:

And many thousands now are sad—
Wait the fulfilment of their fear;
For he must die who is their stay,
Their glory disappear.[1]

Certainly of the "many thousands" no one's sadness was deeper and more genuine than the Prince's. The news of Fox's death came when the Prince was staying in Yorkshire with Lord Fitzwilliam, and for some time he was seriously unwell, losing his appetite and even his taste for wine. To Lady Elizabeth Foster, who was shortly to marry the Duke of Devonshire, he wrote: "It is quite impossible to describe to you all I have gone through of late: such a loss and such a calamity are almost beyond all sufferance: at least it is so to me." He wrote to Grey, who was Fox's natural successor in the Whig leadership, urging that Fox's nephew (Lord Holland) should be appointed Foreign Secretary and ending:

"the regard and admiration with which I have viewed your talents, and the friendship which has always subsisted between us, decide my opinion upon the propriety and wisdom of those duties which rested upon that great and for-ever-to-be-lamented man devolving upon you. It remains only for me to assure you how truly happy I shall be, and what comfort it

[1] Wordsworth.

will afford me, to communicate in the fullest confidence with you, and by every means in my power, to aid and strengthen the views and wishes of the Government.

I am, ever,

Very affectionately yours,

GEORGE P."

He wrote again to Grey on his way south, at Doncaster, on learning that Fox's friends were contemplating resignation, to urge them against such action, and in the course of the letter said, "My dear friend, this is a strange world we live in, and nothing can be done in it without a little temper and a little policy. We must do the best we can, and because we can not have everything our own way, we must not, therefore, instantly throw up the whole game, and by that means become the tool of others."

At the beginning of October, when he had returned to London for Fox's funeral, a ceremony which the King finally refused to allow him to attend, he wrote to Lord Grenville asking him to call and discuss many things in connexion with the Government. He wrote again to Lord Grenville, at the end of October, to say, "If upon any occasion, public or private, you wish me in town, I will readily obey your summons." But the Prince made it perfectly clear both to Lord Holland, who was Lord Privy Seal, and to Lord Grenville that, although he wished the Ministry well he was anxious to retire from the prominent place he had occupied in the councils of the party during Fox's life. But had those Whig noblemen, Lord Grey and Lord Grenville, gone out of their way to consult the Prince, to invite him to London, or to reward some of his friends with minor office, they might have kept him as an ally, though they had lost him as a colleague. Even Lord Holland —a pattern of the zealous party man—laments the impolicy of his leaders' action, and admits that the Prince had considerable grounds for grievance. Lord Moira, a man of honourable character and considerable talents, who was one of the Prince's closest friends and held unimportant Cabinet rank in the Government,[1] said that the Prince "was treated with as continued and mortifying a slight as could have been exhibited towards the most insignificant runner of a party." But it was perhaps most significant of all that

[1] He was subsequently Commander-in-Chief in India, and was created Marquess of Hastings.

Creevey thought that "they were very deficient in ordinary civility to him considering how much it was his due."

At the beginning of 1807 the Ministry fell, in circumstances which hardly redounded to the credit of their intelligence, and which have been generally condemned by historians. Without obtaining the King's consent, they agreed to bring in a measure allowing Roman Catholics to hold rank in the English Army. The King refused to accept the measure, and demanded that his Ministers would sign a declaration never to recommend concessions to the Roman Catholics during his lifetime. They refused, and were dismissed. Their folly was patent, and it was increased by their neglect to consult the Prince, who could have told them of his father's sentiments, and would have reminded them of what had been settled on that issue when Fox took office.

After the Ministry had fallen, the Prince wrote to Lord Moira, and, referring to the cause of the Ministry's fall, he said, "Neither was my advice asked when it might have been of use in the commencement of the discussion, nor my interposition desired when it might possibly have prevented ultimate mischief. Ministers quitting office on this ground of dispute with the King, it was not possible for me to appear as the Advocate and Defender of the ground which they had taken; I decided to resume my original purpose sincerely professed in my own Mind upon the Death of poor Fox *To cease to be a party man*, although in alliance with him it had been the pride of my life to avow myself to be so, and to retire from taking any active line whatever at any rate for the present in political affairs."

X

There was another reason which was drawing him away from his old political friends. In 1805 he formed an intimate friendship with one of the most influential Tory families in the country— the Marquess and Marchioness of Hertford.

He was brought into touch with them through his efforts to prevent Mrs. Fitzherbert's adopted daughter from being taken away from her. Mrs. Fitzherbert had been very close friends with Lord and Lady Hugh Seymour, brother and sister-in-law of Lord Hertford, who were obliged to be much out of England, the former in pursuit of a naval career, the latter as the result of ill health. In 1798 their youngest child Mary had been born, and before leaving England Lady Hugh left the child with Mrs. Fitzherbert. Three years later Lord and Lady Hugh both died. No guardian was appointed for the youngest daughter, as Lord Hugh's will had been made before her birth. Lord Hugh's executors objected to Mrs. Fitzherbert taking charge of the child, because of her religion, and brought an action in the Chancery Division for the appointment of other guardians, which they won. Mrs. Fitzherbert appealed to the Lord Chancellor, and lost, and was going to appeal to the House of Lords when Lord Hertford announced that as the head of the family he would himself undertake the duties of guardian to the child. He then appointed Mrs. Fitzherbert to act for him.

The Prince, who was devoted to "Minnie" Seymour, had been very active in persuading Lord Hertford to take this step, but, as was remarked at the time, if Mrs. Fitzherbert had gained her child she had lost her husband. The Prince had become fatally enamoured of Lady Hertford.

Lady Hertford was the daughter and co-heiress of the last Lord Irvine, and had married the second Marquess of Hertford in 1776. She was very wealthy, and brought in her dowry the magnificent mansion of Temple Newsam, outside Leeds.[1] She was a very intelligent woman, frigid and dignified, and possessed of two seemingly indisputable qualifications for capturing the Prince's heart; she was in the middle forties, and she was a grand-mother. In spite of her age she was an extraordinarily handsome woman, and it was rather cruelly said of her when she was sixty and still in prime favouritism with the Prince:

> All gentle and juvenile, curly and gay
> In the manner of Ackermann's Dresses for May.

The second Marquess of Hertford was one of the most influential peers of the early nineteenth century, with a creditable record of service to the State. The joint income of himself and his wife was at least £150,000 a year, drawn largely from landed estates in Ireland, Yorkshire, Warwickshire, and Suffolk. They lived chiefly at Hertford House in Manchester Square, just behind Oxford Street, at Sudbourne in Suffolk, and at Ragley in Warwickshire. Their only son, Lord Yarmouth, described by

[1] As she had only one son, the third Marquess of Hertford, Temple Newsam passed under the entail, to one of her sisters.

Peel as "a gentleman and not an everyday one," was also a close friend of the Prince's. He was afterwards the third Marquess, and was pilloried by Thackeray as the Marquess of Steyne, and by Disraeli as the Marquess of Monmouth. Certainly his closing days, which were spent in the company of a travelling troupe of prostitutes, himself inarticulate from a paralysed tongue, were hardly the kind of deathbed scenes to which Victorian England was accustomed. But whatever may have been the faults of the third Marquess, in part explained by the insanity which ran in his family, the whole country is under a debt of gratitude to him and his father for forming the magnificent collection of picture now known as the Wallace Collection. One of the finest pictures in this collection is that of Mrs. "Perdita" Robinson, by Reynolds, which was given by the Prince to the second Marquess of Hertford. It is fitting that the Prince's portrait should figure prominently on the walls of the Wallace Collection, since his friendship did much to encourage the collecting zeal of the second and third Marquesses.

There is no doubt at all that it was this common interest in pictures and *objets d'art* in general which bound the Prince to the Hertford family quite as much as his affection for Lady Hertford, which by well-informed contemporaries was always thought to have been based more on admiration than physical passion.

But whatever may have been the precise nature of the spell by which Lady Hertford enthralled the Prince, there can be no two opinions as to his treatment of Mrs. Fitzherbert, "of one," in her own words, "whose life has been dedicated to you, and whose affection for you none can surpass." It was the most discreditable action of his life, made worse by his expecting Mrs. Fitzherbert to act as a "scandal-blanket" and to attend all the parties which he gave for Lady Hertford. It would at least have been understandable if his preference for Lady Hertford had been caused by a sudden burst of romantic passion, but it was simply the outcome of a disagreeable and capricious taste for elderly women.

As Peter Pindar wrote of him

> *The foremost of the royal brood,*
> *Who broke his shell and cried for food;*
> *Turn'd out a cock of manners rare,*
> *A fav'rite with the feather'd fair. . . .*

But though his love was sought by all,
Game, dunghill, bantam, squab and tall,
Among the whole, not one in ten
Could please him like a tough old Hen.

How shallow his passionate feelings for Lady Hertford must have been is shown by his escapade with Lady Bessborough in 1809, whom he had known for thirty years (and who was a grandmother). He went to call on her and made the most violent love to her, offering to break with Mrs. Fitzherbert and Lady Hertford, and to make her his sole confidante and adviser, and that Mr. Canning, to whom she was devoted, should be Prime Minister. Each time the Prince mentioned the distinguished statesman's name he attempted some liberty so that she could scarcely help laughing at the sight of this "immense, grotesque figure flouncing about half on the couch, half on the ground." When his suit, or perhaps suggestions, were rejected, he passed naturally on to a political discussion with Lady Bessborough lasting for three hours.

His breach with Mrs. Fitzherbert is rendered the more unaccountable because, on her own admission, the years just before he became enamoured of Lady Hertford were the happiest of their connexion. The most probable, though hardly the most creditable, explanation is that he never intended a complete breach with Mrs. Fitzherbert, but expected her to be one of several mistresses: it is certain that it was she, and not the Prince, who insisted on a definite separation. The Prince was fond of saying of his ancestors and predecessors who sat on the throne of England that Charles II was the only one of them who could be lived with as a gentleman, but he can hardly have expected that a woman of Mrs. Fitzherbert's character was suited to play the rôle of Lady Castlemaine or Nell Gwynn.

Mrs. Fitzherbert, though she was always devoted to him, took the parting philosophically enough, and used to show her friends an advertisement which had reached her puffing up some lemonade powder, and saying that it was constantly used by Lady Hertford. At the end of the Regency they attended the same party, and, although the Prince spoke very cordially to "Minnie" Seymour, he and Mrs. Fitzherbert showed not the slightest signs of recognition. The Prince regularly corresponded with "Minnie" Seymour, and always sent a message to "my dear old friend, Mrs.

Fitzherbert," or to "dearest Mrs. Fitzherbert," and when he became King he allowed her an additional £4,000[1] a year to the £6,000 which had been settled on her in 1794.

Odd and discreditable as the Prince's treatment of Mrs. Fitzherbert undoubtedly was, it is made even odder by the fact that in other aspects of his life he showed every sign of settling down and of forming regular habits. His parties at Carlton House became much more decorous, and gained their character and enjoyment from the grace and wit of the host. His mimicry of celebrated characters of the day—for instance, the actor Kemble, Dr. Parr (the "Whig Dr. Johnson"), or Mr. Basilico, Fox's black servant—was brilliant, and kept the table in roars of laughter. He said on one occasion, of his imitation of a foul-mouthed old lawyer, "My brother will tell you that my Lord Chancellor Thurlow is very fine though I hardly like to swear up to the mark." But what impressed and gratified his guests was the trouble he took to put each one at his ease, and the facility with which he passed to whatever subject might interest the person to whom he was talking at the moment. Dr. Burney, who was one of the most celebrated musicians of his day, met him at dinner, and wrote an enthusiastic description of him to Fanny Burney. "I was astonished to find him amidst such constant dissipation possessed of so much learning, wit, knowledge of books in general, discrimination of character, as well as original humour. He quoted Homer in Greek to my son . . . and as to music he is an excellent critic. . . . H.R.H. took me aside and talked exclusively about music near half an hour, and as long with your brother concerning Greek Literature." And Dr. Burney's final judgment would surely have pleased the Prince more than anything, "He may with truth be said to have as much wit as Charles II with much more learning."

His taste and knowledge of art are well known and are to be seen to-day in the Royal collection of pictures, but he was always anxious that the general public should be given some opportunity of seeing and appreciating good pictures. He generally attended the Royal Academy dinner, and was always a critical visitor at their exhibition. In 1804 he talked to the artist Farington about

[1] This fact is slurred over by partisans of Mrs. Fitzherbert. Her rather ungracious acceptance of it is described in *Barnard Letters*, edited by Anthony Powell (1928).

his anxiety to advance art in England, and expressed the opinion that there ought long before to have been a gallery for the exhibition of modern artists and also of the works of the old masters. He spoke of the pleasure he derived from works of art, characteristically adding that it was an advantage he had over his brothers, who had no feeling for it.

Like many distinguished patrons of the art of music, the Prince was anxious to show that his interest in it was not purely passive, and he was fond of displaying his vigorous, if not particularly distinguished, bass voice. There was one occasion at the Pavilion when he was singing a trio from *Azioli* with Sir Philip Francis's son and another man, and was thundering out, *Ritorneremo a Clori, al tramontar del dî*, with his heated face rather close to young Mr. Francis, who was overcome with the comicality of the performance and burst into a roar of laughter. Instead of being annoyed, the Prince showed signs of laughing himself, and just said, "Come, come, Philip."

The Prince was one of those easy-going personalities who shone and sparkled, all graciousness and merriment, in the glare of approving publicity. At Brighton, surrounded by a host of admirers, he strutted with all the best side of his nature displayed to the world. We see him at his birthday celebrations, in a tight but resplendent uniform as Colonel of the 10th Hussars (formerly Light Dragoons), jogging out on horseback to a review on the Downs, while the bands play God Save the King, and broadsides are fired from the ships in the distance sailing to a mimic encounter. In the afternoon he takes his daughter—who has driven over from Worthing, wearing a white muslin dress and a gipsy hat, trimmed with roses—and shows her all over the Pavilion. In the evening the townspeople celebrate the occasion with a roast ox, and the Prince is loudly cheered as he drives out to a ball. At Brighton he felt himself a King and the good people, dependent on him for their prosperity, excused much that was flamboyant and disagreeable in his character. As he approached the end of his long apprenticeship as Prince of Wales, to enter a kingdom which was far wider than Brighton and whose people felt that he was dependent on them for the indulgence of all his whims and extravagances, it became doubtful whether the same excuses for him would be made. Yet no one longed more for popularity than the Prince: no one's character was less fitted to endure unpopularity.

Book II

REGENT

I

However lustily loyal Englishmen might sing that their ancient, blind sovereign should be "happy and glorious," there were three events in 1809 which made those words something of a mockery. The King's favourite son, the Duke of York, had been compelled to resign from the command of the Army owing to the public exposure of the activities of one of his mistresses, Mrs. Clarke, in trafficking in military titles. The second event was the Walcheren Expedition, which had set out in brilliant weather in July, and which returned in December, having lost thousands of men in the malarial swamps at the mouth of the Scheldt and having only succeeded in destroying Flushing. The third event was the alarming illness of the King's youngest daughter, the Princess Amelia, who was dying of consumption. She finally died in November 1810, sending from her deathbed a message to her father to "remember me." Many writers have described the result of this message on the King's mind, with an economy of words, but a wealth of effect, by saying "reason fled." Reason did no such thing; at the very most it wavered. He arranged all the details of his daughter's funeral, and it was not until some days afterwards, when he was out riding, that the well-known symptoms of ceaseless chatter alarmed his attendants. Shortly afterwards he began to suffer from delusions, the least remarkable of which was that he was only Elector of Hanover, and the most embarrassing of which was that all marriages were dissolved. It was wisely decided that he must be relieved of all attention to business: bulletins were issued: and at the beginning of December the question of a Regency was once more agitating political parties.

Perceval, who had succeeded Portland as Prime Minister of the Tory Government, decided that the same restrictions should be imposed on the Regent as were suggested in 1788—namely, that he should not be able to create peers, that the Queen and a council should be responsible for the care of the King, and that the King's property should be held by trustees. These limitations on the Regent's power were only to last for a year. Whatever may have been the rights and wrongs of an absolute or limited Regency from a constitutional point of view, Perceval was no doubt influenced in his decision by the physicians, who assured him that the King would certainly recover. The Prince no doubt felt that the limitations were humiliating for a man of almost fifty who had quite as strong an interest as his father in maintaining the prestige of the crown. He summoned all the male members of the Royal Family to Carlton House, and they signed a letter of protest to Perceval against measures contrary to "the principles which seated our family upon the throne of these realms." The Regency Bill finally passed both Houses of Parliament by small majorities (the Whig Opposition voting against the limitations), and in February 1811 the Prince became Regent.

From the moment that the King's indisposition had been announced, Whig mouths had begun to water at the prospect of the sweets of office. Whig noblemen converged on London. Draft Cabinets were drawn up. Mr. Brougham announced that he would not accept the Foreign Office, to which no one but himself had ever felt that he had the least claim: Mr. Whitbread announced that he would accept it, and would conclude a treaty of peace with Napoleon. Faithful, eager, small-minded party men wheedled and intrigued for office. Sedate Whig peers who had last kissed hands in the 1780's polished up their decorous phrases about "distaste for office," and "my only anxiety is to conduct myself honourably to my friends in the evening of my days." Not even a hint, in January, that the Prince was not wholly loyal to Grey and Grenville checked these confident, portentous preparations.

At the beginning of January the Prince sent for Lord Grenville and Lord Grey, asking them to draft a reply from him to an Address from the Houses of Parliament preparatory to the passing of the Regency Bill. Both these Whig leaders had been somewhat lukewarm in their attacks on the proposed limitations, and their reply was not sufficiently vigorous for the Prince. He accordingly sent a reply which had been drafted for him by Sheridan and Lord Moira. The Whig lords then drew up a solemn memorial of protest against "their humble endeavours" being submitted to

the judgment of "another person." These lords acted from the
moment the Regency was first mooted with such sublime confidence in their own indispensability and such frigid pomposity
as to antagonise the Prince and to damage their prospects of office.
Sheridan published a little squib on them, the stinging truth of
which hardly tended to close the breach between the Prince and
his advisers:

> In all humility we crave
> Our Regent may become our slave,
> And being so, we trust that He
> Will thank us for our loyalty.
>
> Then if he'll help us to pull down
> His Father's dignity and Crown,
> We'll make him, in some time to come,
> The greatest Prince in Christendom.

Even after this the Whig certainty of office was undiminished,
and the Tories felt equally certain that they were to be dismissed.
Palmerston, who was then Secretary at War, wrote to his sister,
"We are all, I think, on the kick and the go." There can, indeed,
be no doubt that the Prince had made up his mind to dismiss the
Tory Government as soon as he was installed Regent. But towards
the end of January the King showed unmistakable signs of
recovery and was able to interview Perceval and the Lord Chancellor. The Queen then wrote to the Prince, telling him that, if
the Government was changed, the agitation would inevitably
retard the King's recovery. It was therefore obvious that the
Prince had no alternative but to leave the Ministers where they
were. On February 4th he wrote to Mr. Perceval, telling him that
he was going to keep him in office, but he made it abundantly
plain that only force of circumstances had driven him to this,
because, after explaining that he did not intend to make any
change in the Government, he added:

> "At the same time the Prince owes it to the truth and
> sincerity of character which, he trusts, will appear in every
> action of his life, in whatever situation he may be placed,
> explicitly to declare that the irresistible impulse of filial duty
> and affection to his beloved and afflicted father leads him to
> dread that any act of the Regent might, in the smallest degree,

have the effect of interfering with the progress of his sovereign's recovery. This consideration alone dictates the decision now communicated to Mr. Perceval."

The Whigs were no doubt bitterly chagrined, and indulged in strong abuse of the Regent, but they still hoped that when the limitations on the Regency, which were to last for a year, expired in February 1812, their day would come.

The ceremony of swearing in the Regent, which took place at Carlton House on February 5th, did nothing to diminish Whig hopes. The band of the Grenadier Guards was stationed in the courtyard of Carlton House, and played God Save the King, occasionally relieved by martial tunes, from twelve to five. But while the Tory Ministers were reminded, as they arrived, by these dutiful airs of the filial devotion of their new master, they were reminded of another, and to them less agreeable, devotion of his when they entered the throne-room. Deliberately placed by the Prince in the most conspicuous position in the room, the massive features glowering at them, stood a bust of the Right Honourable Charles James Fox.

As soon as the Prince was installed as Regent, he decided to give a fête at Carlton House to celebrate his accession to power. The question of the date on which it should be held presented some difficulty, as the King's health was constantly fluctuating and he was actually walking on the Terrace at Windsor, in a normal state of mind, as late as June 1811. It would obviously have been ridiculous to hold a fête to usher in the Regency if the state of the King's health suggested that the end of the Regency was imminent. The Prince, accordingly, decided that the fête should be given on June 19th, in honour of the Bourbons and to encourage British trade, the invitation-cards bearing the command, "The company to appear in the costume of the manufacture of the country."

Two thousand invitations were sent out, the guests being asked for nine o'clock. At eight o'clock there was a solid block of carriages reaching from Carlton House to the top of St. James's Street, which by nine o'clock had extended to the top of Bond Street: the empty carriages, in the language of the day, were "ranged in" St. James's Square. The full band of the Guards, in their State uniforms, was playing in the courtyard, and the guests were received in the hall by the members of the Prince's House-hold. They then passed down to the suite of rooms on the ground floor, but were not admitted to the first floor, on which were the principal state apartments including the throne-room.

Few people, apart from the Prince's intimate friends, had been in Carlton House, as, owing to his matrimonial troubles, very little general entertaining had ever taken place there, and the guests were charmed and fascinated with what they saw. At the bottom of the stairs was the large hall, where some of the Prince's Dutch pictures were hung. This led into the library, which had oak bookcases designed in the Gothic style, and was enlivened with buhl cabinets and miniature sculptures of triumphal arches. The library faced south, and leading out of it on the east side was the golden drawing-room, with a clever arrangement of Corinthian pillars, heavily gilded. Leading out of the library on the west side was a small bow-room, where more of the Dutch pictures were hung, which led into the dining-room. The ceiling of this room was painted to represent a summer sky, the doors were painted black and gold, and the furniture was all upholstered in scarlet.

Leading from the dining-room was the principal architectural glory of Carlton House—the Gothic conservatory. This was designed like a cathedral, with a nave and two aisles in the florid Gothic style. An original idea, which added greatly to the light of the building, was that the tracery of the ceiling was per-forated and filled with glass. The ordinary windows were of stained glass, with the arms of all the sovereigns of England from William I to George III, and of all the Princes of Wales, with the notable exception of James II's son, and of all the Electoral Princes of the House of Brunswick. It was lit at night by hex-agonal Gothic lanterns, which hung from the points of the arches.

The windows of the bow-room opened into the garden, and led to a long, covered-in walk, which had been put up for the occasion, and which was decorated with flowers and mirrors, and extended to the wall dividing Carlton House gardens from the Mall. This was divided by three similar covered-in walks, running from east to west, parallel to the Mall, where the guests were to have supper. There were plenty of exits from the main walk into the gardens, the grass of which was covered over with boards and matting.

The Prince made his entrance shortly before 9.15, wearing his

Field Marshal's uniform,[1] the coat of which was rather remarkable as even the seams had been heavily embroidered. A wit remarked that it must have cost and weighed at least two hundred pounds. He wore a magnificent aigrette and the garter star and if perhaps a portly, slightly garish figure, he fitted brilliantly and impressively into the decorations of his house. At 9.15 the Bourbons arrived, and were welcomed by the Prince in a room hung with blue silk, on which were stitched gold fleurs-de-lis. The Bourbon party consisted of the Comte de Lisle (afterwards Louis XVIII), the Comte d'Artois (Monsieur) and his two sons, the Duc de Berri and the Duc d'Angoulême, the Duchesse d'Angoulême, who was Louis XVI's only surviving child, the Prince de Condé, and the Duc de Bourbon. The Prince welcomed them cordially, and himself brought a chair for the Comte de Lisle, saying, *"Ici Votre Majesté est Roi de France."* There was dancing in one of the rooms, but the majority of the guests, as is perhaps inevitable at a Royal party, seemed to prefer to dog the footsteps of their host, or else to admire the rooms, the furniture, and the pictures, particularly a Rembrandt (probably "The Shipbuilder and his Wife") which the Prince had bought a few days before the fête.

At 2.30 there was supper, for which the Comte de Lisle, who, like every Bourbon, was fond of his food, had been evincing some signs of impatience. The supper-table for the principal guests was 200 feet long, and ran straight through the whole length of the Gothic conservatory and the dining-room. The architecture of the conservatory, picked out with innumerable coloured lights placed in the niches, was set off to the best advantage. In the middle of the table, and raised six inches above it, flowed a stream of water, supplied by a silver fountain, which played in front of the Prince. The banks of the stream were decorated with green moss and flowers, a few fanciful bridges were thrown across it, and gold and silver fish swam in it. The Prince sat in a plain mahogany chair with a leather back: on his right hand was the Duchesse d'Angoulême, and on his left the Duchess of York. Queen Charlotte had thought the fête ill-advised considering the King's condition, and had therefore decided not to attend and had refused to allow her daughters to go. This emphasised to the public the extraordinary matrimonial difficulties of the English

[1] One of his early acts as Regent was to appoint himself a Field Marshal.

Royal Family. There were seven Royal Princes, and, deprived of the company of their mother and sisters, they could only muster two Royal ladies, the Duchess of York, and their first cousin the Princess Sophia of Gloucester. As was said of the Prince at the time, "his two wives were sitting at home"—the Princess because she was not asked, and Mrs. Fitzherbert because she was not allowed to sit at the Prince's table.

It should not be imagined that those guests for whom there was no room at the principal table in the conservatory and who were relegated to the supper-tables in the garden were given an inferior entertainment. One who was present wrote: ". . . the extraordinary part of it was, that so large a number should have been served in such a style; tureens, dishes, plates, even soup plates, were everywhere of silver with as many changes as were wanted. There were hot soups and roasts, all besides cold but of excellent and fresh cookery. Peaches, grapes, pine apples, and every other minor fruit in and out of season were in profusion. Iced champagne at every three or four persons, all the other wines also excellent. There was no crowding, hurry or bustle in waiting; everything was done as in a private house." The Prince's own servants wore dark-blue liveries, trimmed with gold lace; the servants of other members of the Royal Family wore state liveries: the assistants wore black suits with white waistcoats.

The fête was only marred by one unfortunate incident. One of the most fashionable, but most ridiculous, figures in London society at that time was Mr. "Romeo" Coates. He was a man of enormous wealth, with a particularly fine collection of diamonds. He used to drive about in a carriage shaped like a kettle-drum and drawn by white horses: prominently displayed on the carriage was a large, brazen cock, beneath which was his motto, "While I live I'll crow." To his surprise and intense gratification he received an invitation to the Regent's fête. He spent days in the preparation of a magnificent suit, and he set out for Carlton House in excellent time, diamonds of the first water flashing on his bosom, his fingers and his sword hilt. The crowd of onlookers gasped at the splendour of his servants' livery as they carried his chair into the courtyard of Carlton House. He presented his card, but it was found to be a forgery, and this brilliant, dazzling figure was turned away. It was always thought to have been a practical joke of Sheridan's. When the Prince heard of it, he was exceedingly annoyed that his servants should have pointed out the forgery, and the following day he sent his secretary to apologise to Mr. Coates, and to invite him to come to see the decorations, which were still intact.

Taken as a whole, the fête was a memorable success, and, in Tom Moore's words, "worthy of a Prince." As the guests sauntered through the rooms admiring the Prince's most creditable collection of pictures, the way in which the furniture was shown to the best advantage, the ornate brilliance of the decorations, and gaping on the gaudy figure itself in its Field Marshal's coat, they could hardly help feeling that the Prince, whom they had been encouraged to regard as an unfilial, reckless debauchee, had at least that spirit of monarchical magnificence which was infinitely refreshing after a century of provincial-minded Hanoverian monarchs. The fête removed much of the upper classes' personal dislike for the Regent. This was fortunate, because he was about to lose the regard of his old political friends and to draw upon himself the execration of the liberal intellectuals who, with soft hearts, but vitriolic pens, were to hold him up to permanent ridicule.

In July 1811, a few weeks after the fête, the King had been taken suddenly worse and assailed with more violent delusions than ever. The physicians were satisfied that complete recovery was out of the question, and it was therefore clear that in February 1812 the Prince would become Regent, with no limitations, and in fact, if not in name, King. Once more the political world was thrown into a ferment at the thought that the Whigs would be recalled to office. But these anxious heart-searchings were as nothing to the distress and tribulation of the Prince. The easy course for him would have been to send for the Whigs, thereby consolidating his popularity with his early friends and winning the affection of the great turbulent masses of his future subjects. But there was one great objection to a Whig Government, which unquestionably weighed with the Prince, and which has not been noticed in the partisan pages of the Whig history books. For twenty years England had been at war with France: in 1811 the first faint signs of victory showed themselves. Wellington was more than holding his own in the Peninsula, and Napoleon had withdrawn 60,000 of his best soldiers from Spain for his fatal enterprise against Russia. Napoleon's hold on Europe in that critical year perceptibly weakened. A strong minority of the Whigs, some of whom would have had to hold office in any Whig Government, was notoriously opposed to the war and in favour of treating with Napoleon. Was it the time to change a Government, which, whatever its faults, was united in vigorous prosecution of the war, for an administration which must have been partially in favour of surrender? In any event, were the Whigs with their brains swimming with ideals of emancipating Roman Catholics and slaves and reforming Parliaments and abuses, well-equipped for the stern and disagreeable business of raising levies, sending money and provisions to Wellington, and carrying through the penal taxation necessary to continue the war? At the same time the Prince was by no means enamoured of Perceval, and was personally antagonistic to some of the members of his Cabinet.

In this exceptionally difficult situation, the Prince showed alarming vacillation and weakness of character. In December he was at Oatlands, the country house of the Duke and Duchess of York, for a dance in honour of the Princess Charlotte. He was showing his daughter how to do the Highland fling, a caper which his bulky figure can have hardly enabled him to execute with grace, when he slipped and slightly damaged his ankle. He took to his bed for a fortnight, existing principally on laudanum while he lay groaning on his stomach, not so much in physical pain as in mental distress over the political situation. He finally decided to try to form a coalition, which inevitably commends itself to Royal minds, but seldom to the country.

Accordingly, at the beginning of 1812, he asked Perceval to draft a letter which he could send to the Whig leaders suggesting a coalition. On reading Perceval's draft, the Prince observed to a friend, "It is a great misfortune to Mr. Perceval to write in a style which would disgrace a respectable washerwoman." He said it was obvious that Perceval intended the overture to be refused, and he sat down, with the help of Sheridan, to write a letter to the Duke of York, who was to show it to Grey. He chose the Duke of York as intermediary so that it might be clear to Grey that no one was fixed on for Prime Minister: if, for example, the letter had been addressed to Moira, the Prince's chief political confidant at that time, Grey would have concluded that Moira was to have been Prime Minister. After emphasising that he had only kept Perceval's Government in office because of the chance of the King's recovery, and after detailing the achievements against Napoleon, he wrote:

"In the critical situation of the war in the Peninsula, I shall be most anxious to avoid any measure that can lead my allies to suppose that I mean to depart from the present system.[1] Perseverance can alone achieve the great object in question; and I cannot withhold my approbation from those who have honourably distinguished themselves in support of it. I have no predilections to indulge, no resentments to gratify, no objects to attain but such as are common to the whole Empire. . . . I cannot conclude without expressing the gratification I could feel, if some of those persons with whom the early habits of my public life were formed would strengthen my hands and constitute a part of my Government. With such support, and aided by a vigorous and united administration formed on the most liberal basis, I shall look with additional confidence to a prosperous issue of the most arduous contest in which Great Britain ever was engaged. You are authorised to communicate these sentiments to Lord Grey, who, I have no doubt, will make them known to Lord Grenville. I am always, my dearest Frederick, your affectionate Brother,

GEORGE P.R."

It seems clear that what the Prince hoped for was an administration composed of his close friends like Moira and Sheridan, moderate Whigs like Erskine and the Duke of Norfolk and intelligent Tories like Canning and Wellesley. Wellesley, who was the Duke of Wellington's elder brother, was a curiously aloof independent personage, and was described by the Prince as "a Spanish Grandee grafted on an Irish potato." Industrious but narrow-minded Tories like Perceval, Lord Castlereagh, Lord Liverpool, and Lord Sidmouth were to be excluded. It was not, therefore, a particularly unreasonable suggestion to Lord Grey, especially when it is remembered that Fox, in 1806, had been content to join a coalition Ministry which contained Lord Sidmouth, and which was not strikingly more liberal than the one proposed.

[1] From the context this referred not, of course, to the Government but to the system of sending troops to the Continent.

Grey immediately conferred with Lord Grenville, and the two Lords then sent a frigid and precipitate refusal based on the fact that differences over the Roman Catholic question made alliance with the present administration futile, though it should be observed that there was nothing in the Regent's letter to suggest that he intended they should form part of the existing Government. The Regent was not suggesting a mere reshuffling of the Cabinet, but the formation of a new Government. Grey's hasty refusal has been generally condemned, with the notable exception of perhaps the most eminent of living historians,[1] who magnificently dismisses the whole incident as "tiresome negotiations." Few of us would disagree, but even the most tiresome of negotiations sometimes warrant unravelling. Grey no doubt refused because he had ceased to trust the Regent. That stately Whig, Lord Grenville, seems to have refused principally on the ground that he was not to be given a free hand "in the matter of patronage, so essential to the situation proposed to me." The Prince was therefore thrown into the arms of the extreme Tories, and had no alternative but to keep Perceval and his Government in office. He opened Parliament in person, and the artist Haydon, who was present, records how admirably he read his speech, in pure English and without a trace of provincialism. However, the rupture with his old political associates was deep and searing. In the very early days this was disguised by that species of stiff politeness which characterises dogs about to fight. At first the Prince was subjected to nothing more disquieting than the pressure of Dukes, though in certain Whig circles there was much private criticism of him. Both His Grace of Norfolk and His Grace of Bedford wrote long letters to him invoking the immortal shade of Mr. Fox, recalling old habits of intimacy, and stressing the importance of meeting the claims of the Roman Catholics. This was followed by an almost abject letter from Lord Moira, couched in terms of humility such as "It grieves me to the soul," "one so insignificant as I" and "deign, Sir, to believe" to the effect that he could not accept the Garter so long as the Tory Government was installed.

A third Duke, more independent than his brethren of Norfolk and Bedford, wrote to warn the Prince against the danger of allowing old friends to "storm the Closet." With these dignified

[1] Professor G. M. Trevelyan, in *Grey of the Reform Bill*.

discharges matters might have continued but for the shocking murder of the Prime Minister in the lobby in May 1812. Perhaps encouraged by his mother who wrote to compliment him on his "steadiness" (a public school virtue with which he can not fairly be credited), the Prince once again set on foot the "tiresome negotiations," and proposed that the Whigs should form part of a Government with Wellesley as Prime Minister, but the Whigs wanted to insist on changes in the Prince's Household, which rendered the overture fruitless. The Prince sent for Lord Liverpool who formed a strong but exclusively Tory administration.

But when it dawned on the Whigs that after all the years of their attachment to the Prince they were not to achieve office through him, they turned on him with a frenzied ferocity unrivalled in English politics. The rewards of public life, official residences, pensions, the deference of Government servants, the distribution of blue and scarlet ribbons, of glittering orders, of strawberry-leaves, coronets, and knighthoods, of prebends' stalls, absentee rectorships, and snug canonries, and all those profoundly obscure offices designed for needy faithful followers like paymasterships, accountantships, and secretaryships were snatched away from them indefinitely. The remembrance of their loss inspired the vigour of their attack. It never once entered Whig minds that they might themselves, by their stiff, uncompromising attitude, be to blame: they could only think of one person who had poisoned the Prince's mind against them—Lady Hertford. On her and the Prince they poured out the embittered vulgarity of their minds. Lord Grey, in the House of Lords, referred to her as an "unseen and separate influence which lurked behind the throne . . . an influence of this odious character, leading to consequences the most pestilent and disgusting." He said that he would never take office until he had come to an understanding with Parliament "for the abolition of this destructive influence." An Irish peer spoke of a figure "issuing forth from the inmost recesses of the gaming house or brothel and presuming to place itself near the royal ear."

In an account in the newspapers of a debate in the House of Commons Mr. Lyttelton, the accomplished author of *Private Devotions for Schoolboys* and the husband of the lady who was later governess to Queen Victoria's family, was reported in a clear reference to McMahon (the Prince's Treasurer and Secretary) to have described him as "a gamester" and "a spendthrift." McMahon wrote an indignant letter to Lyttelton demanding redress for these insults. Lyttelton drily replied: "I now subjoin for *your* satisfaction (at the bottom of this sheet) the whole of that sentence, according to my best recollection of what it was, and this you are at liberty to insert in the newspapers or otherwise to make public in whatever way you may think fit.

"PS. The sentence referred to above—'I had rather vote hundreds of thousands to a Nelson or a Wellington than a single farthing to a Gaveston or a Spenser.' "[1]

For the rest of the Regent's life they were to attack him for his moral character, for his building extravagances, and for his personal appearance, and they were to attack him on information that was notoriously second-hand. It is permissible to ask how Lord Grey would have liked, week after week, to see in the public prints a list of his illegitimate children, how Lord Grenville would have liked the people of England to be constantly reminded of that little auditorship of the Exchequer which he so wisely clung to, and which brought him in £4,000 every year, how Mr. Brougham would have liked his building operations on the castellated mansion at Brougham Hall to be held up to the very proper ridicule of his fellow-countrymen, and how even Mr. Creevey would have liked complete strangers to be reminded of that buxom mistress in Jermyn Street, or of those wounding verses which Hook had written on him:

> I had been a lawyer, but then, but then,
> I had been a lawyer, but then,
>   I hated the fag
>   Of the wig and the bag
> And envied the Parliament men, men,
> And envied the Parliament men.
>
> So I married a widow, and then, and then,
> So I married a widow, and then,
>   Folks wondered to see
>   That a woman could be
> So fond of a face like a wen, wen,
> So fond of a face like a wen.

[1] The notorious minions of King Edward II.

The Royal Family and the monarchical system in England were brought into contempt and jeopardy not by the rag-tag and bobtail of the Whig Party, but by its leaders, by men who in other respects were qualified to be called statesmen. It was hardly surprising that the Prince took seriously an anonymous missive, marked "with speed" which reached him. It said "you black-guard . . . you shall be shot as sure as I remain an enemy of the damned Royal Family." There are very proper signs of remorse in the words of Lord Holland, written long afterwards, "We all incurred the guilt, if not the odium, of charging his Royal Highness with ingratitude and perfidy. We all encouraged every species of satire against him and his mistress." Was it surprising that, after all this, the Regent said to a friend that he would rather sweep the streets than admit to his Government those men who had insulted him in every way?

Even worse than the personal attacks on the Prince was the espousal of the cause of his unhappy wife by a section of the Whig Party. Responsible Whig leaders like Grey, Grenville, and Lord Holland had nothing to do with this, but it is to the eternal discredit of Whigs like Brougham and Whitbread that they should have paraded before the public as chivalrous knights tilting a lance for the injured Princess, whereas they were in fact simply using her as a battering-ram against the English monarchy.

Ever since the Delicate Investigation in 1806 the Princess had continued her odd, rather desolate life at Kensington Palace, seeing her daughter once a week. In 1810 a little brightness, or possibly romance, came into her life, in the shape of two Italian singers—father and son. The father she named, in her agreeable way, "The Old Ourang-Outang," and the son "Chanticleer," and she took a house in Connaught Square so as to be near this melodious couple. She entertained the less respectable members of the English aristocracy, and those sensible social climbers who were anxious to improve their position by a knife-and-fork acquaintance with a Princess. Lord Byron was a frequent visitor at her table, and she flattered herself because "I am rather a favourite with this great bard. . . . I always tell him there are two Lord Byrons, and when I invite him, I say, I ask the agreeable Lord and not the disagreeable one."

It was in the summer of 1812 that she became friendly with

Brougham and Whitbread, who, smarting under their disappointment at not being Cabinet Ministers, were ready for any mischief. The brilliance of Brougham's gifts, the versatility of his mind, his admirable political courage, and his resource in ferreting out abuses should not blind historical judgment to his incredible vanity and selfishness and his contemptible disloyalty to friends and colleagues. Politics and the law were to him merely games which he played with varied skill, but with a constant purpose— "To me the Glory." Although Whitbread's parents had done their utmost to remove the traces of the brewery, from which his fortune was derived, by sending him to Eton, Oxford, and Cambridge, his was essentially a commercial outlook on politics: it was even said that "he spoke as though he had a pot of porter to his lips." For him no means, however trivial and unscrupulous, were to be neglected by which a party triumph might be achieved. The character of his mind is shown by his remark to someone who told him that the Prince was ill with bladder trouble: "God make him worse."

Acting on the advice of these swashbucklers, the Princess began to press to see the Princess Charlotte more often. In the autumn of 1812 she applied to Queen Charlotte to be allowed to visit her daughter more frequently, on the grounds that the Prince was away and of her maternal affections. The Queen refused her consent, and informed the Prince of what had happened. He replied, ". . . Although my poor hand is still so painful that I can scarcely hold my pen, I cannot resist, my dearest Mother, returning you (in my own writing and as well as I am able) my best and most grateful thanks for your communication as well as for the very kind and considerate and (if I may be allowed to express my judgment or opinion) the very well judged and most prudent method that you have adopted to refute and baffle this not only extraordinary (for extraordinary it would be in anyone else) but most impudent fresh attempt on the part of the Princess of Wales to avail herself of my absence by an affectation, and of the most absurd and ridiculous nature, which she never did feel, and is totally incapable of feeling, to create discord or confusion in the family under the pretence of seeing her daughter. . . ." And he goes on to refer to the Princess as "this most mischievous and intriguing Infernale, for such I am sure she has been to me, and to the whole family, ever since we have been cursed in having her in this country."

The Princess's next move was, with the help of her advisers, to draw up a very skilful letter, which was despatched to the Prince. The letter opened by the usual statement of the Princess's innocence, followed by the necessity for her to defend her reputation. "If these ought to be the feelings of every woman in England who is conscious that she deserves no reproach, your Royal Highness has too sound a judgment, and too nice a sense of honour, not to perceive how much more justly they belong to the Mother of your Daughter—the Mother of her, who is destined, I trust at a very distant period, to reign over the British Empire." After stressing how essential it was for the Princess to see more of her mother, the letter closed with stating the Princess's distress "both to my parental and religious feelings that my Daughter has never yet enjoyed the benefit of Confirmation."[1]

The letter was returned unopened by the Regent, and the Princess sent it back to him through the Prime Minister. Whitbread was strongly in favour of publishing the letter in the Press, but Brougham was opposed to this course, and they agreed to consult that great and good statesman Mr. Creevey. He took up a pencil, and scribbled across the draft of the letter. "Publish." The letter appeared in the *Morning Chronicle* of February 10th, to the delight of the vulgar, but to the great harm of the English monarchy. The Prince at once summoned a meeting of the Privy Council, which was attended by the members of the Cabinet and by the leading Bishops. After examining some of the principal documents of the Delicate Investigation, they publicly announced that the Prince was certainly justified in continuing to regulate the visits of his wife to the young Princess. This was a triumph for the Prince, but the publication of his wife's letter had had the desired effect of stimulating popular opinion against him, and he could no longer drive out without the dismal accompaniment of boos and hisses. The Princess, after this disappointment, returned to her life of retirement, and contented herself with making wax figures of her husband, embellished with horns, which she stabbed with pins and left to melt in front of the fire.

[1] George III had expressed a wish that she should not be confirmed until she was eighteen, i.e. in 1814.

II

While the combined efforts of the Princess and the Whigs had succeeded in making the Prince thoroughly disliked by the populace, the verses of a group of brilliant young poets made him ridiculous and unpopular in those intellectual circles where he would have most valued respect and admiration. It is rather pathetic to remember that he told Scott that he preferred Byron's poems to any that he had read, and Scott, describing this interview to Byron, said, "He spoke alternatively of Homer and yourself." The Prince can hardly have read with any particular pleasure the poem which Byron wrote to celebrate the occasion when, in the vault of St. George's Chapel at Windsor, he was present at the opening of Charles I's tomb. This somewhat sacrilegious act was done to set at rest doubts as to where the King was buried. Charles I's coffin was resting near that of Henry VIII:

> *Famed for contemptuous breach of sacred ties,*
> *By headless Charles see heartless Henry lies;*
> *Between them stands another sceptred thing—*
> *It moves, it reigns—in all but name a king:*
>
> *Charles to his people, Henry to his wife,*
> *—In him the double tyrant starts to life:*
> *Justice and Death have mixed their dust in vain,*
> *Each royal Vampire wakes to life again.*
> *Ah, what can tombs avail! since these disgorge*
> *The blood and dust of both to mould a George.*

Few would disagree with Goethe's comment on these verses that they were the "sublime of hatred."

And even the gentle Lamb, in slightly more precious vein, joined the hue and cry, in a poem called, "The Prince of Whales":

> *Not a fatter fish than he*
> *Flounders round the polar sea.*
> *See his blubbers—at his gills*
> *What a world of drink he swills. . . .*
>
> *Every fish of generous kind*
> *Scuds aside or slinks behind;*
> *But about his presence keep*
> *All the Monsters of the Deep.*

Quite as embarrassing as these attacks were the attentions of his principal defender, the *Morning Post*. In 1812, at a dinner at the Freemasons' Tavern, his health was received with partial applause, as well as loud and reiterated hisses and when Sheridan, speaking in defence of him, begged to be allowed to die in the principles of the Prince Regent (a somewhat ambiguous request) he was shouted down. The *Morning Post*, thinking to cover up this unfortunate incident, blossomed out, the next day, in an address to the Prince: "You are the *glory of the People*—You are the *Mæcenas of the Age*—wherever you appear you *conquer all hearts*, wipe away tears, excite *desire and love* and win *beauty* towards you—you breathe *eloquence*, you inspire the Graces—you are an *Adonis* in loveliness." These loyal, lyrical gibberings unluckily caught the eye of Mr. Leigh Hunt, who was editing the *Examiner*, and, in commenting on them, he wrote, ". . . this delightful, blissful, wise, pleasurable, honourable, virtuous, true and immortal Prince was a violator of his word, a libertine over head and ears in debt and disgrace, a despiser of domestic ties, the companion of gamblers and demireps, a man who has just closed half a century without one single claim on the gratitude of his country or the respect of posterity." Most foolishly the Government gave the incident additional publicity by prosecuting Hunt, who was imprisoned for two years and fined £1,000. It was a situation which Hunt's friends thoroughly enjoyed. Shelley was loud in shrill protests, Byron and Moore made a great parade of constant visits to the prison, and Keats composed the line, "Kind Hunt was shut in prison . . ."

It was unfortunate that this chorus of dislike and disapproval should have reached a crescendo just at the most glorious period of the Regency. When Leigh Hunt stood in the dock, in December 1812, the southern provinces of Spain were cleared of the French by Wellington; the *Grande Armée* was in the full rigour of its catastrophic retreat, perishing by thousands. In April 1813, when the Regent stood between the coffins of Henry VIII and Charles I, Wellington's final advance through Spain had begun, the Russians, assisted by the Hohenzollerns, were sweeping back the French from northern Germany. In March 1814, when Byron's verses on the Regent were being secretly circulated and read "with wonderful avidity,"[1] the British army had advanced

1 Moore.

94

on to French soil from Spain, and the armies of Russia, Prussia, and Austria were marching on Paris. After twenty-one years of the misery, privation and anxiety of war, after many false hopes of peace, much muddling, and a wasteful outpouring of gold, the tenacity and stolidity of the British character had enabled them to drive from Europe a brilliant and determined enemy with whom peace was probably impossible, and who was certainly a lasting menace to ordered progress and conservative institutions. When, therefore, the news came that Paris had been occupied by the Allies, and that Napoleon had abdicated, the public enthusiasm and thankfulness were unbounded. Englishmen felt that they had not only saved their own country, but Europe as well.

No one was better qualified than the Prince, with his affection for garish splendour, to give tone to the popular rejoicings. It is very easy to point the finger of scorn at the celebrations that began in March and ended in August; it is very easy to point a parsimonious finger at the money poured out on dinners, fêtes, processions, and balls while the working classes were in the grip of poverty and unemployment; but the series of rejoicings were a fitting close to the war, and a fitting prelude to that long period of British ascendancy in Europe.

An immediate occasion for popular rejoicing was the restoration of the Bourbon dynasty and Louis XVIII's departure from England for France. It was only right that the Regent should have taken a prominent part in this, as he, more than any of the Allied sovereigns, was responsible for the French King's return. The Tsar Alexander of Russia was always liable to sudden frenzies of enthusiasm for Napoleon, and when Napoleon was vanquished he seems to have been struck with remorse at the idea of flinging a fellow Emperor from his throne. The Emperor of Austria was always lukewarm in support of the Bourbons, as he would have preferred a Regency under his daughter, the Empress Marie Louise, until the young King of Rome came of age. But the Prince never wavered in his support of the Bourbons, and it was his action, early in 1814, in sending for the Russian Ambassador in England, Prince Lieven, (which he did quite unknown to his Ministers), and telling him to impress on the Tsar that England would regard any peace as temporary which did not provide for a Bourbon King of France that played a very large part in the eventual restoration.

On April 8th, 1814, news reached England that Napoleon had abdicated: Carlton House was blazing with illuminations, and across the whole front of it could be read, "RUSSIA AUSTRIA VIVENT LES BOURBONS PRUSSIA ENGLAND." The Regent was determined that England should give the French Royal Family a popular send-off after a generation of exile. Louis XVIII had lived for many years at Hartwell in Buckinghamshire, and it was arranged that the Regent should meet him at Stanmore, then a residential village, and that they should from there make a state entry into London. On April 20th the Regent, in his Field Marshal's uniform, plated with English and foreign orders, drove out from Carlton House in his travelling carriage, with his postilions in white jackets, white hats and cockades, in compliment to King Louis, since white was the emblem of the old French monarchy. The inhabitants of Stanmore gallantly dragged the French King's carriage into their village, and he and the Prince met with a warm embrace at the Abercorn Arms.

The procession set off from Stanmore at about three, and was formed by one hundred gentlemen on horseback, six royal carriages, a sovereign's escort of the Life Guards, and a state carriage, surmounted by the Royal Standard of England, and drawn by eight cream-coloured horses. In the state carriage were Louis XVIII, with his niece, the Duchesse d'Angoulême, and the Regent, with his back to the horses. Carriages were placed on both sides of the road all along the Edgware Road and Piccadilly, and enthusiastic ladies stood on the seats of these carriages, cheering and fluttering white tokens. From the houses white flags and fleur-de-lis were hanging in profusion, and in the poorer quarters sheets and even pillow-cases were hung from the windows. The procession drove to Grillon's Hotel in Albemarle Street, where the King was staying.

It was perhaps unlucky for the dignity of the new sovereign that his legs had long ceased to support his enormously bulky body. He had therefore to stagger and stumble into Grillon's Hotel, supported by the Prince. He was immediately conducted to a large armchair in the principal room of the hotel, which had been lavishly decorated with crimson velvet embroidered with golden fleur-de-lis. The male members of the English Royal Family were all assembled in this room, together with one hundred members of the French nobility. The Prince then addressed the King:

"Your Majesty will permit me to offer you my heartiest congratulations upon that great event which has always been amongst the warmest of my wishes and which must eminently contribute to the happiness not only of your Majesty's people but to the repose and happiness of all other nations. I am sure I may add that my own sentiments and feelings are in unison with those of the universal British nation, and that the triumph and transport with which your Majesty will be received in your own capital can scarcely exceed the joy and satisfaction which your Majesty's restoration to the throne of your ancestors has created in the capital of the British Empire." In reply the King attributed his restoration to "your Royal Highness's Councils, to this great country and to the constancy of its people."

The King, assisted by the Prince de Condé and the Duc de Bourbon, then invested the Prince with the Order of the *Saint-Esprit*. The Regent then invested the King with the Garter, himself fixing the insignia round that massive knee: he said afterwards, "When I clasped his knee it was exactly as if I were fastening a sash round a young man's waist." There was no doubt some force in Peter Pindar's rhyme:

> *And France's hope and Britain's heir*
> *Were, truth, a most congenial pair;*
> *Two round, tunbellied, thriving rakes,*
> *Like oxen fed on linseed cakes.*

But the feelings of the crowd were generally sympathetic to a family which had endured much misfortune, and there was great enthusiasm on the following evening when the King went to dine at Carlton House. The Prince sent his state carriage for him, drawn by six black horses in red harness ornamented with white ribbons, and all the servants wore white cockades. But it had become high time for the King to face the reluctant cheers of his new subjects, and he accordingly set out from London on April 23rd, the Duke of Kent and the Duke of Sussex (in Highland uniform) riding at the windows of his carriage. The Prince had set out earlier, and was at Dover to wish him godspeed. The King embarked on the *Royal Sovereign* yacht, and, as the vessel got under way, the Prince, who was standing at the end of the pier, cheered the yacht as she passed, a cheer which was taken up by an immense concourse of sightseers. It was perhaps typical of the character of the new French sovereign that he remained comfortably snoozing below and left the Duc de Bourbon to acknowledge the Prince's politeness. As the yacht passed out to sea the Prince stood bowing at the end of the pier.

He now had to prepare for the reception of the Allied sovereigns who were invited to visit England at the beginning of June. The Emperor of Austria refused the invitation, but the Tsar Alexander and the King of Prussia accompanied by his two sons landed at Dover on June 6th. The Tsar delighted the onlookers by loudly proclaiming at Dover, "God be praised! I have set my foot upon the land which saved us all." Alexander was at this time the dominant sovereign of Europe, and the English crowds cheered themselves hoarse at the sight of this tall, friendly distinguished Emperor: they knew nothing of his wayward, melancholy character; they forgot how at one moment he was a strong Liberal, distributing Bibles to his peasants, and how at the next he was as tyrannical as any Emperor of All the Russias; they forgot those vows of eternal friendship to Napoleon at Tilsit, and then that refusal, five years later, to answer Napoleon's letter appealing for mercy for the *Grande Armée*. In England he was his agreeable, charming, Liberal self, more anxious for the cheers of the populace than for the friendship of his host.

King Frederick William III of Prussia was the least distinguished of that undistinguished trio of monarchs who came between Frederick the Great and the Emperor William I. He had played a very dismal part against Napoleon, though his wife, Queen Louise (the Prince's first cousin), had contrived to give the Hohenzollern family some vestige of heroic conduct. His two sons were much admired by the English crowd, and it is worthy of comment that the younger was, in the dim future, to wrest Hanover from the Prince's nephew (King George V of Hanover), to establish the predominance of Prussia in Germany, and to survive the first Jubilee of Queen Victoria, who was then unborn. But of all the visitors, English people reserved their greatest enthusiasm for a member of the King of Prussia's suite, Marshal Blücher.

After a few days in London, during which both sovereigns had been invested with the Garter, they all paid a visit to Oxford. The Prince arrived first, and alighted from his travelling carriage at Magdalen Bridge. Attended by the University authorities he walked up the High Street, which was lit up by candles in every window, and the simple illuminated inscription from the University Church, "Our prayers are heard." The streets were lined by wildly cheering undergraduates and graduates in evening dress and cap and gown. The Prince stayed with the Dean of Christ Church, the Emperor with the Warden of Merton, and the King of Prussia with the President of Corpus. The following day the Prince, in academic dress, escorted his guests round the University: at the Clarendon Press he was presented with a Bible, and at the Bodleian he gave the Emperor and King copies of the Oxford edition of Aristotle. After honorary degrees had been given to the two sovereigns a banquet was held in the Radcliffe Library, the public being allowed to pass through the gallery and see the eminent persons at their food. When any particular toast met with the crowd's approval they cheered enthusiastically, and the Prince genially waved back to them.

On their return to London the sovereigns were invited by the Lord Mayor to a banquet at Guildhall. The Prince decided to drive in state from Carlton House and it is improbable that a more magnificent spectacle has ever been seen on the streets of London. The procession was headed by an escort of the 11th Light Dragoons. There then followed seven of the Prince's carriages, with officers of his Household and foreign generals, the state carriages of the Dukes of York, Kent, Cambridge, Gloucester, and the Prince of Orange, the Speaker's state carriage, the carriages of the members of the Cabinet, a troop of Horse Guards, followed by a state carriage and six in which were the Prince's officers of state, six royal carriages with the suites of the foreign sovereigns, a hundred yeomen of the guard, the band of Gentlemen Pensioners, the heralds, and finally the Prince's state carriage drawn by eight cream horses with scarlet ribbons, in which were the Regent in Field Marshal's uniform, sustaining English, French, Prussian, and Russian orders, the King of Prussia on his left, the Prince Royal of Prussia and the Prince of Orange sitting opposite to him. The Emperor, accompanied by his sister, the Duchess of Oldenburg, set out in similar state from his hotel a quarter of an hour after the Regent.

A day or two later the Prince and his guests attended the Opera. As they entered their box the curtain rose, and the whole of the cast sang God Save the King. The Prince sat in the middle, with the Emperor on his right and the King on his left, and he was distinguished by the fact that he alone was wearing his hair in powder. They had just settled down when there was a great burst of cheering and the Princess of Wales hurried in to a neighbouring box. She was wearing a black velvet dress, and a black wig on which was perched a diamond tiara and plume. The applause was tremendous, and it has often been confidently asserted that the Prince bowed to the crowd, pretending that the cheers were for himself, but the most reliable account[1] states that he bowed three times "in the direction" of the Princess. The King and Emperor also bowed, the latter gazing at her long and earnestly through his glass. For the Prince it must have been acutely humiliating to see the Tsar's obvious curiosity about this lady to whom he had been strictly forbidden to pay any attention.

Although this was the only apparent hitch in the celebrations, the visit of the sovereigns was not a success. Both the Emperor and his sister disliked the Prince, and took no trouble to humour him. She quickly caused him the greatest offence by visiting Whitbread in his brewery, after which he said to her, "I suppose you would have visited Santerre in Paris." (Santerre gave the order for the roll of drums which drowned Louis XVI's last words from the scaffold.) She had all the music stopped at the Guildhall banquet because she was suffering from a slight head-ache, and only reluctantly consented to God Save the King being played. The Emperor for his part was no less difficult. The Prince made a special point, after a dinner at Carlton House, of intro-ducing Lady Hertford to him, but he merely bowed, said nothing to her, and turned away saying, "She is mighty old." This was an obvious comment, but one which hardly came well from the Tsar, who was just settling down to a romance with an elderly female evangelist. He caused the greatest annoyance to the Royal Family by constantly asking to be allowed to see George III, as though he was one of the sights of Britain. Relations became so strained that he gave out that he would go and see the Princess, whatever the Prince might say. She, poor woman, sat, dressed in her best, for the whole of one afternoon eagerly expecting the call but the advice of the Russian Ambassador and his wife—Prince and Princess Lieven—had brought the Emperor to reason. What

[1] *The Times.*

irritated the Prince more than anything was the Emperor's jaunty, familiar air with the crowd, which made him exceedingly popular —a popularity which was in obvious constrast to the sullen looks and perfunctory cheers which greeted the Regent wherever he went. He was likewise much annoyed by some of the royal rag, tag and bobtail accompanying the sovereigns. In particular he was incensed against Prince Paul of Wurtemberg, stepson of his eldest sister, who made a beast of himself with drink at a dinner at Carlton House. He and the Prince of Orange likewise misbehaved in public at Ascot Races, the latter coming back on the outside of a stage coach in a highly excited state. After a grand review in Hyde Park, and a naval review at Spithead, the kings departed on June 27th: but the tumult and the shouting were by no means dead, as the captains were yet to come. On the following day Wellington landed at Dover.

The Prince always had the greatest admiration for Wellington, though it was not particularly to his credit, because it was obviously only the due of the most successful general that England had produced. He was most generous in acknowledging what Wellington had done for Europe, for England, and for the Hanoverian dynasty. It must be remembered that it was not particularly congenial to a man of the Prince's temperament— nor indeed to any of the Royal Family—to feel that at all public functions the enthusiasm and curiosity of the public were reserved for the Duke, that See the Conquering Hero Comes, with which he was generally greeted, touched the heart of the crowd far more than God Save the King.

The letter in which the Regent wrote to Wellington announcing his appointment as a Field Marshal is a masterpiece of graceful pomposity:

"Carlton House,
July 3 1813.

MY DEAR LORD,

Your glorious conduct is beyond all human praise, and far above my reward. I know no language the world affords worthy to express it. I feel I have nothing left to say, but devoutly to offer up my prayers of gratitude to Providence that it has in its omnipotent bounty blessed my country and myself with such a general. You have sent me, among many other trophies of your unrivalled fame, the staff of a French Marshal,[1]

[1] That of Marshal Jourdan which is now at Windsor Castle.

and I send you in return that of England. The British army will hail it with enthusiasm, while the whole universe will acknowledge those valorous efforts which have so imperiously called for it. That uninterrupted health and still increasing laurels may still continue to crown you through a glorious and long career of life are the never-ceasing and most ardent wishes of, my dear Sir,

Your very sincere and faithful Friend,

G. P. R.

On July 7th the Prince once more drove in state to the City, to offer up thanks for victory at St. Paul's Cathedral. The Duke rode in the carriage with him, and sat on his right throughout the service. Shortly afterwards the Prince was present with the Duke at a large houseparty at Wanstead in Essex. At the dinner given in the Duke's honour he began his speech in reply to his toast, "I want words to express," when the Prince interrupted him with, "My dear fellow, we know your actions and we will excuse your words, so sit down."

The Prince's personal tribute to Wellington took the form of a fête, on July 21st, at Carlton House, which was even more magnificent than the one which had ushered in the Regency in 1811. The guests passed through the house into a great polygon structure, 120 feet in diameter, which had been erected in the gardens. This had been designed by the architect Nash, and was built of brick, with a leaded roof. Inside it was entirely draped with white muslin, decorated with mirrors, and it had an umbrella-shaped roof painted to resemble muslin, so that the whole effect was extraordinarily light. In the centre of the room was a mass of artificial flowers in the shape of a temple, in which were concealed two bands. (This building was eventually moved to Woolwich, where it serves, on the Prince's suggestion, to house the collection of weapons and armour.) Leading from the west side of the polygon room was a long covered walk, decorated with muslin draperies, and ornamented with rose-coloured cords. This walk led to a Corinthian temple on the wall of which was a large mirror, over which was a brilliant star and the letter W cut in glass. On an antique column in front of the mirror was a marble bust of the Duke, which could, of course, be clearly seen from the polygon room, and served to remind the guests of the hero of the fête. From this Corinthian temple opened out two supper tents, decorated with regimental colours in silk. Leading from the east side of the polygon room was a similar covered walk, decorated in green calico. This walk was covered with allegorical transparencies, representing such subjects as, "The overthrow of tyranny by the Allied Powers," "Military Glory," and "The Arts in England." It led to further supper-tents and refreshment-rooms. All the walks and tents were boarded, and particular attention was paid to their ventilation.

The Queen and two of her daughters, the Princesses Augusta and Mary, came over in chairs from Buckingham House, and at 10.30 the Royal party entered the polygon room. The Prince was in his Field Marshal's uniform, sparkling with his English and foreign orders: the Queen leant on his right arm. The Prince and his mother were followed by the Duke of Kent and Princess Augusta, the Duke of Cambridge and Princess Mary, the Princess Sophia of Gloucester (rather pathetically alone), while the Duke and Duchess of York brought up the rear. As they promenaded round the room, the band, from their bower of artificial flowers played, alternately God Save the King and the Prince Regent's March. After supper the Princess Mary, a spirited dancer of thirty-eight, opened the ball with the young Duke of Devonshire to the tune of, *Voulez vous danser, Mademoiselle?* The Queen stayed until half past four, and the party finally broke up at six.

While it was true that the London crowd could gaze and cheer at emperors, kings, and generals as they paraded themselves through the streets, there had been no rejoicings provided in which the crowd itself could join. This the Prince decided to remedy. He accordingly arranged that an enormous fête should be held in Hyde Park, St. James's Park, and the Green Park, to synchronise with the visit of the Allied sovereigns. It was unfortunately found impossible to complete the arrangements in time, so it was decided to hold the fête on August 1st, to celebrate peace and also the centenary of the accession of the House of Brunswick.

For weeks before, the parks had been filled with people watching the preparations. Eastern architecture was at this time in complete possession of the Prince's mind, and a Chinese bridge and pagoda, designed by Nash, were built across the lake in St. James's

Park. The Green Park was reserved for fireworks, and there was much speculation as to the significance of a grim Gothic structure, about 100 feet square, which had appeared there. Admission to St. James's Park was by payment only, but Hyde Park was open to all, and booths and all the paraphernalia of fairs were rapidly springing up. The Whigs, of course, held up their pious hands in horror, and *The Times* was pontifically hostile, when it published the preparations for the fête.

"As other prints have got the subjoined precious piece of nonsense, we are obliged to insert it likewise. The public will first gape at the mummery, then laugh at the authors of it and lastly grumble at the expense. We are chiefly sorry on account of the contemptible light in which it will exhibit us as a people to foreign nations. The Pagoda, the Balloons and Girandoles of Rockets, the Chinese Bridge. . . . Alas! alas! to what are we sinking."

These journalistic forebodings did not reflect the opinion of the public. On August 1st the weather, after preliminary clouds, was brilliant, the crowds were stupendous, and the enjoyment was universal. The Queen and all the Royal Family assembled at Buckingham House, from which they had commanding views of St. James's and the Green Parks. There was a Royal booth in the Green Park, connected with Buckingham House by a bridge across Constitution Hill, but, owing to the enormous pressure of people, the Royal Family watched from the windows and the forecourt of Buckingham House.

The public spectacle began with a balloon ascent from the Green Park by Mr. Sadler. This gentleman was the son of an eminent aeronaut, and, after working in the Liverpool Gas Company, was doubtless well-qualified for his adventure. His start was much delayed owing to the amiable curiosity of the younger Royal Dukes, eager to be classed as patrons of the last and most melancholy of man's conquests. A gallant lady, called Mrs. Johnstone, was to have accompanied the balloon, and she stood by it, clasping to her bosom a dove, which she was to have released from the heavens as an emblem of peace. At the last moment it was decided that the balloon was not safe for two: the ropes were cut, the balloon sprang into the air, and Mr.

Sadler was last observed dropping favours from the sky. He was eventually found on the Essex coast, and only the judicious use of his knife in the bag of the balloon saved him from being carried out to sea.

At eight a mimic naval battle, representing Trafalgar, began on the Serpentine. This, for some reason, had attracted an immense amount of ridicule but, although it was a trifle difficult for the crowd to see, it was much enjoyed, and the greatest enthusiasm was aroused when the French fleet was finally destroyed by a fire ship. A profusion of fireworks of all kinds was fired from the battlements of the Gothic structure in the Green Park, after which the whole building was obliterated by smoke for two minutes. When the smoke had cleared, the Gothic fortress, which had been only canvas, had vanished, and in its place stood a Temple of Concord, brilliantly illuminated. The panels of the Temple were decorated with pictures showing the origin and effects of War, the Deliverance of Europe from Tyranny, the Restoration of the Bourbons, the Return of Peace, and the Triumph of England under the Regency. This was the work of Sir William Congreve—a close personal friend of the Prince's, and the inventor of the Congreve rocket.

The Chinese pagoda on the bridge in St. James's Park was painted yellow, ornamented with black lines, and the roof painted bright blue. It was illuminated with gas and Japanese lanterns and covered with glass reflectors. At ten o'clock it was seen to burst into flames and shortly afterwards topple into the water. The crowd regarded this as part of the fun, but it was actually an unfortunate accident, in which a carpenter and a man who had gone up the pagoda out of curiosity lost their lives.

The fête was a memorable success. Even *The Times,* after referring to its previous criticism, wrote, "It is an indisputable fact that so immense a number of people at large were never brought together in any previous instance by any description of public rejoicings or any of the great events which have so often gilded the pages of British history."

The credit for the fête, for the brilliant entertainments provided for the Allied sovereigns, and for the triumphal entry of the Bourbons into London, belongs primarily to the Prince. The Chinese bridge in St. James's Park, the Temple of Concord, the mimic naval battle, the homage to learning paid by the

Allied sovereigns at Oxford, the splendour of the procession from Stanmore, and the white decorations on postilions and horses were all obviously inspired by his taste—ever eager for fresh adventures in the realms of æsthetics. He was the ideal patron of victory. And as he watched from the windows of Buckingham House, and saw the rockets fizzing, the Chinese pagoda glittering with its gas lamps, the smoking Temple of Concord, the balloon sailing off on its perilous flight, and heard the shouts of the people and the hum of their enjoyment, he would have been less than human if he had not felt that he was in some way responsible for bringing the country to victory, and that the inscription on the Temple of Concord, "The Triumph of England under the Regency," was not merely an empty compliment but a sober, demonstrable fact.

III

Triumph followed triumph, and in the month following the fête the Princess of Wales, deprived of any share in the rejoicings or of any compliment from the visiting sovereigns, left for what was generally regarded as a permanent visit to the Continent. She embarked from Worthing, wearing a dark-coloured satin pelisse with gold clasps, and a cap of violet and green satin adorned with green feathers. Her taste in dress certainly did not qualify her to be the Prince's wife. She was accompanied by a motley crew of attendants, with Sir William Gell ("topographical Gell"), a gouty, amusing knight, with a hankering for patrician life, as her chamberlain.

Many writers have been eager to condemn the Prince for virtually driving his wife from the country. Our hearts have been torn, and such feelings of chivalry as we possess roused, by descriptions of this hapless, innocent stranger hounded from our shores at the instance of a selfish voluptuary. An examination of the facts may perhaps stifle sentimental indignation.

No doubt the Prince must be roundly blamed for having ever agreed to be a party to a *mariage de convenance*. His character, though in some respects curious and perverse, was too open and kindly to admit of his masking misery by that species of icy politeness in which some unhappy marriages are shrouded. The subtle philosophic turn of mind which enabled King Charles II to tolerate the society of Queen Catherine was completely lacking in King George IV; he had rather the intolerance, without the savagery, of King Henry VIII for company which was incompatible. But all this he should have appreciated before accepting a bride of his father's choosing. To this extent he must be held responsible for the deep and murky waters in which the middle years of his life were passed. Indeed, the evil consequences of his marriage pursued him far beyond the grave and his character and personality are still distorted by those who abetted the machinations of his wife. For this purely domestic issue need not have convulsed the country and shaken the monarchy to its foundations had it not been for the character and personality of the Princess. On these no judgment can be too harsh, no words too severe. Her mind, which was at once flighty and vulgar, was absorbed by three things—scandalmongering, romancing about sexual matters and magnifying her grievances and wrongs. The English Royal Family—including her own daughter—were convinced that she was the mother of two bastard children. Princess Charlotte used often to meet William Austin, the elder of these children, on going to see her mother and described him as "a sickly child with fair hair and blue eyes." The affection which her mother lavished on the boy and the knowledge that he always slept in her bedroom convinced Princess Charlotte of his parentage. She likewise believed that a baby girl, whom the Princess of Wales christened in her fanciful way Edwardina Kent, after her favourite brother-in-law, Edward, Duke of Kent, was also a bastard of her mother's. Whether these changelings were in fact children of the Princess will now never be known for certain; it is likely that they were, but the important fact is that the Princess took a wanton pleasure in making people believe that they were hers.

The follies of the Princess's personal conduct became almost insignificant in comparison with her choice of friends, associates and advisers. By reading the diaries of Lord Glenbervie or of Lady Charlotte Bury, anyone can sense the surroundings in which the Princess passed her days. The tuft-hunters, the gossips and the disaffected flocked to her house; by people of standing and integrity her company was shunned.

Condemnation of the Princess and irritation with her antics must be tempered by the knowledge that she was abnormal. The members of the House of Brunswick from which she sprang were remarkable for their instability of mind and character. Her great-aunt had married Frederick the Great with results not materially different from her own marriage with the Prince. The Prussian Royal Family, always somewhat outspoken, described Frederick's wife as "just an animal," with the agreeable emphasis that she smelt like one. The Princess's aunt married King Frederick William II of Prussia, but this marriage was dissolved after a few years because her brothers-in-law objected to the risk of "some accidental bastard" of hers cutting out their rights of succession. Her nephews—the sons of the illustrious Duke of Brunswick, killed at Quatre Bras—were notoriously strange, the behaviour of the elder agitated all the Courts of Europe during the 1820's. The truth was expressed with forceful poignancy by the Princess's own mother, the Dowager Duchess of Brunswick. "Her excuse is, poor thing, that she is not right here"—tapping her forehead, the Duchess burst into tears.

Too often the Prince has been portrayed as the heartless persecutor of his wife, but in order to judge this matter it is necessary to set it against a far broader canvas than has been previously attempted. As was perhaps inevitable the squabbles of the parents fell with all their force on the only child of the marriage. Her education had been much neglected and her manners were coarse. Even as a girl of seventeen she had a marked partiality for both food and drink. In 1812, when she was sixteen, she had grown into a handsome, voluble, showy, full-blooded, fearless and bouncing miss with a slight stammer; she was in fact a larger and somewhat coarsened edition of what her first cousin, Queen Victoria, was to be, with a generous portion of that same Hanoverian zest for life which was to startle Court circles in the early years of the Queen's reign. Everyone concerned with the child's welfare was clearly determined that she should see as little as possible of her mother and that her upbringing must be entrusted to others.

Her father was fitted neither by temperament nor inclination for this task. Though affectionate towards his daughter, he was too absorbed by his own life to allow her to disrupt his routine of pleasure. He was likewise antagonised by a certain restlessness and querulousness in his daughter which in his experience, made it very difficult to please her. He thought that these defects sprang from a perversity of temper which could have been easily corrected when she was a child, and he felt that the only hope of overcoming them now was by an appeal to the heart. In writing to his mother he let fall in this connexion, a characteristically amusing comment "but there again, there must be a heart to be able to appeal to, and how alas! can we flatter ourselves with any such ameliatory hope . . . especially if we reflect and recollect, *that part* of the stock from whence this has sprouted forth. . . ."

There was in consequence no alternative but that her grand-parents and aunts should be responsible for her upbringing. Owing to the insanity of the King, this really meant that she was in the hands of the old Queen,

When King George lapsed into final madness Queen Charlotte was sixty-seven. For too long this lady has been relegated to the shadows of history; in fact her influence over the Royal Family was more potent than that of the King. Her character and person-ality were masterful and lively; her temper was vile. She exercised her sway over the family with ease, and their feelings for her were a nice admixture of affection and awe. Never a handsome woman, she had grown very stout, especially in front, and it was said that she looked in middle life as if she were bearing simultaneously all her fifteen children. Though she was devoted to the King, she aggravated his disorder by being incapable of showing him any tenderness or warmth and by an understandable nervousness of being left alone with him. In fact, it had been the object of his life, as one of his daughters once said, "to keep from the world all he *suffered* and *went through*" with his wife's temper. No doubt the remorseful realisation of this made her determined that she and her daughters, after the King's final madness, should behave as if they were in perpetual mourning. Any gaiety was stamped on and she fought hard to prevent her daughters from even visiting their brothers. Any effort on their part to attend a State ceremony, such as the opening of Parliament, was made the occasion for a tumultuous row. "We were brought up in a cloister rather than a Kingdom," said one of the Princesses. With Shakespeare, the Queen might have said, "For my daughters they shall be praying Nuns not weeping Queens." This life, as enclosed and secluded as any monastic order, was the background for the youth of Princess Charlotte.

Although she herself lived outside the Castle with her own

establishment, her only recreation, apart from the dubious society of governesses, was at the Castle or at Frogmore in the company of her grandmother and aunts. Not unnaturally, the comfortable, easy-going licence of her mother's house shone with something of the same alluring charm as does Paradise for more orthodox inmates of convents. Undoubtedly the Princess was sorry for her mother, but it was primarily a desire to escape from Windsor which made her seek her mother's company.

As will be seen from the following letter, written to the Princess when she was seventeen, the Prince was constantly trying to circumscribe these meetings.

"*16th May*

I cannot express to you how much delighted I am with your most kind and affectionate letter. I shall not object to your visiting your mother upon the occasion of her birthday, but I confide so much in your own discretion, sense of propriety and what you must feel is the delicacy of both our situations at the present moment, that you will see how desirable it is to make this merely a morning visit, and not to extend it to that hour of the day when you might be subjected to society, of the nature of which I cannot be apprized, which I might not approve of and which consequently I have every reason to rest satisfied that you would not wish to meet."

This letter must have been in part inspired by the knowledge freely canvassed in society, that the young Princess had met Sir William Drummond at her mother's table. This worthy, a diplomatist turned sceptic, was seized with that sudden desire to spout flashy absurdities which often attacks intellectuals in the company of their social superiors. He asked the girl if she was interested in history; without waiting for any reply, he gabbled on about the Scriptures, saying: "I can assure your Royal Highness there is nothing in it; it is all an allegory."

However, the company which the young Princess met in the dining-room of her mother's house was as nothing compared with the company encountered in the more private parts of the house. On Christmas Day, 1814, she told her father and her Aunt Mary something of what she had been through. She started by saying that in spite of the strict injunction of her grandfather (the King) never to see her mother alone, she had in fact often seen her alone "and had witnessed many things in her mother's room which she could not repeat." She went on to say that when out driving at Windsor with her elderly governess she had met Captain Hesse of the Light Dragoons. This dashing officer, who was reputed to be the bastard son of the Duke of York, regularly met the Princess for six weeks and rode by her carriage. When his regiment was moved from Windsor, her mother arranged meetings between them frequently in her own bedroom. She would turn the key on them as she left the room saying, "*A présent je vous laisse amusez vous.*" Through her mother, she was able to carry on a regular correspondence with Captain Hesse. She said with the simplicity of a girl, "God knows what would have become of me if he had not behaved with so much respect to me." With all the wisdom of fifty, the Prince replied, "My dear child, it is Providence alone that has saved you." She then added that she could never quite make out if Captain Hesse was her lover or her mother's. The Prince closed the interview by saying to his daughter, "My object must be to save you, not now to reproach you, but to prevent the possibility of such a thing ever happening again."

The affair with Captain Hesse had happened during 1813 and against this highly coloured background must be set the remarkable events of 1814. Although the Prince Regent did not say so to his daughter, some rumours of the Hesse affair had reached him and were the main reason for his anxiety that the Princess should quickly settle down by making a suitable marriage.

At a dinner party at Carlton House at the end of 1813, the Princess accepted an offer of marriage from her distant cousin, Prince William of Orange, a somewhat colourless and uninteresting prince. No official statement was made, but there existed between the young people what might, in other walks of life, be called an understanding. In the summer of 1814, when London was filled with the jangling gaiety of young martial princes, fresh from their triumphs over the French, the Princess decided that she did not after all love Prince William and broke the engagement. Her father was enraged, gave her a sound rating and dismissed her ladies, whom he suspected of encouraging this step. When the interview was over, the Princess rushed out, hailed a hackney coach from the Charing Cross stand, and gave the driver a guinea to take her to her mother's house in Connaught Place. After long consultations between her mother, Brougham, the Archbishop of Canterbury and the Dukes of York and Sussex, she was at last persuaded to return, but not before the news of the escapade had become public property. In reference to the Prince's treatment of his daughter, a Whig Member of Parliament, Mr. Francis Horner, asked, "Could a Prussian corporal have behaved worse?" But Greville notes that all parties were united in blaming Princess Charlotte's behaviour.

When the incident was over, the Prince spoke to a friend for an hour of his love for his daughter, emphasising his affection with characteristic bursts of sobbing. The explanation for his harsh treatment of the girl undoubtedly lay in the fear that her impetuous jilting of the Prince of Orange coupled with rumours of her affair with Hesse might fatally damage her chances of attracting a suitable and respectable Prince. Relations between father and daughter settled down during the latter half of 1814, and by the close of that year they were on terms of affection and confidence which were never afterwards disturbed.[1]

They were even able in the spring of 1815 to discuss the possibility of reopening the negotiations with the Prince of Orange. In February the Princess wrote to her father: "Happily for me, we are now upon the most comfortable and confidential terms possible. We have broken through the awkwardness of talking upon one subject, which is a very delicate and painful one,[2] and I should grieve if there was anything left to make us less open with each other." She then stated "my strong and fixed aversion" to the Orange match because she was unable to feel for the Prince "those sentiments of regard which surely are so necessary in a matrimonial connection."

The Regent's answer was typical. His letter began with a series of elaborate and flowery compliments at the satisfactory

---

[1] Anyone familiar with "the last letter" written by Princess Charlotte to her mother may feel that the relations between the Princess and her father were not as I have stated. In this last letter she refers to "illustrious relatives who offer me no kindness," and in a reference to "my adored mother" she says that "in a better world our congenial spirits will rush to meet each other." In alluding to her husband, Prince Leopold, she says that his attentions "are insufficient to supply the chasm in my bosom." Neither the style nor the sentiments are those of the Princess; the letter is evidently a forgery by political associates of her mother. It is printed from a copy at Windsor in Professor Aspinall's *Letters of George IV*, Vol. II, p. 203.

[2] The affair with Captain Hesse.

sentiments expressed by "my dearest Charlotte." He then devoted a whole paragraph to announcing with infinite circumlocution that he was going to lay before her his views, which were not "the effect of prejudice nor dictated by any retrospective or splenetic feeling upon the painful and unfortunate occurrences of the last year." He emphasised that "my confidential servants" were wholly ignorant of the correspondence. After saying that the character of the Prince of Orange was unblemished, he went on:

"It could only, therefore, be the result of the counsel and advice of mischievous, false and wicked persons plotting equally against your happiness and mine, and the welfare of the country, that could have raised these (I might, and with inexpressible grief, my dearest Charlotte, I do say) unreasonable and groundless prejudices in your mind. But thank heaven you are now withdrawn from all communication with such counsellors and justly rely upon me, as your best friend, and most anxious and most dispassionate adviser. . . . Our station compels us no doubt to enter into matrimonial connections guided by a superior sense of the duty which we owe to the country, and if we are so far fortunate as to be allied to virtue, it is proved by experience that the comfort of matrimonial union will follow in such a reasonable degree as to render life comfortable, and the high station which we are destined to fill, respectable in that relation.

You have no reason to apprehend in a union with the Prince of Orange the grievous calamity, which I alas! my dearest child, have experienced from a marriage with a person whose character we have had occasion so recently, so fully and so freely to gather, and from the contemplation of which, it is so much my wish, always to abstain."

He then went on to emphasise the dangers of her position, how she was completely in the power of her mother who, as they were both agreed, was bent on besmirching her character in order to bring forward William Austin. "In such a sad predicament when I am gone you can have no protector but a husband, and that husband can not be protector unless he shall have a name, a station, and a character in Europe, calculated to repel, what may be and what you and I now do clearly see, will be attempted."

H   113

He referred to her situation as *"most critical . . .* for the Princess of Wales has but to make known the documents so unfortunately in her possession to render it impossible for you to form a marriage alliance not only with the Prince of Orange but with any other Prince of character, power and respectability, and then reflect, my dearest child, how the whole happiness, credit and honour of your life will be destroyed, and how the very means of your discharging your exalted duties hereafter when I am no more, will not only be embarrassed but entirely frustrated."

With a bland superiority which was truly characteristic, he went on: "We cannot marry like the rest of the world, for both our elevated rank, and our religious faith limit our choice to few indeed." He also said that his desire for a marriage with the Prince of Orange had been strengthened "by the melancholy and frightful disclosures you made to me last Christmas Day."

He urged her to discuss the whole question with anyone fully in her confidence, and assured her that he would not take any active steps to renew the union, closing this long effusion of some two thousand words by a typical flourish "with the warmest feelings of my heart, with the most earnest and anxious wishes for your happiness, and with my most fervent prayers that providence may direct you to a right and due consideration of your situation in the awful circumstances in which you are placed, I remain my dearest child, ever, etc."

The Regent was somewhat mortified when his daughter, with a hastiness which marked her temperament, dashed off an answer maintaining all her objections to the marriage, but he replied affectionately enough that she need have no fears of his pressing the matter further.

When, in 1815, the young Princess fell in love with the handsome face, agreeable manners, and determined attentions of Prince Leopold of Saxe-Coburg, the Prince readily agreed to the marriage, although Prince Leopold's oily character, indigence, and lack of territorial possessions hardly commended him to any father-in-law. He gave them Claremont, the Princess's favourite house, to live in, and encouraged his Government to settle the enormous income of £50,000 a year (which was to be paid even if the Princess died) on the fortunate Prince.

Certainly the Regent's behaviour on that fatal November day in 1817, when the Princess died giving birth to a still-born son,

in the dust
The fair hair'd Daughter of the Isles is laid,
The love of millions . . .

suggests that he was mourning a personal loss quite as much as
a dynastic one.

He was staying with Lord and Lady Hertford, at Sudbourne
in Suffolk, when a message reached him that his daughter's
labour had begun. He set out at once for Carlton House, asking
at each stopping-place whether there was a messenger for him.
He was told at one point that the labour was prolonged, and a
messenger, bringing news that the child was dead, passed him in
the dark. He reached Carlton House shortly after three in the
morning, when he was told that the child had been born dead,
and he retired to bed, thinking no doubt that there was plenty
of time to remedy this misfortune. At four he was roused by the
Duke of York, who came to tell him of the Princess's unexpected
death. There is no reason to believe that the following announce-
ment, which was put in the papers two days later, was inaccurate:
"The Prince Regent received the tidings of the death of his
Beloved Daughter with the greatest grief. His Royal Highness
was bled in the course of the day." He went down to Brighton,
and lived in retirement for some months, where his dejected
appearance was the subject of comment, and he had a severe
illness which was described as being of "the worst nature,
founded on religion and despondency."

The public, who idolised the Princess, regarded her death as a
judgment on the Prince, and could never forget what they
regarded as his tyrannical treatment of her, but it was most unfair
when they extended their animosity to the old Queen Charlotte,
and even suggested that she had poisoned the Princess. She had
done her best to bring up her granddaughter strictly (which she
regarded as essential for the Princess's rather skittish disposition),
and at the same time to give her such gaiety as was possible at
Windsor having regard to the unfortunate state of the King's
mind. When the Princess was in London she was always ready
to advise the Prince as to what parties she might, and what
functions she should, attend, and she even gave the Prince advice
on such an abstruse subject as the correct mourning (black
bombasine) which the Princess should wear when the Duchess

of Brunswick died. But the public regarded her as aiding and abetting the Prince, and as a cruel enemy of her granddaughter, and on one occasion, when she was going from Buckingham House to Carlton House, a large crowd surrounded her sedan chair, shouted out insults, and shook her in the chair. The Queen's behaviour was perfect, and she let down the glass and called out, "I am an old woman of seventy: for over 50 years I have been Queen of this country. I was never so insulted in my life." The crowd was so abashed that they allowed her to proceed.

There can be no question but that she was genuinely fond of the Princess and deeply grieved at her death. She was staying at Bath, where messengers describing the progress of the labour reached her. She was at dinner when the final message came, and she read the tragic news in the look of horror as one of her gentlemen advanced to speak to her. She rose from the table, covered her face in her hands, and gave way to a fit of convulsive sobbing. She wrote to her great friend, Lady Harcourt, "God knows from the moment I saw the poor deceased Charlotte advance in Her Pregnancy, I had a bad opinion of it, and named it to my Daughter: for her Figure was so immense (to me not natural) that I could not help being uneasy to a considerable degree." And who, with those fifteen children to her credit, could be a sounder judge of what was natural on such occasions?

The old Queen belonged to a stern generation, to whom the happiness or desires of children were naturally subordinate to the whims and fancies of parents. The matrimonial prospects of her own daughters were entirely sacrificed, because George III could not face the prospect of parting from them whom he once described as "All Cordelias, all Cordelias, no Regans or Gonerils." It was therefore natural that to the Queen the Prince's treatment of his daughter should seem kindly and generous, and she wrote, "He granted and accomplished Her Wish to marry the man she chose Herself, and gave Her the place to reside at, she was always partial to. . . . God be praised that the Prince can have nothing to reproach himself with, but can say with truth, 'I made her Happy.'"

Where his family was concerned, he showed in all his dealings the true kindliness of his nature. His mother and sisters respected and adored him, although his mother's difficult temperament and the sad, frustrated lives of "the dear sisterhood" (as he always called them) were a severe test on both his tact and his good nature.

As has been previously explained in connexion with Princess Charlotte, the Queen was determined to mark the tragedy of her husband's madness by living a life of rigorous seclusion. She was also determined—and when her mind was made up it assumed an almost Elizabethan resistance to advice or suggestion—that her cheerful, middle-aged daughters should conform to her dolorous isolation. In 1812 the Duke of York, who had lost a curl in a duel, who had faced the armies of revolutionary France and who had won renown in many an affair of gallantry, went into action on behalf of his sisters against his mother. With the loud rhetoric of the family, he outlined the sorrows of his sisters' lives, but his mother interrupted him, saying, "I had not adverted to this circumstance," and changed the subject. In reporting this to the Regent, the Duke said: "It is now perfectly open to you to speak to her . . . she will be easily got the better of." He added that "our sisters are determined to be stout, and trust that you will support them." A few weeks later two of "the dear sisterhood" attended the State opening of Parliament, without the permission of the Queen, and this resulted in a shocking outburst of tantrum and temper. The Regent wrote to her: "I do implore you, my dearest Mother, for your own happiness, for that of my sisters, and for the peace of the whole family, not to suffer the repetition of scenes so distressing and painful to all of us." A little later he wrote that he was particularly grieved that she had been so critical of the princesses, "whose conduct has been so truly proper and affectionate and whose one object has been to meet wishes expressed by me." He then asked his mother to come up to dine at Carlton House, and with a mixture of tenderness and firmness, which was typical of his adroit character, he coaxed her round to a more reasonable point of view. This helps to explain the enthusiastic feelings of all his sisters for him, why all their letters are couched in the most affectionate terms, unceasingly invoking God's blessing on him, as is shown by the following characteristic letter from the Princess Sophia, headed "The Nunnery":

"As I know how difficult it is to you, My dearest Brother, to read my scrawls, I was determined to send you a few lines in a legible hand trusting to your kindness to forgive my troubling you at this busy time, but my heart *overflows* with gratitude for all Your noble and generous intentions towards us. . . . How good you are to us which however imperfectly expressed I feel most deeply. *Poor old wretches* as we are, a *dead weight* upon You, *old lumber* to the country, like *Old Clothes,* I wonder you do not vote for putting us in a *sack* and drowning us in The Thames. . . . God bless You, my dearest G.P. Ever your unalterably attached Sophy."[1]

He was deeply attached to his brother the Duke of York, who was only a year younger than he was, and had been the companion and confidant of his boisterous youth. In later life he raised £50,000 which he gave to the Duke to help him with his debts, accompanying the gift with the advice that his brother should shun the turf. He added: "In this suggestion I have no motive, no feeling but what arises from the purest source; do not therefore answer this, nor recur to it in conversation, because I wish that the few years which may be left to either of us, should be passed in uninterrupted friendship and the warmest affection."

Nor did he show less consideration and feeling over the vexed question of the marriages of his brothers, which, in the middle years of the Regency, agitated the hearts of those amorous princes and broke up the happy home lives of their mistresses. Writers often suggest that it was the death of Princess Charlotte and the absence of an heir to the British throne which impelled them towards wedlock. This is not correct. Princess Charlotte, as a woman, could not succeed to the throne of Hanover, and it was that secondary but none the less desirable crown which was their objective. When the disaster of Princess Charlotte's death occurred, the prize was, of course, enhanced by the British crown, as were the matrimonial exertions of the Royal Dukes. The subject was in itself distasteful to the Regent, because it brought to notice his own matrimonial misfortunes and his own failure to provide the House of Hanover with an heir. The most embarrassing suitor among his brothers was the Duke of Clarence, whose proposals to various princesses rang round Europe with the speed of machine-gun fire, but with far less accuracy of aim than is generally associated with that instrument. Cousins and heiresses

[1] Quoted by Miss D. M. Stuart in *The Daughters of George III*, Macmillan, 1939.

in England likewise came under the fire of his frequent proposals. He solemnly wrote to the Regent that as no son of his cousin, the Princess Sophia of Gloucester, who was a faded spinster of forty-two, could sit on the throne of Hanover, he must positively decline that union. Yet the Prince took it all in good part and put forward great exertions to provide the Duke with a bride. In 1817 he wrote to Queen Charlotte asking her to tell the Duke to come to see him at once about the possibility of a German princess. Knowing the impetuousness and the capacity for chatter which marked the Duke, the Regent wrote:

"Pray, pray, pray, three times pray, do inculcate and enjoin silence in the first place, and in the second a prompt visit to me here. . . . Forgive all this repetition, but I really feel so anxious about him and as this is probably, considering his time of life, the last opportunity that will offer itself, in which one can do anything, that may be of any very essential service to him, I could not endure the thoughts, if he was to fail at last, and perhaps too from some little and very trifling mistake *misentendu.*"

The marriage of another brother, the Duke of Cumberland, caused the only serious break in good relations between the Prince and his mother. This Duke, who had a genius for stirring up trouble for himself and who, by brutal disregard for the feelings of others was the most detested member of the English Royal Family since the days of King John, selected a lady, widowed and divorced, who had families by both her previous marriages. This princess was a niece of Queen Charlotte, and for a reason which will now never be clearly known the Queen absolutely refused to meet or receive her. She shut her ears to reason and appeals, nursing a sulky and indignant rage with all her family. The Regent's reply to one of her letters during this difficult time is very characteristic of the patience and good humour with which he faced these family trials:

"I have this moment had the happiness to receive your most kind letter which, being filled with such parental affection, could not fail to give me great pleasure.

My devotion to your peace and comfort must ever make me studious to avoid anything that could agitate or disturb that sensibility which I know to be so intimately connected with your health and tranquillity. I therefore ever wish to forbear from anything which could possibly tend to the slightest controversy or discussion of an unfortunate subject, that has for the first time in our lives forced upon us a shade of difference which never could have arisen but in fulfilling the duties peculiar to and imperious upon our respective stations and which we cannot fail mutually to deprecate and to deplore.

It is, therefore, my dearest mother, with the deepest regret that I beg merely to observe that towards the conclusion of your letter I can perceive that there seems still unhappily to prevail in your breast the feeling that I had not done enough on my part to bring this unfortunate transaction to a different termination; whereas upon carefully reviewing all the circumstances (which are too voluminous to detail in a letter) of my conduct throughout the entire business, I am unaware of having in any one single instance withheld from your Majesty the slightest particular connected with this embarrassing affair, and I can conscientiously here add that it has been the ruling principle of my life, by every means within my power, to promote the happiness and preserve the harmony and uninimity [sic] of the family. I can not, my dearest mother, conclude without assuring you that my prayers to heaven are fervently offered up for the full restoration of your health and that every blessing may attend you."

That the flowery civilities of this letter were no idle compliments is suggested by the way in which the Prince received his mother when she came to stay with him. After she had been to stay with him at the Pavilion, he wrote:

"One and all of us after dinner yesterday could not help, after drinking your health in a bumper, expressing how cordially we wished from the very bottom of our hearts that we had the happiness of seeing you again at the head of the table here, as well as my dearest sisters, for you cannot conceive the sensation your visit has made upon everyone here, or of the regrets which your departure has occasioned."

At the beginning of 1814 he heard that his mother was thinking of coming to London on business, and he wrote at once to say that she must on no account think of coming up and down in the day "at this very, very, very severe and inclement season of the year." Though he was away from Carlton House and "not able personally to attend you and wait upon you," he had given orders to his servants to expect her at any hour and to be prepared for anything she might care to give in the way of dinners, suppers and evening parties. His use of the words "wait upon you" was not a fashion of speech, for even his enemies commented favourably on the way in which he never allowed a servant to wait on his mother at a party at Carlton House, but always himself handed her tea and refreshments. When it was obvious that the King could never recover and she was reconciled to the inevitable, she allowed herself the pleasure of entertaining for him, always giving a fête in his honour on his birthday at Frogmore, her house in the Home Park at Windsor. For his birthday in 1814 she had the tents which has been given to her by Tippoo Sahib—they were decorated on the outside with half-moons and covered inside with chintz—erected in the gardens at Frogmore. The band of the Grenadier Guards, concealed in a shrubbery, played "God save the King" alternately *forte* and *piano*. Thus accompanied the Queen and Prince walked arm in arm round the garden, which was softly illuminated with Chinese lanterns. They shone on the old Queen, plain, snuff-stained, but a regal personality exchanging forceful, pungent witticisms with her favourite son, bland, smiling, full of gracious banter. In the same winter and for each succeeding winter until her death she went to stay with him at Brighton. She died at the age of seventy-three in 1818, clasping his hand.

IV

Although the average English history book contrives to make all its pages proud reading for English boys and girls, there are only two periods of English history which are completely and gloriously triumphant—the age of Elizabeth and the Regency. There are, of course, other periods when the English whack the French or whack the Dutch or whack the Spaniards, but the Elizabethan age and the Regency are peculiar in that a brilliant achievement of arms was accompanied by a leap forward in English civilisation. While Wellington was driving the French from the Spanish Peninsula, Byron, Shelley, Keats, and Wordsworth were writing their poetry, Jane Austen and Scott were publishing their novels, and manufacturers were everywhere taking advantage of new inventions to increase trade and add to the comfort of life. While Nelson was sweeping the French ships off the sea, noblemen, gentlemen, and important rectors throughout the length and breadth of England were rebuilding their houses, laying-out lawns, walled gardens, flower gardens, and shrubberies, developing prospects and vistas, buying pictures, stocking cellars, and filling libraries, and ordering their local furniture dealer to provide them with tables, chairs, sideboards, secretaires, commodes, chests of drawers, and washing-stands— all in the latest style. There are many intelligent people who look back to the Regency as a model for the art of living, when comfort and elegance were the joint deities of home life, before the Victorians thought to increase comfort by slaying elegance.

There can be no question but that this age was rightly called after the Prince Regent. It is true that he had no share in the triumphs by land and sea, although, with his rather attractive conceit, he undoubtedly attributed them all to himself, as he wrote to his mother that he had the heartfelt consolation, without unbecoming vanity, to ascribe them "to my own original and indefatigable endeavours." But he did more than any other man before him, or after, to develop the art of living in England. It was his example which inspired much of the rebuilding and redecoration undertaken by his fellow-countrymen from the proudest noble to the most pious rector. Carlton House, which was really finished before the Regency began, has already been described, but since the fête in 1811 the Prince had employed Nash there, who was responsible for much gilding and garish embellishment. The only structural alteration was the building of a Gothic dining-room at the east end, to balance the Gothic conservatory. This room was divided into five compartments by Gothic arches, and the walls were of highly varnished wood, which were decorated with the royal arms of the Kings of England from Edward the Confessor to Queen Anne. There remain to be discussed two notable examples of the Prince's taste—his cottage at Windsor, and the Pavilion at Brighton.

It was rather natural for him when he became Regent to look round for a country home in fairly easy reach of London. Windsor

Castle was fully occupied by the King and Queen and their daughters; two or three country houses in Berkshire were considered but turned down. He therefore decided to build what was originally called the Cottage, and afterwards the Royal Lodge, in Windsor Great Park.

The Cottage was built on the site of a small lodge, about half a mile to the south-east of where the statue of George III (known as the Copper Horse) now stands. It was designed by Nash, and was begun in 1812, and was probably finished at the end of 1814, as in August of that year *The Times* records that the Queen, the Prince, and two of his sisters drove in an open carriage down the Long Walk to view the Prince Regent's cottage "which was nearing completion." He first stayed there in the summer of 1815 for the Ascot races, just before the battle of Waterloo was fought. The word cottage which we rather naturally associate with agricultural labourers or bright little maiden ladies must not be taken as a literal description of the building: the Whigs were nearer the mark when they contemptuously described it as the Prince's "Thatched Palace." It was officially known as the Royal Lodge. No adequate description of the building survives. We only know that it was in the Gothic style, that it was thatched with reeds and that it had mullioned windows and that Nash had used trees and shrubberies with great skill in order to give it the appearance of being smaller than it was. A thatched verandah, with wooden supports covered with creepers and honeysuckle, extended along the whole of the south front. It was surrounded by a fence of wooden palings, and from outside this nothing but the chimney-tops were visible.[1]

The Pavilion at Brighton, with its pinnacles and domes, its oddly irregular, but yet effective, outlines, rising from the heart of the town, is a far more familiar example of the Prince's taste.

It is often stated that at the beginning of the nineteenth century he was given some Chinese wallpaper, which started his craze for *chinoiserie*, and decided him to convert the Pavilion into an eastern palace. This seems improbable when it is remembered that he had a Chinese drawing-room at Carlton House from as early as the 1780's. This drawing-room had always been greatly admired, and it seems probable that this encouraged him to experiment with eastern decorations.

[1] It is now the home of King George VI.

In 1802 he added two rooms to the Pavilion, one at each end—one was to be a music-room, and the other a dining-room. Although for the next twenty years the Pavilion was being constantly altered and embellished, the essential plan remained the same: that is, three large rooms—the drawing-room in the middle, and the dining- and music-rooms at either end. These rooms were connected by ante-rooms, small drawing-rooms, and saloons, which are rather confusing and were being constantly altered. The two new rooms which were built in 1802 were decorated entirely in the eastern style, and at the same time considerable quantities of eastern furniture were sent down to Brighton. The alterations were not finished until 1805, when the building, brilliantly lighted with Argand burners—recently invented oil-lamps—was the scene of a large ball. The following evening Mrs. Fitzherbert's adopted daughter, Miss Seymour, aged eight, gave a ball and supper to the "Juvenile nobility."

It is rather pointless to describe the decorations of the Pavilion at this period, as all the best features, with one exception, were incorporated in the later alterations. The exception was a passage leading from the music-room to a small drawing-room. This passage was 12 feet long by 8 feet wide, and was formed entirely of stained glass decorated with Chinese figures, which was lighted from outside, so that it gave anyone the impression of being inside a Chinese lantern.

For the next few years, although many structural alterations at the Pavilion were contemplated, none actually materialised. It was probably in 1807, when the Prince was staying with Lord and Lady Hertford at Ragley, that he drove over to see Sezincote at Moreton-in-the-Marsh some twenty miles away. Sezincote had been built in the Indian style, by Repton, for a wealthy nabob who, unlike most Anglo-Indians, was not content with describing his dull experiences in that brilliant country, but desired some more permanent and suitable reminder of the best years of his life. The Prince, in company with more distinguished critics, greatly admired this eccentric example of romantic architecture. He immediately ordered Repton to draw up designs for converting the Pavilion into an Indian palace. These designs still exist, and are much admired, but lack of money made it impossible to put them into effect. When he became Regent, the Prince felt that he had sufficient money to justify the rebuilding of the Pavilion.

The work was however entrusted to Nash, in whose skill he had implicit confidence, and the result is the Pavilion as it stands to-day, a curiously effective blend of Indian, Chinese, and Moorish styles.

From 1812 onwards Chinese furniture, ornaments, wallpapers, and fittings poured into Brighton. Most of them were removed to Buckingham Palace by Queen Victoria, and it is only possible for the visitor to the Pavilion to-day to form a shadowy idea of what the rooms looked like when, in 1822, they were finally finished in all their tinkling magnificence.

The music-room was 42 feet square, and the walls were decorated with crimson and gold paintings of Chinese scenes. This room did not have a flat ceiling, but a dome painted with green and gold shells, which gradually diminished in size and gave thereby an added sense of height. There was an enormous lustre, suspended from the apex of the dome, in the shape of a lotus, from which darted golden dragons in attitudes of flight. In one of the recesses of the room stood a fine organ built by Lincoln in 1818. The carpet, which was manufactured at Axminster, was bright blue, ornamented with golden stars, serpents, dragons, birds, and insects.

The Chinese gallery, which ran behind some of the smaller rooms and connected the dining- and music-rooms, was 162 feet long by 17 feet wide. The doors at either end were faced with mirrors, so as to increase the impression of length. The walls were painted the colour of peach-blossom, ornamented with blue, and the furniture was principally of ivory. The centre division of the gallery projected through the first floor to the roof, and was illumined by a horizontal piece of stained glass, 22 feet long by 11 feet wide, on which was represented the Chinese God of Thunder, flying and surrounded by his drums. The god was wielding a mace, wherewith to strike the drums and arouse the thunder. From his other hand a lantern was suspended.

Probably the finest room of all was the banqueting room which was described by an observer as of "quiet and chaste beauty which is almost intellectual." Like the music-room, it had a dome, on which was painted an eastern sky partially obscured by the foliage of a fruiting plantain-tree. From this issued a brilliantly coloured dragon, from which in turn was suspended a magnificent lustre measuring 30 feet in length and weighing a ton. The walls were divided into eleven compartments, bordered by scarlet and gold trellis work, in turn surrounded by blue and silver paper. Each of these compartments was filled with paintings on canvas of the domestic manners of the Chinese—feasting, receiving guests, playing with children, music, gardening, and love-making. The backgrounds of all these canvases, as well as the doors, were painted to resemble mother-of-pearl.

The Prince's private apartments were on the ground floor, and consisted of a library, a bedroom, and a bath-room. The bedroom had light green walls, on which stars and dragons were drawn in white. The bathroom was lined with white marble, and the bath was 16 feet long by 10 feet wide, and was 6 feet deep. It was supplied with salt water from the sea. There was a private chapel, which was 80 feet long by 40 feet wide, and although no very satisfactory description of it has come down to us, we gather that China and the east stopped abruptly at its door.

The whole building with Chinese cabinets, mandarins, dragons, jars, ornaments, weapons, and musical instruments, must have accurately resembled the words of the nineteenth-century nursery jingle:

> *Ching-a-ring-a-ring-ching! Feast of Lanterns!*
> *What a crop of chop-sticks, hongs and gongs!*
> *Hundred thousand Chinese crinkum-crankums,*
> *Hung among the bells and ding-dongs!*
> *What a lot of Pekin pots and pipkins,*
> *Mandarins with pig-tails, rings and strings,*
> *Funny little slop-shops, cases, places*
> *Stuck about with cups and tea-things!*

It is wrong to think that the Prince gave *carte blanche* to Nash to produce an eastern palace and then took no further interest in it himself. He carefully went over the plans, he was constantly at Brighton supervising the work, and tradition has it that he encouraged a young workman, who was graining the doors, to introduce dragons into the grain. It was natural that a building of this kind should lend itself to a certain amount of ridicule, and the following verse was repeated with a good deal of relish at the time:

> *The outside—huge teapots, all drill'd round with holes,*
> *Relieved by extinguishers, sticking on poles.*
> *The inside—all tea-things and dragons and bells,*
> *The show rooms—all show, the sleeping rooms—cells.*

And Miss Berry, the friend of Horace Walpole, who had consequently some familiarity with architectural oddities, wrote, "The effect is more like a china shop *baroquement* arranged, than the abode of a Prince. All is gaudy, without looking gay; and all is crowded with ornaments without being magnificent." Against this view must be put the opinion of countless guests at the Pavilion who were lost in admiration of it. But there is no doubt that the Pavilion was one of the reasons for the unpopularity of the Prince with subsequent generations. There could be no greater contrast between its architecture and furnishings, and the grim little villas stuffed with padded furniture and adorned with faded photographs which to later generations were synonymous with breeding, good taste and virtue.

It is impossible to avoid reflecting upon the reactions of the hundreds of people who now see over it every year. Many are doubtless genuinely puzzled, some are shocked, a few think it "amusing"; while some, we may hope, sincerely and intelligently admire it in company with all who understand the architecture of the eighteenth century.

There is a danger that, as the ridicule and horror with which the Pavilion was so long regarded gives place to appreciation and admiration, the Prince will be regarded as simply a dabbler in exotic extravagances. He has, in fact, far more solid claims to the gratitude of those who are concerned with the architectural beauties of England. His name is associated with one of the few intelligent pieces of town planning in London. It was his encouragement which made the building of Regent Street possible —"the royal mile" which was to connect Carlton House with a pleasure pavilion, which never materialised, in Regent's Park. It is clear that Nash would not have been able to carry through such a large undertaking as the building of the new street and the lay-out of the Park without the influence of the Prince and his authority over that lethargic, troublesome body, the Commissioners for Crown Lands.[1] The fact that public opinion in the decade after the War, when it has never been so craven and mischievous, allowed Regent Street to be "rebuilt," and much of Nash's work in Regent's Park to be ruined, should not blind

---

[1] All this is clearly brought out in Mr. John Summerson's life of Nash which has been recently published. I am grateful to him for permission to see his book in proof.

a later generation, which is alive to the wisdom of planning cities, to the credit which is due to Nash and the Prince for attempting to make a district of London both grand and beautiful.

It would also be a great mistake to regard the Prince's experiments in Chinese furniture, and the fantastic decorations of the Pavilion, as his only claim on the gratitude of those who now live in his houses and enjoy his purchases. The French, Regency, and lacquered furniture in Buckingham Palace and Windsor Castle, the bronzes, the clocks, and the china, were practically all collected by him. During, and just after, the French Revolution, when Louis-Quinze and Louis-Seize furniture was neglected, the Prince, assisted by the expert advice of the third Lord Hertford, bought on a large scale. Acting on the advice of M. Benoit, who had been *pâtissier* to Louis XVI, he also bought magnificent examples of Sèvres porcelain, so that the Royal Collection of Sèvres is to-day the finest in the world. Apart from a very few examples which date from the seventeenth and early eighteenth centuries, the Royal Collection of gold and silver plate was all acquired by him. This was principally bought in the early years of the Regency, and his account with Messrs. Rundle & Bridge, the Court silversmiths, amounted to £15,840 for the four years 1812–1816.

But probably posterity has most cause to be grateful to him on account of his taste in painting. Even before the Regency he had been attracted by Dutch pictures, and had been a regular buyer of Rembrandt, Rubens, and the Cuyps, but in 1814 he bought the whole of the magnificent Baring collection of Dutch pictures which contained several examples of such artists as Gerard Dou, Gerard Ter Borch, Gabriel Metsu, Jan Steen, and Vandevelde. He was also a great admirer of Greuze and Watteau, several of whose paintings are in the Royal Collection. It would be easy to think that the Prince just gave a *carte-blanche* order to his agents to buy up all the pictures they could: in fact each purchase was carefully considered and discussed with Lord Hertford, and the whole collection is clearly the work of someone who really appreciated works of art and understood what he was buying. One of the Keepers of the King's Pictures,[1] with that prudent, commercial outlook of those brought up in Victorian England, has written, "The colossal extravagance of George IV has justified

[1] The late Sir Lionel Cust.

itself because his pictures are worth three or four times what he gave for them."

The Prince's expenses during the Regency, with his purchases of pictures and furniture, the building of the Royal Lodge, the rebuilding of the Pavilion, and the improvements at Carlton House, were, of course, tremendous. At the end of 1811, his debts were estimated at £522,000, which was made up as follows:

To English Creditors:

	£
Under liquidation at the rate of £30,000 per annum	153,000
Remainder of the Princess of Wales's debt	17,000
Arrears not on any fund of liquidation	125,000
To the purchase of plate and pictures	67,000
	£362,000

To the Landgrave of Hesse:[1]

	£
Contracted before 1795, and not paid at the settlement of his debts on marriage	71,000
Borrowed in 1799	40,000
Total Principal	111,000
Interest to 1811	113,000
	224,000
Deduct from this the share which the Prince had re-lent to the Duke of York who had agreed to repay him	64,000
	160,000
Total Debt to English Creditors and the Landgrave	£522,000

He also owed £96,000 for income-tax. The arrears of his payments to English creditors at this period were partially explained by his having had to bear all the expenses of the Regency without any increased income, and by his having had to pay off £45,000 of the Princess of Wales's debts.

The Prince urged the Government to apply to Parliament to

[1] This very accommodating creditor was the grandson of George II, being the son of the Princess Mary of England.

vote a lump sum for the liquidation of the whole debt, but Mr. Perceval, who was Prime Minister, was opposed to this course, and in 1812, when the limitations on the Regency expired, the Prince had to be content with an increased income, and with paying an increased annual sum in liquidation of the debt. By 1814, the debt had been reduced to £350,000, and by the end of the Regency it was virtually paid off.

There were throughout the early and middle years of the Regency constant increases in the Civil List to provide for the Prince's various building schemes. As both the Pavilion and the Royal Lodge were the Prince's private property, as distinct from Carlton House, which was Crown property, the Treasury very properly objected to finding large sums of money which ought to have been paid by the Prince himself, and they only agreed to a payment of £50,000 for furniture for the Pavilion on condition that the furniture became Crown property. In 1816 the Prime Minister, Foreign Secretary and Chancellor of the Exchequer sent a memorandum to the Prince stating that unless all new expenses at the Pavilion were abandoned the existence of the Government would be jeopardised. They felt that, in view of the general distress in the country, the unfavourable impressions made by the Prince's demands "may never be effaced." But the groans and head-scratchings of Chancellors of the Exchequer and Treasury officials were as nothing to the acid, vituperative speeches of the Whigs when the Civil List came under discussion in the House of Commons. The storm finally broke in 1816, when it was announced that the Prince was going to erect a monument in Rome to the memory of the exiled Stuarts. This was finally finished in 1819, and was placed in St. Peter's, Rome. It was designed by Canova, and inscribed:

IACOBO III
IACOBI . II . MAGNAE . BRIT . REGIS . FILIO
KAROLO EDVARDO
ET . HENRICO . DECANO . PATRUM. CARDINALIUM
IACOBI—III—FILIIS
REGIAE—STIRPIS—STVARDIAE—POSTREMIS
ANNO M.DCCC.XIX.

The responsibility for erecting the monument was the Prince's —a singularly gracious act—but it was actually paid for by the surplus of the French Government's contribution for the removal from Paris to Rome of statues which Napoleon had looted. It was too good an opportunity for the Whigs to miss, and Brougham, speaking in the House of Commons, said, "Much better would it be instead of doing honour to that Family to profit by its example, to recollect that by thwarting the prejudices, opposing the wishes and pressing on the sore places of this nation, they were at length ousted from the throne. ['Hear! Hear! Hear!'] And yet their conduct was comparatively harmless and innocent. They were in a great measure betrayed by the tenderness of their consciences, by the nicety of their religious scruples. Far otherwise must those be estimated who entertained no scruples of religion, who experienced no tenderness of conscience: who, in utter disregard of the feelings of an oppressed and insulted nation, proceeded from one wasteful expenditure to another: who decorated and crowded their houses with the splendid results of their extravagance, who associated with the most profligate of human beings . . . yet desired the House of Commons to lavish on their favourites the money extracted from the pockets of the suffering people of England. [Loud cries of 'Hear! Hear! Hear!']."

Even after 120 years we can hardly fail to be fascinated by the boldness and felicity of Brougham's phrases, and nineteenth-century moralists would accept his argument as equally fascinating. There are, however, to-day those economic wizards who would hail the Prince as one who really understood finance because he appreciated that personal extravagance was the proper weapon with which to combat a post-war depression. But even without invoking their aid, we need not be overwhelmed by Brougham's argument.

Supposing that the Prince had incurred no debts at all, who would have benefited? Certainly not "the suffering people of England," who were groaning under an iniquitous system of indirect taxation, notably on food. There would have been no suggestion to lighten the taxes that bore so heavily and unjustly on them. The only people who would have benefited would have been the rich and middle classes, from whose well-lined pockets rather less money would have been taken in direct taxation. As a result of a reduction in income tax Mr. Brougham might perhaps have felt that he was justified in giving up those slashing articles in the *Edinburgh Review* (a respite from labours which were not of inestimable value to English literature), or perhaps Mr. Whitbread might have felt that he was justified in putting another vat into his brewery to the permanent enrichment of the great House of Whitbread. At this distance of time we can feel thankful that the money was spent by a Prince who, from our point of view, used it far more generously and effectively than if it had been left to fructify in the pockets of the middle classes, and swallowed up in the great maw of commercial England.

Naturally it was not possible for those who had actually to provide the money to judge the question with the same detachment as we can. They saw, on the one hand, the Pavilion rising in all its fantastic glory, furniture, plate, and pictures pouring into Carlton House, money being freely spent on the Royal Lodge at Windsor while, on the other hand, the distress among the working classes was unparalleled, thousands of soldiers who had returned from the war finding no possibility of work, and nothing but starvation for them and their families. It is probable that no ruler in England, not excluding King John, has ever been so unpopular as the Prince in the years immediately following Waterloo. The reason for this was that, although a large part of the population was living in misery, he contrived to give the impression that it was no concern of his. In 1817 the fact that it was some concern of his was forcibly brought home to him.

In January of that year he drove to Westminster to open Parliament. As his sister-in-law, the Duchess of Cumberland, had on the previous day given birth to a still-born child, no guns were fired, and there was no band. The Prince met with a very hostile reception, the hisses being painfully audible as there was nothing to drown them. It was observed that he read his speech in a very depressed voice. On the return journey his carriage was pelted with gravel and stones, and the horses had to be put to a quick trot. On arriving at Carlton House, the Prince complained that he had been shot at. It was found that there was a neat hole, such as a stone could not have made, in one of the windows of the carriage, but as no report had been noticed it was concluded that he had been fired at with an air-gun.

The Prince sent a message, complaining of the outrage, to the Houses of Parliament, and on the following Sunday a prayer was ordered to be read in all the churches:

"Almighty God—Merciful God, who, in compassion to a sinful nation, hast defeated the designs of desperate men, and hast protected from the base and barbarous assaults of a lawless multitude the Regent of the United Kingdom, accept our praise and thanksgiving; continue, we implore thee, thy protection of his Royal Person. Shield him from the arrow that flieth by day and from the pestilence that walketh in darkness; from the secret designs of treason and from the madness of the people. . . ."

This incident was the high-water-mark of the Prince's unpopularity during the Regency. He gradually became more popular, partly owing to improving conditions of trade, and partly owing to his giving up £50,000 a year out of the Civil List. In 1819 he held a Drawing-Room, which was largely attended, even by the Whigs, and on the way to which he was loudly cheered by the crowd.

V

"I look through all his life, and recognise but a bow and a grin." As *The Four Georges* was composed to titillate republican audiences in America, we should not be too critical of Thackeray for not looking through the life a trifle more industriously, and for leaving his own question unanswered—"There may be something behind, but what?" Criticism should hardly be so generous to the many writers who, since Thackeray's day, have lavishly expended their ink in description and condemnation of the Prince, but have not troubled to unswathe what Thackeray calls "the royal old mummy." He appears as a central, but strictly impersonal, figure. We see him in many books—and doubtless in the future we shall see him in many "historical" films—in his Field Marshal's uniform, gaily emblazoned with orders, driving through the streets of London, or receiving a distinguished company of guests at Carlton House, patronising a race meeting, or watching a boxing match, handing a silver cream-jug to his mother, explaining the beauties of his pictures to his friends, poring over the plans of houses, acquiring furniture, suffering mental distress over politicians, his wife, or a hostile public, driving in his yellow Berlin, with the purple blinds, to spend the afternoon with Lady Hertford, writing his tortuous letters, joking, chatting, drinking and overeating: but the intelligent observer is still left with the question, "What was he really like?"

The difficulty of answering this question is not lessened by the strident replies from the Whig diarists and memoir writers— "a drunkard," "a spendthrift," "an adulterer," "a soulless sot," "a traitor," not even by the dulcet, wheedling tones of Mr. Creevey, "Ah, Prinney, Prinney." The question is made especially difficult because no reply to it has come down from those who really knew and appreciated him.

The popular conception of him as a plump satyr in a state of perennial tipsiness is ridiculous. The facts of the Prince's sexual life are neither particularly interesting nor particularly edifying, but they are certainly not outrageously scandalous. He was unfaithful to his wife, he was unfaithful to Mrs. Fitzherbert; when he was forty-five he settled down to a life of domestic bliss with an aged marchioness, who, after some fifteen years, was supplanted by a second aged marchioness. As a young man he was undoubtedly promiscuous in his attachments, but he did not in that respect differ from the majority of his generation. His name has become almost a synonym for adultery, and this popular view of him is well illustrated by a tradition, treasured, suitably enough, in Thackeray's family. A young lady of the family had been sent down from Yorkshire to stay with an aunt at Brighton: when the sweet young thing was strolling along the Steyne, the Prince came riding by and looked at her through his spy-glass. The aunt immediately packed the young lady straight back to Yorkshire. This story is surely only a proof of the alarming prudence of maiden aunts, not of the wickedness of princes. But popular traditions die hard. And there is now almost a vested interest in maintaining the wickedness of the Prince, because there are many people to-day who like to fill in a gap in their pedigrees, or to explain away the honourable obscurity of their origin, by claiming a dishonourable descent from the Prince. It is only possible to say that family tradition is not proof, nor even the Royal characteristics of a tumble of fair hair and a wide mouth: such descendants may exist, but proof appears to be uniformly lacking.

Possibly an exception should be made for the daughter of

Mrs. Elliot, who was the Prince's mistress in the 1780's. This child was given the convincing names of Georgiana Frederica Augusta[1] and her mother undoubtedly thought she was the Prince's daughter, but others, including apparently the Prince, regarded Lord Cholmondeley as the father.

In the same way his drunkenness has been grossly exaggerated. Thackeray, with logic which seems difficult to follow, attributes his drunkenness to his having a beautiful voice. As a young man he used to get fairly frequently drunk, and he had always a taste for wine, being very fond of lingering over some old brandy which he called "diabolino." When he rose from the dinner-table, he was never perhaps strictly sober, but his condition was not materially different from that of thousands of his future subjects in country-houses and parsonages up and down England.

"Lax, maudlin, slip-slop." Thus Thackeray on the letter-writing style of the Prince. In this charge there is, of course, much substance. There is, for example, the extraordinary letter which the Prince wrote to his mother from Ragley—the country home of Lord and Lady Hertford—and dated, significantly enough, Tuesday night, with all the implications of composition after one of those rich Regency dinners, washed down with those bumpers in which the Prince delighted. The absurdity and vivacity of the opening paragraph are matchless:

"What a kind, oh! what a kind kind very kind dear letter I have been favoured with from you; never no never never can I find words sufficiently strong or powerful to express to you the full tide of all my gratitude for your affection, kindness, goodness and attention to me and to my wishes. But since I feel myself wholly unequal to the task, I will not presume to trespass upon your precious time with weak and fruitless attempts at such expressions as can only be really felt by the heart, and do not admit of being traced by the pen, therefore, I must and I do throw myself upon your indulgence, to fancy to yourself, to interpret to yourself and to say to yourself for me *all* that heart can feel or that pen can trace."

A somewhat closer examination of the Prince's letters suggests

[1] She married William Charles Augustus Cavendish-Bentinck and had an only child Georgiana Augusta Frederica Cavendish-Bentinck, who died unmarried in 1883.

that Thackeray's heavy condemnation missed some of the finer points of the Prince's style. As is well known—indeed, Thackeray's own Miss Pinkerton drives the lesson home—at the end of the eighteenth century it was the hall-mark of culture and politeness to write letters in a style as straight and trim as a *parterre*, in which each sentence was stiff, formal and balanced. The Prince Regent could, of course, write in that style, but in writing to his family and intimates he regarded it as only polite to drop formality and write, as he once explained to his mother, "every thought as it occurred in its own misshapen and crude state, preferring writing to you in this natural and easy way to any studied language."

No doubt he wrote these letters in much the same fashion as he spoke, the same obtrusion of himself and his feelings, the same solicitation for his own comfort and well-being, the same long and rambling jests, but all faults redeemed and the whole character illumined by a sense of the oddity of life and by a true sympathy with the feelings of others. In 1814, at the end of a prodigious letter to his mother filled with little splashes of scholarship and gallicisms, he indulges in an unexpected tribute to laughter which was especially important in winter because "it generally makes one shake one's sides somewhat," which in turn "contributes in no small degree to make one warm." He went on to say that laughter was also very valuable because it quickened the circulation of the blood—"a most excellent thing when or if one is a little benumbed or torpid."

He then asked his mother to guess a new nickname which he had made up for a certain courtier. This was Sir Thomas Tyrrwhit —a very short gentleman of whom the members of the Royal Family were very fond and by whom they were greatly amused. The question asked was why Sir Thomas Tyrrwhit was like June 23rd. The answer, making allowance for a slight confusion in the proper date, was that the shortest knight was like the shortest night. He then went on that he had thought of sending to Hunter's Museum for one of the large glass jars "containing one of the little embryos (*ou peutêtre ce que l'on peut appeller aussi fausse couche sans se tromper beaucoup de nom*) in order to tie a little bit of blue string round the neck of it, and then a little bit of red ribbon over its shoulder and then to have sent it as a cadeau to you to have ornamented the mantle piece of the chimney of your sitting-room. . . . Forgive with your usual indulgence and kindness this momentary bit of farrago and nonsense."

Hardly less entertaining is his description of a minor illness with which he was seized shortly after the death of Princess Charlotte:

"I do not know under what denomination to class the attack, or by what name regularly to define and call it, for it seems to me to have been a sort of mishmash, Solomongrundy, Olla podrida kind of a business in itself that is quite anomalous; a good deal of rheumatism, as much of cold, with a little touch of bile to boot, not a very pleasant mixture on the whole and composed of as unpleasant ingredients as can be well thought of or imagined. In short all that pot pourri has rendered me both bodily as well as mentally very unfit indeed."

He clearly disliked dwelling on anything painful or disagreeable. In reply to a letter of Lord Anglesey of sympathy on the death of Princess Charlotte, he wrote: "The visitation has been most severe, as it was unexpected, but we are all bound, great as well as small, to bow with resignation to the rule and dispensation of Providence, and it would be distressing to your feelings as it must be to mine to dwell upon a subject so afflicting in all its bearings." He then dropped into French for a playful criticism of Anglesey's character, closing his letter by saying, "My bile is now all discharged."

His vanity was constant, though tinged at times with pathos. He felt that he had made a personal contribution to the overthrow of Napoleon by maintaining the Tories in office in 1812 rather than gratify his personal predilections by sending for the Whigs. He deeply felt the savage attacks of his old friends, but viewed them as a necessary consequence of the patriotic line which he had followed. In a letter to his mother dated September 22nd, 1813, he wrote to announce a great victory over the French, heading his letter: "Great Events! Great Events! Great Events!" He asked his mother "to drink a bumper" on this occasion "and do not quite forget poor me, who have I think some little merit at having been the first to set them all at work." After the Battle of Leipzig, he sent his mother a snuff-box with a portrait of himself on the lid who "I hope you will *now* think is *no disgrace to you,* to his family or to his country." Finally, after Napoleon's overthrow in 1814, he could write: "perhaps I may be vain enough to hope that you may feel a little proud of your son."

Thackeray is of the opinion that all the Prince's private letters were spelled for him by others. This is, of course, a gross travesty of the truth, and on one occasion the Prime Minister asked him if he would mind translating an English letter into French, "because your Royal Highness understands the idiom of that language."

It may be as well here to dispose of one other of Thackeray's inaccuracies. With many blasts on his moral trumpet, with many pats on the back to the age in which he lived, because "Play is a deposed goddess, her worshippers bankrupt and her table in rags," the eminent novelist calls the Prince "a great practitioner" of gambling, and a "pigeon for the playmen." The Prince spent money like water and lost large sums racing, but there is no evidence at all that he gambled to any extent with cards or dice. The Duke of York was a gambler all his life, but there is no reason for disbelieving the Prince when he said that he himself did not care for it. Further proof of this is afforded by his rebuke to Lord Kenyon in 1799. Lord Kenyon, who was Lord Chief Justice, was one of those tiresome members of the judiciary who regard the bench as a platform for airing their banal views on behaviour and morality, and he referred in the course of a case to a rumour that one of the parties to the action was to keep a subscription gaming-house "under the patronage of a very high and illustrious personage." The Prince wrote to him at once:

". . . I am confident that your lordship could never have used *the expression*, which in the notion of everyone so decidedly alludes to me. . . . But if these were really your lordship's words (which I cannot for a moment suppose) give me leave to tell you that you have totally mistaken my character and turn, for of all men universally known to have the least predilection to play, I am perhaps the very man in the world who stands the strongest and the most proverbially so upon that point. . . ."

It should not be imagined that because the Prince did not spend every night under the table, or in the arms of a mistress, or rattling a dice-box, he was consequently an estimable character. He was, as Wellington said, "the most extraordinary compound of talent, wit, buffoonery, obstinacy and good feeling—in short a medley of the most opposite qualities, with a great preponderance of good—that I ever saw in any character in my life."

The misfortune has been that although many books have been written on the Prince they all have harped on the violence and caprices of his passion to the exclusion of much that was fascinating in his character, much that was more important. There can be no doubt that his talented and expansive nature is to be seen to the best advantage and at its most natural, not struggling with politics, not sobbing his heart out to Fox about Mrs. Fitzherbert, not sitting at Lady Hertford's feet, but entertaining a party of his friends at the Pavilion, charming comparative strangers by his attentions, and shining as a gracious, intelligent host. That most voluminous of Victorian writers, Mrs. Pitt Byrne, the talented authoress of *Social Hours with Celebrities*, *A Collection of Serious and Whimsical Wills*, and *A Glance behind the Grilles of the Religious Houses of France*, has summed up in three foolish sentences what is unfortunately still the prevailing belief of what the Prince's life at the Pavilion was really like. "The unbridled license the future monarch allowed himself in this sybaritical palace was, however, the cause of grave scandal throughout the country. It is perhaps better to make no more than a shadowy allusion to the character of the company harboured beneath the Pavilion Domes. Riot and unrestrained festivity were the order of the day; and it may be added also of the night." A moment's reflection should have shown this virtuous lady that the place was far too brittle for any very tumultuous festivities. A number of drunken "Regency bucks," reeling among the mandarins and vases, would have done irreparable damage. Nor did the decorations of Carlton House lend themselves to the antics of the pothouse.

In fact, the Prince's life at Brighton was what his mother would have called "Hum-Drum." In the morning he dressed late, and then went out for a ride, but towards the end of the Regency, particularly after his illness following the Princess Charlotte's death, he practically gave up riding. This was one of the reasons why he became unwieldy and lethargic, but his answer to someone who urged him to take exercise was rather convincing, "Why should I? I never had better spirits, appetite and health than when I stay within and I am not so well when I go abroad." And on another occasion he explained that his ankle-bones were too slender to support his body, and that they swelled after he had taken any exercise. The afternoon was generally spent quietly with Lady Hertford, and he preferred not to see his other guests until the evening, but if he happened to meet them he took a delight in showing them over the Pavilion, particularly the kitchens. Croker, who saw over them, wrote, "Such contrivances for roasting, boiling, baking, stewing, frying, steaming and heating; hot plates, hot closets, hot air and hot hearths, with all manner of cocks for hot water and cold water and warm water and steam and twenty saucepans all ticketed and labelled, placed up to their necks in a vapour bath."

The guests assembled for dinner shortly before 6.30, the ladies seated, and the gentlemen standing. When the Prince came in, the ladies rose, and he passed round, shaking hands with all. He then led the lady of highest rank in to dinner, or if there were two of equal rank he gave an arm to each. After dinner the Prince generally played at Patience, and Croker was amused on one occasion to hear him say, "Damn the King."

When he was at Brighton there was always a number of distinguished people staying at the various hotels, and he used to give a dinner-party for some of these at least twice a week. The Prince generally chose the *menu* himself, as he took a great interest in wine and food. He was fortunate in being able to secure Carême for his *chef*, though home-sickness drove him back to Paris after a few months' employment with the Prince. One of Carême's *menus* has fortunately survived:

TABLE DE S.A.R. LE PRINCE REGENT
Servie au pavillon de Brighton, Angleterre,
15 *Janvier*, 1817
Menu de 36 entrées

QUATRE POTAGES

Le potage à la Monglas   Le potage d'orge perlée à la Crécy
La garbure aux choux   Le potage de poissons à la Russe

QUATRE RELEVÉS DE POISSONS
La matelote au vin de Bordeaux
Les truites au bleu à la Provençale
Le turbot à l'Anglaise, sauce aux homards
La grosse anguille à la régence

QUATRE GROSSES PIÈCES POUR LES CONTRE-FLANCS
Le jambon à la broche, au Madère
L'oie braisée aux racines glacées
Les poulardes à la Périgueux
Le rond de veau à la royale

TRENTE-SIX ENTRÉES, DONT QUATRE SERVENT DE CONTRE-FLANCS
Les filets de volaille à la maréchale
Le sauté de merlans aux fines herbes
La timbale de macaroni à la Napolitaine
La noix de veau à la jardinière
Les filets de volaille à l'Orléans

Le Jambon à la Broche
La darne de saumon au beurre de Montpellier
Le sauté de faisans aux truffes
La fricassée de poulets à l'Italienne
Le turban de filets de lapereaux

Les Truites au Bleu
Les boudin de volaille à la Béchamel
Le sauté de ris de veau à la Provençale
Les ailes de poulardes glacées à la chicorée
Les galantines de perdreaux à la gelée

L'Oie Braisée aux Racines Glacées
Les petites canetons de volaille en haricots vierges
Les poulets à la reine, à la Chevry
Les petites croustades de mauviettes au gratin
Les côtelettes de mouton à l'Irlandaise
Les filets de bécasses à la royale
Les filets de sarcelles à la Bourguignotte
Les petits poulets à l'Indienne
Les petites pâtés de mouton à l'Anglaise
L'épigramme de poulardes, purée de céleri
Le faisan à la Minime, bordure de racines

Les Poulardes à la Périgueux
L'aspic de blanc de volaille à la ravigote
Les filets de perdreaux à la Pompadour
L'émincé de poulardes au gratin
La côte de bœuf aux oignons glacés

Le Turbot à l'Anglaise
Le sauté de poulardes à la Provençale
Le salmis de cailles au vin de Madère
Les escalopes de volaille aux truffes
La salade de filets de brochets aux huîtres

Le Rond de Veau à la Royale
Le pain de carpes au beurre d'anchois
Les côtelettes d'agneau glacées à la Toulouse
Le vol-au-vent de quenelles à l'Allemande
Les ailerons de poulardes aux champignons
Les pigeons à la Mirepoix financière

POUR EXTRA, DIX ASSIETTES VOLANTES DE FRITURE

5 De filets de soles
5 De filets de gelinottes à l'Allemande

HUIT GROSSES PIÈCES DE PÂTISSERIE

La brioche au fromage
Le nougat à la Française
La ruine d'Antioche
L'hermitage Syrien
Le biscuit à l'orange

Le croque-en-bouche aux pistaches
L'hermitage chinois
La ruine de la mosquée turque

QUATRE PLATS DE ROTS

Les coqs de Bruyères
Les canards sauvages

Les poulets gras bardés
Les gelinottes

TRENTE-DEUX ENTREMETS

Les truffes à la cendre
La gelée d'oranges moulée
Les épinards à l'essence
La Brioche au Fromage
Les homards au gratin
Les petits pains à la duchesse
Les sckals au beurre
Le pouding de pommes au muscat
Les mirlitons aux citrons
Les Canards Sauvages
Les bouchées perlées aux groseilles
Les oeufs brouillés aux truffes
Le Nougat à la Française
Les pommes de terre à la Hollandaise
La gelée de punch renversée
Les champignons à la Provençale
Les navets glacés à la Chartre
La gelée de liqueurs des îsles
Les concombres à la Béchamel
Les Biscuits de Fécule à l'Orange
Les laitues farcies à l'essence

Les Coqs de Bruyères
Les gâteaux glacés aux abricots
Le fromage bavarois aux avelines
La purée de haricots
L'Hermitage Chinois
Les petits paniers aux confitures
Les Poulets Gras Bardés
Les génoises glacées au café
Le charlotte à l'Américaine
Les choux-fleurs au Parmesan
L'Hermitage Syrien
Le céleri en cardes à l'Espagnole
La crême française à l'ananas
Les petits soufflés d'abricots
Les Gelinottes
Les gâteaux de feuilletage pralinés
Les huîtres au gratin
Les Croques-en-Bouche
Les petites carottes à la Flamande
La gelée de citrons moulée
Les truffes à l'Italienne

POUR EXTRA, DIX ASSIETTES VOLANTES

5 De petites soufflés de pommes
5 De petits soufflés au chocolat

Dinner would be followed by an evening party, to which invitations were of a more general character, when there might be 100 guests present. The principal entertainment after dinner was provided by the Prince's private band, composed only of wind instruments, which played in the music-room, according to Croker, rather *bruyant*. Occasionally a private person would be asked to play on the pianoforte, and one evening Viotti played on the violin. At twelve o'clock supper, consisting of sandwiches and wine, was brought in, after which the Prince shook hands all round and retired. William Wilberforce, who was staying at Brighton in 1815, was invited to dine by the Prince, and described how the Prince, like any other English gentleman, sat at the head of his own table, and added, "Really had I been covered with titles and ribands, I could not have been treated with more real, unaffected, unapparently condescending and therefore most unostentatious, civility." But the great philanthropist could not help giving vent to his moralising nature, and added, "How ill-suited to the baptismal engagement to resist the pomps and vanities of this wicked world."

Nor was the Prince's time passed very differently in London, though he was more occupied with public affairs and with official receptions. He was generally to be seen riding in the Park, attended by a member of his household, in the late morning, and he would often stop to talk to a friend whom he happened to recognise. After he gave up riding he used to drive out in the Park in a tilbury, a light two-wheeled carriage, with his groom sitting by his side. Greville said that "grave men are shocked at this undignified practice." In the afternoon he would drive up in his yellow Berlin to Manchester House to pay a call on Lady Hertford, which inspired Moore's lines:

> *Through Manchester Square took a canter just now—*
> *Met the old yellow chariot, and made a low bow.*

His principal recreation at the end of the Regency, particularly after he had to give up riding, was sailing, and in the summer he always spent several days at sea, generally crossing the Channel and cruising along the French coast. On these occasions part of the Fleet accompanied the Prince, and a sham battle would be staged for his benefit. In the early part of his reign and for the last three or four years of the Regency he always spent a fortnight at Cowes. His favourite yacht was the *Royal George*, 330 tons, which was built at Deptford in 1817, and was finally broken up in 1902. The accommodation for the Prince consisted of a state cabin, a dining-room and small bedroom, all simply furnished, though the state cabin was well lined with books, particularly those dealing with naval history. Members of the public were allowed to go over her when she was in dock and it shows that the members of the crew had both an affection and admiration for their master that when a visitor, surveying the staircase leading to the King's cabin, called out, "Ah, just the thing for fat George when beastly drunk to roll down," they caught hold of him and popped him overboard.

The mistake made by those who have tried to rehabilitate the Prince's character from these venomous exaggerated attacks has been that they have considered it sufficient to reply to every charge against him by the parrot cry, "He was a Patron of the Arts." So was Nero. The point is that the Prince was far more than a mere patron—than one who merely gave august encouragement to a school of artists. He was a discriminating collector and an intelligent critic of pictures, he thoroughly understood music, and was not an indifferent performer. A mind bounded by self-indulgence could have had no room for such occupations, still less for the Prince's wide range of literary interests. He was well grounded in the classics, and he was discriminating reader of current literature. Political antagonism cut him off from many of the brightest ornaments of the literary world like Byron, Moore, Shelley, and Keats, but his encouragement of Scott, and more particularly of Jane Austen, is to his lasting credit. In 1815 Jane Austen had come up to London to nurse her brother in Hans Place. The doctor who attended him happened to be one of the Prince's physicians and told her that the Prince was a great admirer of her novels: that he read them often, and kept a set in each of his houses. A few days later the Prince's librarian, Mr. Clarke, called to say that he had the Prince's instructions to show her over the Library at Carlton House, and over the whole building if she cared to see it, and that he was to pay her every possible attention. Miss Austen went, and the librarian told her that the Prince would be very pleased if she would dedicate her next novel to him. Accordingly *Emma*, which to many is the most perfect novel in the English language, bears the inscription:

To
His Royal Highness
The Prince Regent
This work is,
By His Royal Highness's Permission,
Most respectfully
Dedicated,
By His Royal Highness's
Dutiful
and Obedient
Humble Servant
The Author

In thanking Miss Austen for the dedication, Mr. Clarke repeated that "the Regent has read and admired all your publications," and added, not from the Prince but on his own account, that "an historical romance illustrative of the august House of Coburg would just now be very interesting and might very properly be dedicated to Prince Leopold." Fortunately the rise to eminence of that august but rapacious House and even the opportunity of dedicating it to that subtle, scheming Prince, so different from the simple heroes and straightforward rascals of her own creation, did not tempt her to desert what she called "my own style" and "my own way." It is obvious from her letters how delighted she was by the Regent's patronage, and it must be remembered that, although her novels were in her lifetime much admired, she received very little personal encouragement.

Scott was in a far more assured position and therefore less in need of royal approval. The Prince offered Scott the poet laureateship in 1813, which was refused, and when he came to the throne he made him a baronet, on his own initiative, saying, when Scott kissed hands, "I shall always reflect with pleasure on Sir Walter Scott's having been the first creation of my reign." He always called him "Walter," and he used to arrange what he called "snug little dinners" for Scott when he came to London. It is pleasant to think of him quoting to Scott Moore's lines on what he called "me at breakfast":

> Methought the Prince in whisker'd state
> Before me at his breakfast sate;
> On one side lay unread petitions,
> On t'other hints from five physicians;

Here tradesmen's bills, official papers,
Notes from "my lady," drams for vapours;
There plans for saddles, tea and toast,
Death-warrants and the Morning Post.

The Prince was gifted far in excess of most members of the Hanoverian family, but his character was marred by a selfishness which would have been remarkable in a private citizen but which was fatal in a public man. It was clearly this consideration of self which enabled him to organise all the rejoicings of 1814, with himself as the central figure, but it was this characteristic which made him so impossible as a politician, and so capricious and uncertain in his dealings with the leading statesmen. It is difficult to absolve him from some share of the blame for the treatment of Napoleon after Waterloo, which was so seriously condemned by contemporary Whig opinion. When he read Napoleon's letter, throwing himself on his mercy, he simply said, "Upon my word, a very proper letter: much more so I must say than any I ever received from Louis XVIII." That was because Napoleon had addressed him as *Altesse Royale* instead of *Monseigneur*.

As he grew older, this selfishness was unquestionably accentuated by his loneliness. His unfortunate marriage, his early squabbles with his mother, and his disagreements with his brothers cut him off from any very close companionship with members of his family. He had, of course, many friends but few intimates, and no one, with the possible exception of Lady Hertford, who had any real influence over his character. The friends of his youth like Fox, Burke, his uncle the Duke of Cumberland, the Duchess of Devonshire, *Philippe Egalité*, and even rakish friends like Lady Lade and the Barrymores who from long association could have treated him almost as an equal, were all dead by the time he became Regent. The only close friend who remained from the days of his youth was Sheridan, who undoubtedly had great political influence with him during the early years of the Regency—a friendship which so infuriated the Whigs that they applied to Sheridan his own words:

Friends, fortune, fame itself I'd lose
To gain one smile from thee.

Although the Prince and Sheridan never actually quarrelled, they ceased to see one another after 1812. Thanks to the very prejudiced life of Sheridan written by Moore, and thanks to an equally biased statement by the Prince, biographers of Sheridan have found the circumstances of their rupture baffling and confusing. The Prince gave his version of the story with a recollection of detail and an attention to *minutiæ* which was remarkable, but with a slurring over of more important matters which is regrettable. His description to Croker of the last occasion on which he saw Sheridan is typical: "I sometimes, however, heard of him, and I once saw him by accident, as I shall tell you presently. He now took to live in a very low and obscure way, and all he looked for in the company he kept was brandy and water. He lived a good deal with some low acquaintance he had made—a harness maker; I forget his name but he had a house near Leatherhead. In that neighbourhood I saw him for the last time on the 17th August 1815. I know the day from this circumstance, that I had gone to pay my brother[1] a visit at Oatlands on his birthday, and next day as I was crossing over to Brighton, I saw in the road near Leatherhead old Sheridan coming along the pathway. I see him now in the black stockings and blue coat with metal buttons. I said to Blomfield 'There is Sheridan'; but, as I spoke, he turned off into a lane when we were within about thirty yards of him, and walked off without looking behind him."

In 1812 the Prince gave or lent Sheridan £3,000. There is no doubt that Sheridan believed that this money was to pay off his debts, which he did, and there seems little doubt that the Prince at the time also understood that the money was for that purpose but realising that Sheridan's debts were like the sand on the sea-shore, he decided that he must break with him as he could not afford to be so closely connected with him. Subsequently, therefore, the Prince said that he had given Sheridan the £3,000 for the specific purpose of paying his election expenses at Wootton Basset, and when he found he had squandered the money in paying his debts he refused to have anything more to do with him. This was probably an excuse, and Sheridan's version was probably correct. But even after this the Prince offered Sheridan an apartment in Carlton House to keep him safe from arrest for debt or, in Sheridan's own words, "to avoid all possible risk of personal insult on the score of debt." There would not seem to be sufficient ground for the savage attacks which Moore

[1] The Duke of York.

and the Whigs made on the Prince for his treatment of Sheridan.

When Sheridan was dying amid considerable privations, the Prince sent him £500, which was returned: an incident which was celebrated by Moore in the savage stanzas:

> *And Thou, too, whose life a sick epicure's dream,*
> *Incoherent and gross, even grosser had pass'd,*
> *Were it not for that cordial and soul-giving beam,*
> *Which his friendship and wit o'er thy nothingness cast:—*
>
> *No, not for the wealth of the land that supplies thee*
> *With millions to heap upon Foppery's shrine;—*
> *No, not for the riches of all who despise thee,*
> *Though this would make Europe's whole opulence mine;—*
>
> *Would I suffer what—ev'n in the heart that thou hast—*
> *All men as it is—must have burn'd,*
> *When the pittance which shame had wrung from thee at last*
> *And would found all his wants at an end was return'd.*

Few could say that the Prince behaved shabbily over this incident, particularly as the Whigs, so eager to label his £500 a pittance, showed no alacrity to succour their unfortunate colleague. In the Prince's own words, no one took any notice of Sheridan on his deathbed except Lady Bessborough, who sent £20, and Lord and Lady Holland, who sent some ice and currant-water from Holland House, which the Prince characterised as "an odd contribution." But whatever may have been the circumstances of the Prince's quarrel with Sheridan, it was most unfortunate, as it removed someone on whose judgment, though often erratic, he relied, and who was a link with his old deferential relationship with Fox.

In addition to his selfishness the Prince lacked stability of character, and brought to bear on grave matters of state a wayward and trivial mind. As he grew older and lazier he allowed himself to become more and more swayed by trivialities, which greatly added to the embarrassments and difficulties of his Ministers. He had once written to his father, "In these unhappy times, the world, Sir, examines the conduct of princes with a jealous, a scrutinizing, a malignant eye." It was profoundly true, and most unfortunate, that he failed to see that the "unhappy times" called for princes to sacrifice whims and prejudices and indulgences.

Book III

KING

I

As 1820—the tenth year of the Regency—opened, there were no grounds for supposing that the dissolution of the King was at hand. He was completely blind, completely deaf, and completely mad, but it seemed as though his system, relieved of the anxieties and fretfulness of sentient man, would run on for ever. From time to time the Prince visited his father at Windsor, and he would have been less than human if he had not begun to wonder whether the bearded figure, in its long violet gown, strumming on the harpsichord, singing in a high, detached voiced, chattering of Mr. Pitt and of forgotten statesmen and gentlemen-in-waiting, would not stand for ever between him and the crown.

But, at the beginning of January 1820 the King refused to eat, and was rapidly reduced to a skeleton. By the end of the month, although he still got up, it was clear that he was dying, and at half past eight on January 29th the crown came, in the words of the proclamation, "solely and rightfully to the high and mighty prince, George, Prince or Wales." As the following day January 30th, was a fast day, being the anniversary of the execution of King Charles I, it was decided to postpone the official proclamation until Monday, January 31st. At twelve o'clock on that day, the King, supported by all the Royal Dukes and by Prince Leopold, stood in the forecourt of Carlton House while Garter King at Arms, a venerable gentleman of ninety, read the proclamation, which was followed by much acclamation and cheering.

The new King had been seriously unwell at Brighton before his father's death, but the excitement over his accession and the exposure at the proclamation brought on a serious attack of inflammation of the lungs. The following day he became critically ill and in the evening was in "imminent danger." The public bulletin spoke of his being "severely indisposed." For four days two bulletins were issued daily, and it was several weeks before he fully recovered his strength. According to the best medical opinion of the day, his life was only saved by his losing 150 ounces of blood. He had been so seriously ill that his physicians took the unusual course of sending him a memorandum appealing to him not to attend his father's funeral—an undertaking which they dubbed "a dangerous effort of respect and piety." They drew attention to the fact that everybody noticed the "anguish of mind" suffered by him at Queen Charlotte's funeral.

Prayers for King George IV's recovery ascended to heaven from some very unexpected quarters—Brougham, for example, praying with the utmost fervour and heartiness that his life might be spared. The explanation of this sudden religious activity on Mr. Brougham's part is not difficult. The accession of the King placed the Ministers, that noble Tory hierarchy of Lord Liverpool, Lord Eldon, Lord Castlereagh, and Lord Sidmouth— or, as Brougham preferred to call them, "these villains"—in a position of unexampled difficulty, from which his death would have rescued them.

For a proper understanding of their difficulty it is necessary to go back six years to that August day in 1814 when the Princess of Wales, accompanied by her motley crew of English admirers, embarked for the Continent. The next six years of the Princess's life were spent travelling in Germany, Switzerland, Italy, and the East. So much has been written of these travels, most of it violently biased either for or against her, so much was to be said over and over and over again about them during 1820, that the actual facts were blurred by the dust of controversy. It may therefore assist to a clearer view to set out a brief outline of what the Princess actually did during those six years, as admitted by even the staunchest of her partisans.

On leaving England she went straight to Brunswick. From Brunswick she went to Milan, stopping in Geneva for some weeks. At Milan she took into her service an Italian, of obscure birth but handsome appearance, called Pergami. His original name was Bergami, but the B was changed to P because Pergami was thought to be more aristocratic. Shortly afterwards all her English attendants left her. In 1815 she took the Villa d'Este on Lake Como, and here she made Pergami her Chamberlain, admitted him to her table, and expected those who had been his fellow-servants to wait upon him. In November 1815 she set out for the East, accompanied by Pergami, with Pergami's sister as lady-in-waiting, and with Pergami's little daughter Vittoria to amuse her. There were also a number of raffish Italians with her. Her adopted son, William Austin, was naturally of the party. He had always slept in the same room with the Princess, but it was about this time, when he was fourteen, that he ceased to share her bedroom. When she reached Jerusalem she established the order of St. Caroline—of which she appointed Pergami Grand Master. She returned to Lake Como at the end of 1816: after which she sold the Villa d'Este and settled down at Pesaro on the Adriatic, travelling to Germany from time to time, but always with the same companion, always with Pergami in attendance.

From those facts which were well known in Italy, France, Switzerland, Austria, Brunswick, and England at the time, and have never been disputed by subsequent writers, it is only possible to draw one of two conclusions. Either the Princess had a taste for low company, or else her partiality for Pergami arose from an adulterous connexion. Whether the Princess committed adultery with Pergami can never now be proved: according to our estimate of human nature, and of the Queen's character, we must form our own opinion on that point. But on one matter there is no room for speculation or ambiguity. The Princess's conduct scandalised Europe. Even the Italians, accustomed as they were to displays of royal oddity from the Habsburgs who still ruled in Lombardy, from the Bourbons who reigned over the two Sicilies, and from the Borgias who were sovereigns of Modena, were outraged by the Princess's behaviour.

It was not only her attentions to Pergami, but her general conduct which amazed those who saw her. The people of Genoa, for instance, were naturally startled to see a gilt and mother-of-pearl phaeton, resembling a sea-shell, drawn through their streets by two piebald horses driven by a child dressed like an operatic cherub in flesh-coloured tights. In the phaeton lounged the Princess, a fat woman of fifty, wearing a pink hat with several pink feathers floating in the wind, a pink bodice, cut very low, and a short white skirt which showed two stout legs and a pair of top-boots. The phaeton was preceded by Pergami, dressed to resemble King Murat, and riding on a small piebald horse. Nor was her visit to Baden in 1817 any more edifying. She was described by an eyewitness as "an elderly stout little lady in a scarlet riding habit," who did not hesitate to give a bold display of her underclothing when she mounted her horse. One evening she was to have been the guest of the Margravine at the Opera.

The Margravine, as became widowed royalty, was dressed in dark velvet, sitting in a box draped in purple. As the Princess did not arrive, she gave orders for the opera to start. Suddenly the door of her box was flung open, and with a great, coarse laugh the Princess strode in, wearing an enormous head-dress, as worn by the Oberlander peasants, and decorated with flying ribbons and glittering spangles. The poor, aged Margravine was seen to be nearly swooning.

Unfortunately the Princess lacked the appearance to carry off the girlish extravagances in which she indulged. At the age of fifty, with a head too large for her body, her figure like a ball, and her countenance wearing an expression of defiance and boldness, she must have looked anything but attractive. Even her staunchest supporters must doubt whether she was showing herself to the best advantage when she danced at Geneva dressed *en Venus*, i.e. naked to the waist. The Princess's latest biographer[1] valiantly sums up all these activities as "a life of charity and usefulness." She herself summed up the position with a good deal more accuracy when she said, "Since de English neither give me de great honour of being a Princesse de Galles, I will be Caroline, a happy, merry soul." Unhappily merriment, as the Princess understood it, could only be paid for by loss of respect and reputation. In England, a sedate country clergyman entered in his diary in 1816: "I hear that the Princess of Wales has been brought to bed of a fine boy in the harem of the Bey of Algiers.'

Whatever may have been the sins of George IV's private life we can hardly be surprised if he began to fret against the bonds which tied him to this woman. As early as July 1816 he approached the law officers of the Crown, who gave their opinion that there was sufficient evidence to support a divorce, but that its success would depend on the credibility of the Italian witnesses. In 1817, when the Princess Charlotte died, he was strongly urged to marry again in order to provide the country with an heir. Prince Alexander of Solms wrote to him suggesting that he should strengthen his title by marrying a daughter of the King of Sardinia, who, now that the Cardinal-Duke of York was dead, was the Stuart claimant to the throne, being descended from Charles I's youngest daughter. But it is not likely that he ever seriously considered remarriage: all he wanted was to be free. The

[1] His Honour Sir Edward Parry.

danger was that when George III died the Princess would return to England to claim her husband, her crown, and all the patronage which in those days was attached to a Queen-consort.

In 1818 what was known as the Milan Commission was appointed in order to collect evidence for a divorce. Thirty-one Italian witnesses were examined, and the case was then submitted to counsel for opinion, who advised, in July 1819, that "the great body of Evidence establishes the fact of a continued adulterous intercourse."[1]

The Milan Commission is often erroneously described as if it had been officially appointed by the Government. It was actually arranged, though not conducted, by Sir John Leach, who was vice-Chancellor and one of the law officers to the Regent. Leach was not popular with the legal profession, chiefly because he wisely preferred a fashionable party to the society of his brethren of the bench, but he had great influence with the Regent, and had from the first pressed for a divorce. The task of collecting the evidence was actually undertaken by two barristers.

In the circumstances, the appointment of the Milan Commission was not only foolish but cruel to the Princess. When she left England, and when reports of her behaviour began to trickle through, her husband and his advisers should have done one of two things. They could either have ignored her completely, allowed her to be received at foreign Courts and trusted that the enjoyment of complete freedom would have prevented her wishing to return to England, or, as soon as they were convinced that she had sufficiently committed herself, i.e. in 1816, they should have instituted immediate proceedings for divorce. Instead of this she was constantly annoyed, harassed, and frightened without definite proceedings being taken against her. She knew perfectly well that she was being spied on in Italy, she knew perfectly well that her husband had begged none of the foreign Courts to receive her. (He wrote to the Emperor of Austria, who had refused to receive her, "My gratitude will last to the tomb.") She was given no intimation of the death of her daughter, but was left to learn it casually, and no one could avoid some sympathy for her when she sadly decked herself out in a white gown, with bright lilac ribbons, and a black crape cap,

[1] These papers are at the Record Office, and it would be difficult for any impartial reader not to form the same opinion.

and said, "What an ugly thing mourning is!"—which, of her idea of mourning, was perhaps true. When she heard that the Milan Commission was being sent out to Italy, she wrote to Brougham that she was "more dead than a life . . . Oh Mr. Brougham if my ever beloved daughter was still a life such proceedings would never have taken Place to make such fals and foul accusations upon my character."

There is no doubt that the Princess was perfectly correct in her reference to "my ever beloved daughter," as the following important letter from George IV to the Lord Chancellor shows:

The letter was written a few months after the Princess Charlotte's death, and after referring to the scandal on the Continent to which his wife's conduct had given rise, he continued:

"You cannot, therefore, be surprised (much difficulty in point of delicacy being now set aside in my mind by the late melancholy event which has taken place in my family) if I, therefore, turn my whole thoughts to the endeavouring to extricate myself from the cruellest, as well as the most unjust predicament that ever even the lowest individual, much more a Prince, ever was placed in by unshackling myself from a woman who . . . Is it, then, my dear friend, to be tolerated, that . . . is to be suffered to continue to bear my name, to belong to me and to the country, and that that country, the first in all the world, and myself its sovereign, are to be expected to submit silently to a degradation, under which no upright and honourable mind can exist? This, then, was my main object for collecting certain of my confidential servants here. . . .

I shall now take my leave of you, wishing you from my heart many happy returns of the season, and assuring you that if it depended upon me alone, your happiness should never know interruption.

I remain, my dear friend,

Always most affectionately yours,

GEORGE P.R.

Pavilion, Brighton,

Jan. 1st, 1818.

PS. I hope that you will be able to make out my scrawl."[1]

[1] Unfortunately the editor of Lord Eldon's papers evidently thought it best to omit the Prince's exact description of his wife.

It is therefore perfectly clear that after the death of the Princess Charlotte the King was anxious for a divorce. The fatal delay in taking action was none of his doing. It was the Ministers, principally Lord Liverpool and Lord Eldon, who were reluctant to resort to divorce, because they were nervous of the scandal and popular clamour, doubtful of the adequacy of the evidence, and certain that the King's "marriage" to Mrs. Fitzherbert, his affection for Ladies Jersey and Hertford, and his neglect of his wife would all have been paraded before an eager, gossiping public. All this, as the King constantly explained, he was prepared to encounter "if only he might be free." In those spacious realms, where come neither hurry nor mental bustle, in which Cabinets have their being, the Tory Ministers at the end of 1819 settled down, in Lord Castlereagh's words, "to take the whole case into their mature consideration." This dilatoriness of the Cabinet was to prove fatal. Having irritated the Princess, the Government should have proceeded to action while the initiative was theirs and while the Princess was still only Princess of Wales. The moment that she became Queen any action that they took was bound to appear dictated by the necessity of keeping her from the exercise of her rights and not by a genuine belief in her guilt. The comparatively unexpected death of George III made the whole matter urgent and imminent, and found the Government unready for action and unprepared to advise the new King. His anxiety and distress prolonged and aggravated his illness; Lord Castlereagh said that the subject haunted his imagination and distracted his rest.

On the morning of February 5th the following bulletin was posted outside Carlton House. "The King has had a good night. His Majesty is recovering. Under the present circumstances there will be no evening bulletin. H. Halford, W. Knighton, M. J. Tierney." At the same time passers-by were embarrassed to see that some wit had chalked up on one of the walls of Carlton House:

Long live the King
His Majesty
George the Fourth
And the Queen Consort
Her Majesty
Caroline
May they live and reign together
For ever and ever
Huzza! Huzza!

With returning health came the realisation of the full horror of his position with regard to the Queen. The following day, February 6th, was a Sunday, and he remembered that no steps had been taken with regard to the exclusion of his wife's name from the prayer-book. They had formerly been prayed for as "their Royal Highnesses George, Prince of Wales, and the Princess of Wales." He sent for every prayer-book in the library at Carlton House, and spent the evening studying the precedents for the prayer for the Royal Family. When Sunday came the Whiggish clergy prayed for the Queen by name, and asked God to bless her, to endue her with the Holy Spirit, to enrich her with heavenly grace, to prosper her with all happiness and to bring her to "thine everlasting kingdom," while those clergy who were Tories and favourable to the King prayed simply for "all the Royal Family." The Archbishop of Canterbury and part of the Cabinet were opposed to deleting the Queen's name from the prayer-book, but the King was adamant, and told them that "if she was fit to be introduced as Queen to God she was fit to be so introduced to men."

On February 10th the Cabinet, which had been sitting some days until as late as two in the morning, submitted a forty-page memorandum to the King on the whole question. With the distinguished exception of Canning, who was at the Board of Control, the Ministers were unanimous in believing in the Queen's guilt and would have certainly echoed Castlereagh's description of her as, "This infamous woman," and his advice "to stamp upon her conduct the stain which the voice of Europe affixes to it." They described it as "the most delicate and distressing subject upon which they have ever been called to tender their advice." They could not recommend a divorce, but they suggested that "the Princess" should be given an annuity "payable only during her Residence abroad": that she should not be named in the Liturgy, and that she should be refused the honour of coronation. The King replied that he had read their Cabinet memorandum "with some surprise and much regret." He thought that divorce would have settled the matter, and that the publicity arising from it would not have been greater than that which would arise from "the qualified measure" proposed by them. They replied that they could not introduce a Bill of Divorce without a previous judicial decision, which meant that the King would have to sue for divorce in the Ecclesiastical Courts, where the defence would be able to indulge in "recriminations of every kind." Their discreet insinuation that unedifying details about Mrs. Fitzherbert and his former mistresses would have been raked up would not have affected the issue of the action; damaging as they would have been to the King's reputation, they would not have affected the question of the Queen's guilt. The whole case turned on the reliability of the Italian witnesses.

Sir John Leach, who was familiar with all the evidence, and had considerable legal experience, was pressing the King to insist on divorce. The King, emboldened by this advice, and loudly asserting that his honour demanded a divorce, threatened to retire to Hanover, threatened to dismiss his Ministers, insulted them, and told Lord Eldon that "your conscience always interferes except where your interest is concerned." Leach actually sounded various public men as to the possibility of their forming an alternative Government, but naturally even moderate Whigs like Lord Wellesley, whom he approached, would not have dreamt of taking office conditionally on obtaining a divorce, and the King was obliged to accept the terms of the Tory Ministers, saying that he made "this great and painful sacrifice of his personal feelings for the sake of public decorum."

Provided the Queen stayed abroad their advice was sound. In justice to the Tory Ministers it must be said that they, who had seen all the evidence, were confident of her guilt, and never imagined that she would return to risk a public enquiry. In fact they agreed privately with the King that if the Queen came back to England they would meet his wishes. If her return to England was inevitable, then the King was right in contending that a divorce was more final and no more scandalous than "their qualified measure." He, knowing her character, could not share his Ministers' confidence that she would not return. He was right.

At the end of 1819 she was writing to Brougham that if the country would protect her she would come to England, but if not she would prefer to live in obscurity for the few years "I am to remain upon this wild globe." Certainly for the remainder of her life she was to do nothing to diminish the wildness of the globe. However, when news came of George III's death, it found her and her advisers, like the King and his Ministers, prepared with no plan of action. At two o'clock in the morning after the

King's death the innocent slumbers of Mr. Brougham were disturbed by an important visitor, and he had to hurry into a dressing-gown to interview His Royal Highness the Duke of Sussex. The Duke, who was fortunately untroubled by feelings of grief at his father's death, or of affection for his eldest brother, had come to urge that the news should be sent at once to his injured sister-in-law in Italy. That morning a courier set out for Italy to urge the Queen's immediate return to England.

It seems clear that, but for a series of unfortunate incidents, the Queen would never have decided to return. After George III's death she was treated with studied contempt by all the foreign Courts through which she passed, as the various sovereigns and their representatives, believing that a divorce was imminent, thought that any recognition of the Queen would annoy George IV. She was always referred to as the Princess of Wales, sometimes by her maiden name as Princess Caroline of Brunswick, and she had a great deal of trouble in getting her passports signed. It was those petty insults, which were certainly not done on the instructions or in accordance with the wishes of the English Government, which decided her, in the month of April, to return and assert her rights. She reached Geneva in May.

All those who had the real interest of the Queen at heart and who had some knowledge of her behaviour during the last six years must have seen the folly of her courting a public exposure. It is naturally difficult to belief that there was room in Brougham's heart for anyone's interests but his own, yet it seems clear that he, who knew the Queen as well as anyone and knew all the facts, did genuinely try to prevent her from coming. He was completely in the confidence of the Government, but it would seem that the Government made a grave blunder in not sending an intermediary to the Queen so soon as their plan of campaign was settled. By waiting about for Brougham they lost precious time. In fact it was not until April that they arranged that he and Lord Hutchison, a Whig but a close personal friend of the King, should go and meet the Queen to discuss terms. The Government proposed, with the full approval of the King, that the Queen should be paid £50,000 a year provided that she remained abroad, and that while she was abroad she should take some other title than Queen, though this was to be regarded as no renunciation of her title and rights. It was, as it still is, usual for the King or Queen of England when travelling privately abroad to adopt some secondary title. It was the greatest possible mistake that Brougham did not set out immediately he was in receipt of those terms. This fatal delay was caused by a reluctance to throw up many profitable briefs rather than by chicanery. He actually set out on June 1st, when the Queen had already almost reached the French coast. He and Lord Hutchison found her determined to go to England, so that instead of acting the part of plenipotentiaries they could only threaten her with the terrible consequences of her decision. They were but sorry negotiators, because Brougham seems to have lacked the courage to tell her what the terms were, and Lord Hutchison appears to have been unable to recollect them. Hutchison saw the Queen on June 4 at St. Omer and was immediately repelled by her deportment. Writing to the King's secretary he said, "It is impossible for me to paint the insolence, the violence and the precipitation of this woman's conduct. I never saw anything so outrageous, so undignified as a Queen or so unamiable as a woman."

As a result of this bungling between Brougham and Hutchison the wrong terms were sent to the Queen. She was told that the Government would pay her £50,000 per annum if she lived abroad, which was perfectly correct, and then "the Queen is not to assume the style and title of Queen of England or any title attached to the Royal Family." She could never have been expected to agree not to use any title of the English Royal Family. But this was not the Government's proposal. Their condition was that she should take "some other title" than Queen, which did not exclude a subsidiary English title—for example, Duchess of Cornwall. The Queen naturally refused to listen to the terms as submitted to her, and replied "It is quite impossible for Her Majesty to listen to such a proposition." Lord Brougham, being a lawyer, regarded the negotiations as just beginning, and wrote off to England for improved terms. The Queen, however, posted to Calais, and embarked for England on the following day.

Brougham, who had known for weeks, since April 15th, what the correct terms were, said afterwards that he was prevented from delivering them by "strange unaccountable accidents." The only reason that prevented him from delivering the terms was neither an "accident" nor "strange" nor "unaccountable," but simply his own pusillanimity because he was afraid that if he told the Queen the terms to which he had tentatively agreed, she would dismiss him from her councils, and that he would lose his main hope of advancing his political, legal, and financial interests. He had boasted to the Government of his complete influence over the Queen, but when he met her he found that his influence was gone; as Lord Hutchison wrote to Lord Liverpool, "In my opinion Brougham has acted with great sincerity. . . . but I am convinced at the same time that he possesses no real authority or power over the mind and decisions of the Queen."

In fact Brougham's influence over the Queen was completely eclipsed by an even less reliable person, Alderman Wood, M.P. Wood, after a most exemplary and industrious youth, was making a very satisfactory fortune out of a chemist's shop. He was a member of Parliament for the City, and an advanced radical, who was never so happy as when visiting some extremist in goal, or suffering agonies of sympathy for some murderer condemned to the gallows. Lord Hutchison described him as "an enlightened mountebank." He had twice been Lord Mayor of London and was the type of man who was admirably suited for the slightly risible pomp and circumstance of civic life. But in 1820 he left the pestle and mortar, which he had wielded so profitably for so long, to espouse the cause of the Queen. He met her at Montbard, and long before Brougham had set out from England he was pouring into her wild, distracted brain visions of the great popular welcome that would be hers (and his) if she came to England with him. The responsibility for the Queen's return rests primarily with Alderman Wood: it was on his advice that she had made up her mind to return long before Brougham had set out from England. Wood deserved well of neither his Queen nor his country. He did more than anyone else to imperil the monarchy, and it is true to say that, although the Queen was on his lips, revolution was in his heart. Yet Queen Victoria, although she was perhaps too young to know better, rewarded his services to republicanism and his loyalty to her uncle by making him a baronet in 1837. It is an ugly blot on the fair pages of Debrett.

She landed at Dover in the afternoon of June 5th, wearing a puce-coloured sarcenet pelisse lined with ermine, and a white willow hat in the style of the then fashionable Leghorn hat, and she was thought by observers to look "interesting." She was rapturously received. The crowd drew her carriage, an impromptu band was provided, and the principal tradesmen of the town, carrying garish banners, headed the procession to her hotel. A similarly enthusiastic reception was waiting for her at Canterbury, and as news of her approach reached London an immense concourse of people lined the streets from Greenwich to Westminster Bridge. Greville rode out to Greenwich to see the sights and was amazed at the fervour with which she was everywhere greeted. It was exactly a quarter of a century since, as a bold and rather vulgar bride, she had landed at Greenwich to claim her husband's hand. She now drove into London, like some second-rate election candidate, to seek the favours of what Croker called "the lower and middling classes."

She drove over Westminster Bridge in an open landau, with Alderman Wood sitting beside her and Lady Anne Hamilton and an Italian woman opposite. There were a couple of seedy carriages behind, in which rode her adopted son Mr. William Austin, Alderman Wood's son, and some rather ferocious-looking Italians. As the cavalcade passed Carlton House the sentries rather sheepishly presented arms, and Alderman Wood, intoxicated with self-importance, stood up in the carriage and frantically cheered. Respectable people, and those well versed in etiquette, were amazed that Alderman Wood should have assumed the place of honour and allowed a Duke's daughter (Lady Anne Hamilton) to ride with her back to the horses. Nothing astounded and infuriated the King so much as the seating arrangements in this triumphal landau, and he was heard to say, "That beast Wood rode beside her in the carriage."

She reached Alderman Wood's house in South Audley Street, where she was to stay, and after hours of cheering the mob dispersed to spend an enjoyable evening smashing windows. That evening she repeated over and over again, "If they wished me to stay abroad, why not leave me there in peace?" This showed the folly of the Cabinet in the policy they had pursued, ever since 1814, of rousing and irritating her without either intending or being able to crush her. Events had now forced their hands, and, while the mob was still roaring through the West End of London, a messenger was carrying down to the House of Lords the evidence against the Queen, contained in the famous green bag.

A Secret Committee—secret not because their names were

unknown, but because their proceedings were private—of the House of Lords was appointed to examine the papers. The members were the Archbishop of Canterbury, the Lord Chancellor (Eldon), the Lord President of the Council (Harrowby), the Duke of Beaufort, the Duke of Northumberland, the Marquess of Lansdowne, the Marquess of Buckingham, the Earl of Liverpool, Earl Beauchamp, Viscount Sidmouth, the Bishop of London, Lord Redesdale, Lord Erskine, and the Earl of Lauderdale. The Marquess of Lansdowne and Lord Erskine had Whiggish sympathies and refused to serve, so the Earl of Hardwicke and Lord Ellenborough were appointed in their place. The Committee reported at the beginning of July that ". . . these charges appear to the Committee to be calculated so deeply to affect, not only the honour of the Queen but also the dignity of the Crown and the moral feeling and honour of the country, that in their opinion it is necessary that they should become the subject of a solemn enquiry. . . ." During June there had been a series of meetings between Wellington and Castlereagh, representing the King, and Brougham and Denman, as the Queen's Attorney-General and Solicitor-General, to try to settle the case without the scandal of a public enquiry. But it was obvious that once the Queen had arrived in England, and once the charges had been examined, even if she left as Queen, and with a handsome annuity in her pocket, her departure would have been interpreted by the nation, and even by the "lower and middling classes," as a confession of guilt, as a refusal to face the evidence which had been collected against her. To do the Queen credit, she realised this more clearly than either of her distinguished advocates, and she resolutely set her face against any terms. The time for *pourparlers* had gone by; as she stepped on English soil at Dover war was declared. As Lord Hutchison said "The Queen has thrown down the gauntlet of defiance. The King must take it up."

Accordingly, as soon as the Secret Committee had reported, a bill, known as the Bill of Pains and Penalties, was introduced in the House of Lords by the Prime Minister. In the preamble to the Bill the Queen was said to have carried on "a licentious, disgraceful and adulterous intercourse," and her conduct was stigmatised as "scandalous, disgraceful and vicious." The object of the Bill was to deprive her of the title and rights of Queen

Consort and to dissolve her marriage with the King.[1] On July 5th the Bill was read for the first time, and the second reading was fixed for August 17th, and it was agreed that the Queen should be represented by counsel and should be allowed to appear herself. She, in the meanwhile, was becoming rather nervous, and announcing that it would be all Mr. Brougham's fault if her head was on Temple Bar, she redoubled her efforts to consolidate her position in the affections of "the lower and middling classes." At the beginning of August she took Brandenburgh House, on the river at Hammersmith, which, having been built by Prince Rupert for his mistress, was no doubt a suitable residence for her, and here day after day addresses from various public bodies poured in, to the accompaniment of cheering and bellowing from the rag-tag and bobtail who swarmed across the gardens of the house. It was this eager cordiality to anyone who cared to go and see her which inspired Theodore Hook's verses:

> *Have you been to Brandenburgh—heigh, ma'am; ho, ma'am?*
> *Have you been to Brandenburgh, ho?*
> *—Oh, yes; I have been, ma'am,*
> *To visit the Queen, ma'am,*
> *With the rest of the gallanty show—show,*
> *With the rest of the gallanty show.*

> *And who were your company—heigh, ma'am; ho, ma'am?*
> *And who were your company, ho?*
> *—We happened to drop in*
> *With gemmem from Wapping,*
> *And ladies from Blowbladder—row—row,*
> *And ladies from Blowbladder—row.*

On the day before the second reading of the Bill, August 16th, the Queen moved off from these elegant surroundings to St. James's Square, in order to be near the House of Lords. She stayed with Lady Francis, widow of that Sir Philip Francis who had been a close friend of George IV as Prince or Wales, and who was the reputed author of the "Junius Letters." She set out from

[1] The ordinary procedure in the case of adultery by a Queen-consort or Princess of Wales would be the trial of both parties for high treason under an Act of Edward III. As Pergami was an Italian, and therefore not subject to the laws of England, he and the Queen could not be proceeded against for high treason, and it was consequently necessary to proceed by Act of Parliament.

St. James's Square on August 17th, shortly before ten, and drove to Westminster, rousing the onlookers to a frenzy of enthusiasm, who cried out, "God bless you," and, "We'll give our blood for you." She sat in a new state coach, drawn by six horses, accompanied by Lady Anne Hamilton. She was dressed rather ostentatiously in black, as the English Royal Family was in mourning for the Duchess of York, though hers was a tribute of sympathy with which they could gladly have dispensed. It cannot be said that as she waddled into the House of Lords she looked the picture of a persecuted Queen or of a modest, wronged wife. She had chosen a coal-black wig, with a profusion of girlish curls (her hair had originally been fair), and she had heavily painted eyebrows and cheeks. She carried herself boldly and defiantly, conscious of her wrongs, but revelling in the battle.

The examination of witnesses, the hearing of counsel, and the speeches of peers lasted for over eighty days. The witnesses, as was inevitable, were mostly of the servant class, though it may be questioned whether they were deserving of Brougham's subsequent description as "pimps of hideous aspect, whose prurient glance could penetrate through the keyholes of rooms, where the rat shared with the bug the silence of the deserted place." The evidence was of the usual kind in such cases; what this servant saw when the Queen and Pergami were together, what that one heard when he passed the Queen's bedroom door, and what another saw when he took hot water to the tent in which the Queen and Pergami lived by day (if not by night) on board the ship that was carrying them to Constantinople and the East. There was the famous "*non mi ricordo*" of the principal witness, when pressed in cross-examination, which Brougham brilliantly characterised as "the felicity of his forgetfulness." Whatever he may have thought in private of his client, Brougham fought for her manfully in public, and would appear to have had serious thought of trying to prove that Pergami was impotent through his vital parts having been frozen in the Russian Campaign.

If there was the usual mass of sordid filth for the public to discuss, and for subsequent dabblers in the period to rake over and enjoy, the "trial" was redeemed by two persons. Lord Liverpool conducted the Government's case with a dignity and impartiality which was recognised by his opponents and which was wholly admirable, and Brougham's conduct of the Queen's case amazed the Tory peers, and was one of the most brilliant pieces of advocacy which has ever adorned the English Bar. When he came to the end of his opening speech and appealed to the peers to save the country, the crown, the aristocracy, and the altar, the effect was so tremendous that one nobleman was seen to rise in his place and rush from the House in a burst of sobbing. Denman, who also appeared for the Queen, undid much of the effect of Brougham's speech, and showed the Bar at its worst. His speech was full of inept and pedantic comparisons, pompous and long-winded. He compared the King and Queen to Nero and Octavia, not a very fortunate comparison considering that Octavia was a charming young girl of eighteen. He introduced a filthy quotation, which was generally considered to apply to the King, but which he seemed to hope might be slurred over as it was in Greek, and he did untold damage to the Queen's cause by applying to her the fatal words of the Founder of the Christian religion to the woman taken in adultery, "Go, and sin no more," which scarcely fitted in with his whole argument that she had not sinned at all.

On November 6th the House of Lords gave the Bill a second reading by a majority of twenty-eight. Four days later, on the third reading, the majority fell to nine. Lord Liverpool realised that so slender a majority in the Lords made the passage of the Bill through the Commons most unlikely, and he immediately announced that it would be dropped. London was illuminated for three nights in succession, and the mob went round smashing the windows of those who refused to join in the illuminations. Bond Street and all the West End were decorated, and one of the illuminations which attracted much attention was a transparency adapting Genesis, which read, "And God said, 'It is not good the King should reign alone.'" Naturally in the neighbourhood of the royal palaces darkness prevailed, except that people were surprised to see Marlborough House, between the black outlines of Carlton House and St. James's Palace, blazing with light and with flambeaux burning on its garden walls. The explanation of this humiliating spectacle was that Prince Leopold of Saxe-Coburg, who frugally lived there on his £50,000 a year, was naturally to be found struggling to curry favour with the popular side.

Unluckily something of this carnival spirit has found its way to the pages of history, with the result that to the average reader the Queen's "trial" is a gay, triumphant jumble. It has to be remembered that there were three distinct issues before the Lords: first the question of the Queen's guilt; secondly the constitutional propriety of proceeding against her by Act of Parliament, and thirdly the advisability of proceeding against her at all in view of the existing state of popular opinion. It was never a trial in the sense that the peers were simply deciding the issue of whether the Queen was guilty or innocent of adultery. Had it been, there is good reason to suppose that the majority against her would have been very large indeed. The great majority of the peers, including the moderate Whigs, were convinced of the Queen's guilt, particularly after the evidence about her living with Pergami in the tent on the deck of the ship which was carrying them to Constantinople. Of the ninety odd peers who voted against the Bill not a score believed in the innocence of the Queen. Lord Ellenborough, who was a Whig and voted against the Bill, said, "The Queen of England was the last woman in the country which a man of honour would wish his wife to resemble, or the father of a family would recommend as an example to his daughters [Loud Cheers]." The "lower and middling classes" acclaimed the dropping of the Bill as the triumph of "immaculate innocence": those who read the speeches of the peers more carefully could hardly disagree with the supporters of the King who shouted in reply, "Immaculate In No Sense." When everything that can be said for and against her guilt has been said, one remark of a woman—Charles Lamb's sister—remains profoundly true: "They talk of the Queen's guilt, I should not think the better of her if she is what is called innocent."

But apart altogether from any question of guilt or innocence, one fact emerges quite clearly from "the trial"—a fact which now that more than a century divides us from all the bitterness and animosity of the case is even plainer—that she was ill-suited to be the wife of any man, and totally unfit to be the Queen of a civilised country to be prayed for, admired, revered, honoured, and imitated by a proud, moral people as "our gracious Queen Caroline."

No reign can ever have begun more dismally than George IV's. For thirty years, ever since his father's first attack of madness, his inheritance had appeared imminent; and being human he must have often thought of the days when he would be King, often dreamt of the proud achievements of his reign, and often planned scenes of magnfiicence and splendour. He may well have longed for the day when it would have been possible for him to echo the words of Henry V:

> *The tide of blood in me*
> *Hath proudly flow'd in vanity till now:*
> *Now doth it turn and ebb back to the sea,*
> *Where it shall mingle with the state of floods*
> *And flow henceforth in formal majesty.*

But when at last the crown came to him, he began to reign at a more advanced age than any English sovereign before him, and any pleasure in his inheritance was completely destroyed by the antics of his wife. For a few weeks after his recovery from his serious illness, and when it was still uncertain whether the Queen would come to England, he was able to enjoy himself making arrangements for his Coronation, which was to take place in August 1820 with particular magnificence. The Duke of Wellington's brother was able to refer in writing to the King's secretary to "his hourly augmenting popularity." On May 30th it was announced that the public would be excluded from the Abbey owing to the preparations for the Coronation. A week later the Queen arrived, and it was announced that "for divers good and sundry reasons" the Coronation would not take place for the present. The hourly augmenting popularity had come crashing into the dust.

What the King really felt, and what depressed him for the rest of his life, was that, as a result of the Queen, he had been held up to ridicule and mockery not only in London, but throughout the length and breadth of his kingdom. As we look back over the first thirty-five years of the twentieth century and the last eighty years of the nineteenth, we cannot find any single domestic event which roused public interest and stimulated the pencils and pens of caricaturists and lampoonists as did the case of "the Queen."

It was as though Queen Victoria's Diamond Jubilee, the reform of the House of Lords, and the Tichborne case had all been rolled into one. The summer of 1820 was one of those dry burning seasons when sleep in London is impossible, and in those long evenings, unnaturally prolonged, groups of fashionable people were seen strolling in their gardens or the parks discussing the eternal question; in the heavy, commercial quarters of Bloomsbury and the City the modest, moral merchants and their wives revelled in the latest details of the case; and in the squalid streets of Westminster, or in the dingy alleys by the river, the Queen and her doings were bandied from mouth to mouth. People talked till they were sick of it, and Greville lamented "how great an evil it was when a single subject of interest takes possession of society; conversation loses all its lightness and variety."

The interest in the case spread far beyond the confines of London. Lord Eldon, who, next to the King and Lord Liverpool, shared much of the odium for the Bill, was greeted at a remote village, where he stopped to change horses on the way to his country house in Dorset, by what he calls "a collection of people," who put their heads into his coach, calling out, "Queen Caroline for ever." In almost every church in England, after the prayer for the Royal Family had been read, the voice of the local radical would call out, firmly but devoutly, "And God bless the Queen too." But perhaps most terrible of all was the case of the loyal Lincolnshire clergyman who, after the dropping of the Bill, was detected posting up in his parish, under cover of the dark, the following handbill—

ADULTERY TRIUMPHANT
ILLUMINATION IN HONOUR OF AN ADULTERESS

Light up your windows; shout long live the Queen!
Than whom a greater whore was never seen.

As soon as the Queen landed at Dover, the King very wisely slipped down to the seclusion of the Royal Lodge, where he stayed until September, only appearing in public at the Ascot races. If he had appeared in London, the authorities could not have been responsible for his safety; he was as effectually barred from entering his capital as ever Charles I was in the Civil War.

The King was mortally distressed by the whole lamentable

business. When he heard that the Queen was advancing through France, he wrote to Sir William Knighton:

"I must implore of you, my dear friend, *if you have any regard for me*, to call upon me as soon as possible after your return to London to-morrow morning, as I *cannot* think of going to Church, nor of *stirring out* of my house until I shall have seen you. *My mind* is in a state that is *not to be* described, therefore, I shall add no more at present than that I am, etc.

PS. Pray do not *you also suffer me to linger.*"

What agitated him beyond measure was the feeling that Liverpool and the Government were lacking in determination. He believed that one member of the Administration—Canning— had in earlier days maintained an adulterous connection with the Queen; he likewise believed that Liverpool was modifying his policy against the Queen in order not to offend Canning, who, with his liberal-minded associates, was a powerful force on the Government side. In almost every letter to Liverpool, the King repeats with an emphasis which is petulant and pathetic that he cannot allow his honour and the honour of the country to be sacrificed "to political expediency."

He even went so far as to consult a prominent politician outside the ranks of the Government as is shown by this letter which he wrote to Lord Wellesley in June, 1820:

"Pray come and breakfast here tomorrow morning at C(arlton) H(ouse) with Bloomfield at *nine o'clock*. Come on *foot* and enter through the *stables* by the gate where the sentinels are, the *nearest* to Spring Garden Passage.

I want your private advice and your support, as an *old and attached friend*, and there is *much* to be communicated to *you*. . . . . .

PS. You will understand me I am sure when I stop at these few words of our old friend Cum *tot* sustineas et *tanta negotia solus.*[1] *Ver. sap.*"

Like all people with a fastidious mind, the King felt acutely the parade of ridicule and obscenity of which he was made the central and ludicrous figure day after day in the public prints. Occasionally he could rise above it and look down on it with characteristic whimsicality. Writing to his favourite brother, the

[1] Horace, *Epistles*, Book II. i. 1.

Duke of York, at the height of the proceedings against the Queen he said:

> "You must my dearest Fredk. be so bored upon other matters [i.e. the Queen] that I shall say no more to you upon them, than, that though I have now lived a good many years in the world, still I never thought that I should have lived to witness so much prevarication, so much lying, and so much wilful and convenient forgetfulness. . . . But, for certain, it is a very strange world that we do now live in where everyone now thinks that he has a right to say if he pleases, and in defiance of all truth and reason, that black is white and white is black."

When, as the result of long months of fumbling and bungling, Liverpool's Cabinet decided to close the proceedings against the Queen, the indignation of the King knew no bounds and he plainly enjoyed drafting a letter—though it was not despatched—to Liverpool. This closed with the sentence: "But it would not at the same time be consistent with that honour and fairness with which the King has always acted towards his confidential servants, if the King were not to declare to Lord L that however painful it may be to the King's feelings, he considers himself under the necessity of taking measures for the formation of a new administration."

A few days later the King set down on paper the advantages which he would gain from a change of Government, notably that a Whig Government might be able to come to speedy and final terms with the Queen. He then set out the evils likely to follow from such a course which arose from their principles being what he called *Liberaux*. Would such a Government press him to free Bonaparte, to smash up existing European friendships or to emancipate the Catholics in defiance of the wishes of "the pure and exalted spirit of my ever revered father"? He thought that Liverpool's Government had sacrificed "my feelings" and "my happiness," but that "they have been a good Government for the country." Then, not without pathos, he sets out all that he has suffered at the hands of the Whigs "the vindictive persecutions, the lowering abuse to my character, the wanton aspersions upon all those principles most sacred and dear to me, in short whatever of estimation I may have lost among my subjects . . . I may justly date to them." Though it will not accord with the prevailing view of George IV it is clear that he felt not only for himself but for the future of the English monarchy, fearing that a false step by him might lead to a loss of "all political and moral influence, weight and authority to the Crown, for ever."

The effect of all these turbulent and humiliating events on the health of the King was serious. His constitution, though strong, was highly nervous. In a private memorandum of the early years of his reign his physicians emphasised that he must avoid "everything calculated to produce anxiety of mind"—a prescription easy to write but impossible for a king to follow.

However, the state of his health and his nervousness about himself explain his comparative retirement after coming to the throne. A new influence in his life made his semi-invalidish life more congenial to him than might at first sight appear. His home life was more comfortable.

For some time he had been seeing much less of Lady Hertford, who was then sixty and perhaps even to the King past the first blush of beauty, and people were consequently not wholly taken by surprise when he transferred his affection to another aged Marchioness—Lady Conyngham. The swan song of Hanoverian passion is a very formidable affair, and although the King was fifty-eight he was as absorbed by the charms of Lady Conyngham as ever he had been by Mrs. Robinson or Mrs. Fitzherbert forty years earlier. Lady Conyngham was the daughter and heiress of Joseph Denison, a banker who lived in the City and who had also a property in Dorking called Denbies. She married, in 1794, Viscount Conyngham of Mount Charles, who, in 1816, was created a Marquess. In 1820, when she was fifty-one, Lady Conyngham presented no very obvious attractions; she had never been a great beauty, she was neither witty nor brilliant, but simply a plump matron with five grown up children.

In a pamphlet which went into two editions, and in which she figures as "Q," her appearance was treated somewhat scurvily:

> *Give the devil his due, she's a prime bit of stuff,*
> *And for flesh she has got in all conscience enough.*
> *He'll never need pillows to keep up his head,*
> *Whilst old Q and himself sleep and snore in one bed.*

However there could be no doubt of the effect of these homely charms on the King. A member of the Austrian Embassy in London wrote to Metternich to say that the King had lost thirty pounds due to dieting himself in an endeavour to make his figure *plus svelte* and consequently more attractive to *sa nouvelle passion*. On one occasion, when she was staying at Brighton, Lady Conyngham gave orders that the saloon should be illuminated, and the King came up to her and said, with the greatest tenderness, "Thank you, thank you, my dear; you always do what is right; you cannot please me so much as by doing everything you please, everything to show that you are mistress here."

It is difficult now to realise the vehemence and scurrility with which the King was attacked during the Queen's "trial" on the score of his connexion with Lady Conyngham. A further example from the pamphlet quoted above, which was typical of thousands disseminated all over the country, with the same excruciating disregard for the laws of metre and the canons of good taste, may help to show this:

> 'Tis pleasant at seasons to see how they sit,
> First cracking their nuts, and then cracking their wit;
> Then quaffing their claret—then mingling their lips,
> Or tickling the fat about each other's hips.

> 'Tis pleasant besides, too, to hear their discourse,
> Which is, more or less, touching the wish'd for divorce;
> To hear their soft tales and each smart repartee
> But most when her Ladyship squats on his knee!

> Then he's prime, then he's up, then he's spooney no more;
> Then he looks like a something a nymph might adore:
> Then Cupid and Bacchus get pleasant and merry,
> And drench the OLD BOY with their kisses and sherry.

> The lady is blinkey—she's full half-seas over,
> And He like a Mutton pot-bellied with clover;
> 'Till having both feasted as long as they're able,
> They fall, like dead muttons, both under the table.

Yet in spite of all this, and in spite of Lady Hertford's reply to a friend, who asked her about Lady Conyngham, that "intimately as she had known the King . . . he had never ventured to speak to her upon the subject of his mistresses," it is improbable that there was connexion between the King and Lady Conyngham beyond the need in one of his naturally affectionate disposition for sympathy and companionship. It seems to have been very generally overlooked that Lady Conyngham never left her husband to go and live with the King, but when she went to live with him at the Royal Lodge or at the Pavilion, she was accompanied by her husband and by all her children, which, to say the least of it, was a very unorthodox arrangement. It may, of course, be argued that the smiles and favour of a King dispel the ordinary rules which propriety lays down for an injured husband and his scandalised children, and that they should share the same roof, sit at the same table, and welcome the endearments of the seducer of their wife and mother because he is the King. Lord Conyngham himself was a distinguished nobleman with a long record of public service to the State, his eldest son died as a young man, his second son, afterwards Lord Conyngham, had also an honourable and distinguished career in front of him; his third son, famous as a connoisseur, was created Lord Londesborough by Queen Victoria; his elder daughter married Lord Huntly from the Royal Lodge, and his younger daughter married Lord Athlumney. It is hardly probable that any one of this distinguished family would have countenanced the adultery of Lady Conyngham. Lady Conyngham was moreover an exceedingly religious woman, and the Princess Lieven speaks of her limited mind "being occupied with religious questions."

It is far more likely that the King's affection for Lady Conyngham and all her family sprang less from sexual impulses than from the extreme loneliness of his position. He was parted from his wife, his only child was dead, he was fond of the Duke of York, but he naturally had his own interests; his other brothers, with the exception of the Duke of Sussex whom he disliked, were all in the first bliss of their belated marriages, his spinster sisters, with the exception of the Princess Augusta, with whom he used to sing glees at Frogmore, had little in common with him, and most of his old friends had died. A King is necessarily debarred from mixing with people with the same easy familiarity as a Prince of Wales or even a Prince Regent. There is no doubt that he found in Lord and Lady Conyngham and their children agreeable company and a pleasant antidote to the isolation of old age.

Croker has described the life of the King and Lady Conyngham
at the Pavilion, which to the most prudish will hardly seem of
abandoned viciousness. By day the King never left his private
suite of rooms except in the afternoon to stroll across to Lady
Conyngham's house. At six those staying in the Pavilion, together
with a few guests from outside, met for dinner, which was served
at 6.30. The King sat at the side of the table, with Lady Conyngham, dressed in a white cashmere shawl, on his right, and Lady
Elizabeth Conyngham, dressed in a scarlet cashmere shawl, on
his left; Lord Conyngham sat at one end of the table and Lord
Francis Conyngham at the other: the King's Secretary (Sir
Benjamin Bloomfield) sat opposite him, and two other ladies and
ten gentlemen completed the party. When the King took wine
with Lady Conyngham, he touched glasses with her.

The King was in excellent spirits during the evening, and
discoursed on the superiority of fowl to pheasant, advised Lady
Conyngham to read Tickell's *Anticipation* (a learned work which
her Ladyship had certainly not the understanding to enjoy), gave
the most brilliant imitation of an old French Duke mumbling
about ballet dancers, and asked Croker, "Why did you not bring
that dear little girl of yours to my children's ball last Monday?"
After coffee the gentlemen followed the King to the music-room,
where he sat down, and, with two Miss Liddells (daughters of
Lord Ravensworth), sang Italian trios, "Life's a Bumper," and
"The Friar of Orders Gray." After this the King settled down to
a game of Patience with Lady Conyngham, and retired to bed
at 11.30.

On the following day dinner was rather later, as the King was
busy trying on a new coat, and he discussed Lady Hervey's
Letters, which Croker had just edited, and regretted that Croker
had not consulted him, because "I am a great reservoir of
anecdote." After dinner the King sang, with two boys from the
choir of the Chapel Royal at Brighton, "Glorious Apollo,"
"Mighty Conqueror," Lord Mornington's "Waterfall" (*encored*),
and "*Non nobis, Domine.*" Although his bass voice was not
particularly good, Croker thought he sang with more gaiety and
spirit than the professionals. His life with Lady Conyngham
was domestic rather than vicious and was totally different from
the picture of it formed in the public mind as the result of
scurrilous squibs and lampoons.

Two years before he came to the throne, the King first took into his service Dr. Knighton, who was soon afterwards made a baronet, and who had won his confidence through the discretion with which he had acted as executor to MacMahon, who had been private secretary to the King when Regent. Sir William Knighton strengthened his hold over the King by the skill with which he managed his finances, and his influence became quite as great as that of Lady Conyngham. Knighton was competent and sympathetic; though his power over the King was absolute, it was benign. His style of treating the King is well illustrated by the following letter written by him to the King in 1822:

"I trust that the Almighty will give you peace, and that your afflicted mind will cease to be tortured by the overwhelming inquietudes which have of late made such painful inroads on your health.

I feel assured all will be well. In the meantime let me implore of your Majesty to *guard your* health, and to use every means to protect it in your power. . . . If you knew, Sir, what I really and sincerely felt your Majesty would scarcely believe the *extent of my anxiety* and *misery respecting you.*"

As some indication of the King's reliance on Knighton's judgment in all matters, personal and public, it is only necessary to quote the closing words of the King's memorandum on the advantages of dismissing Liverpool's Government "These also I submit for thy dear consideration, but will do whatever you will desire." In any difficulty or worry the King immediately turned to Knighton, and when he heard of the death of the Princess Elizabeth, the three months old daughter of the Duke of Clarence, he wrote at once to Knighton:

"MY DEAR FRIEND,

For God's sake come down to me to-morrow morning, at latest by ten o'clock. The melancholy tidings of the almost sudden death of my poor little niece has just reached me, and has overset me beyond all I can express to you. Poor William's[1] letter, which is all affection, and especially towards you, refers me to you for all particulars; therefore pray come to me with as little delay as possible. I have not time to add a word more

[1] The Duke of Clarence.

about myself, or upon other subjects *most dear and important to
all my happiness and very existence.* You will be *a great consolation
to me.*

Ever your most affectionate friend,

Brighton, *March* 4, 1821."

G. R.

Unfortunately Knighton became an object of general suspicion,
being regarded by everyone as a master of intrigue, and by many
as a pander to the King's pleasures. This reputation has been far
too glibly accepted. Knighton was in fact a very devout person
who brought up his children to read the Bible, which he described
as "the *only thing* to be relied upon," and, with Lady Conyngham,
undoubtedly was responsible for the increasing attention paid to
religion by the King in the last ten years of his life. He had had
to make his own way in the world, and is not to be regarded as
an immoral man because he owed everything to having acted as
accoucheur to Lord Wellesley's mistress. He had the soothing
amiability and elegant accomplishments of the very best type of
provincial medical man, which impressed, and possibly imposed
upon the King. If the rapid way in which he wormed himself
into the confidence and counsels of the King is surprising, and
may have disgusted his contemporaries, at any rate the dis-
interested way in which he served the King is deserving of the
highest praise.

It was in the seclusion of the Royal Lodge, and consoled by the
Conynghams and Sir William Knighton, that the King passed
the most humiliating months of his life. But as soon as the Bill
was dropped, and popular excitement had begun to die down, the
King attempted to recover, if not the affection, at least the respect
of his subjects. He accepted defeat, and pressed Lord Liverpool
to arrange for an allowance for the Queen, and also to offer her
one of the Royal houses, so that the whole business might be
finally settled. Although popular enthusiasm spluttered rather
dangerously until the Queen died, it had really burned itself out
in the three days' illumination which followed the dropping of
the Bill, and the Queen undoubtedly was correct when she wrote,
"This business has been more cared for as a political affair, dan
as de cause of a poor forlorn woman." With the subsidence of
popular feeling the King returned to London, and at the end of
January opened Parliament in state. In the speech from the throne

he said: "I well know, that, notwithstanding the agitation produced by temporary circumstances, and amidst the distress which still presses upon a large portion of my subjects, the firmest reliance may be placed on that affectionate and loyal attachment to my person . . . and which, while it is most grateful to the strongest feelings of my heart, I shall ever consider as the best and surest safeguard of my throne." These were brave words, for at the moment there were very few signs of "affectionate attachment."

At the beginning of February he decided to put his popularity to the test and to drive in state to the theatre. On February 7th he went to Drury Lane, accompanied by the Dukes of York, Clarence, and Wellington. He was loudly applauded for two or three minutes, and stood bowing in his box while the cheering lasted. The following night he went to Covent Garden, where he was even more enthusiastically received, and he rose and bowed with his hand on his heart. There were audible noises of interruption from the gallery during the performance, and a man's voice was distinctly heard calling out, "Where's your wife, Georgie?" He drove rapidly to and fro in a closed carriage with an escort of Life Guards, and there was a certain amount of hostility from the crowds lining the streets, but it was clear that the King was rapidly regaining popularity, and he decided that it was possible for him to go forward with arrangements for the Coronation, which was fixed to take place on Thursday, July 19th.

The preparations lasted for months and exactly followed the precedents for the coronation of James II. The Coronation banquet was to be held in Westminster Hall, and a wooden flooring was put down about 14 inches above the stone flags, the walls were draped, and tiers of wooden galleries for spectators and distinguished guests were erected along the sides. The dining tables, at which the bishops and peers were to sit, ran down the length of the Hall, and at the south end was a platform heavily draped in scarlet and gold, where the King was to sit with the Royal Dukes on his right and left. At the north end, facing the Royal platform, was a triumphal arch, executed in the Gothic style, some 30 feet high by 36 feet wide, above which was the gallery for the King's band.

The Abbey was similarly transformed. The west aisle was entirely filled with galleries, boxes, and benches, decorated with crimson cloth, from which the procession could be seen, the seats in which were sold to the public. Galleries were also put in the choir for spectators, and the north and south transepts were fitted with benches for peers and peeresses. There was a box for members of the Royal Family in the *sacrarium*, and facing this was a box for the foreign Ministers, and also accommodation for gentlemen of the Press.

At half past eight on Wednesday, July 18th, the King drove down in a closed carriage from Carlton House to the Speaker's house, where he spent the night. At midnight the bells of St. Margaret's rang a merry peal, which was continued at half hourly intervals throughout the night, guns fired at similar intervals, and the tramp of soldiers, the clatter of horses' hooves, the rolling of carriages, and the excited clack of tongues turned night into day. Many of the spectators had arrived by one o'clock in the morning, and at seven all ticket-holders had to be in their places.

The Coronation procession was to form in Westminster Hall, and to move along a covered walk to the Abbey. This walk, which was 25 feet wide, was raised three feet from the ground so as to be plainly visible, and was covered with a blue carpet. Between Westminster Hall and the Abbey, advantage had been taken of every possible site for galleries for spectators, seats in which were sold at prices ranging from two to twenty guineas. These galleries were all gaily decorated, and given such names as, "The Royal George," "The Royal Cambridge," and "The Ladies' Fancy." The duties of doorkeepers at Westminster Hall were undertaken by eminent pugilists.

At ten o'clock everyone who was to take part in the procession was waiting in Westminster Hall, but the King was twenty-five minutes late, as Lord Gwydyr, who was acting as Lord Great Chamberlain, unluckily tore his clothes while getting into them. At 10.25 the King entered the Hall, preceded by the great officers of state, an entrance which was described by the artist Haydon: "Something rustles, and a being buried in satin, feathers and diamonds rolls gracefully into his seat. The room rises with a sort of feathered, silken thunder. Plumes wave, eyes sparkle, glasses are out, mouths smile and one man becomes the prime object of attraction to thousands. The way in which the King bowed was really royal. As he looked towards the peeresses and foreign ambassadors, he showed like some gorgeous bird of the East."

After a short pause the procession set out, headed by the King's herb woman and six maids strewing flowers. After the household band came the dignitaries of the City of London, and it is pleasant to have to record that that great master of publicity, Alderman Wood, who, one might have imagined, would have been prevented by indisposition from attending, was received with general jeers and groans. The whole of the peerage walked, according to their rank, in their state robes, and privy councillors who were not peers wore Elizabethan fancy dress of white and blue satin with trunk hose. As Sir Walter Scott said, "Separately so gay a garb had an odd effect on the persons of elderly or ill made men: but when the whole was thrown into one general body all these discrepancies disappeared." Immediately in front of the King walked three bishops carrying the paten, the chalice and the Bible, and in front of them walked the great officers of state, carrying the crown, the orb, the sceptre, and the sword of state. The King walked under a canopy of cloth-of-gold, borne by the barons of the Cinque Ports. His train was nine yards in length, and was of crimson velvet ornamented with golden stars. He wore a black Spanish hat, with a spreading plume of white ostrich feathers, surmounted by a heron's plume and under it a wig, the curls of which fell over his forehead. In his progress to the Abbey he was received with the utmost enthusiasm, and it must be confessed that for a man of almost sixty he had contrived to appear as an extraordinarily regal and virile figure. It was this assumption of youthfulness that inspired Leigh Hunt's brilliantly cruel "Coronation Soliloquy":

> Yes, my hat, Sirs,
> Think of that, Sirs,
>   Vast and plumed and Spain-like,
> See my big,
> Grand robes; my wig,
>   Young, yet lion-mane like.
> Glory! Glory!
> I'm not hoary;
>   Age it can't come o'er me;
> Mad caps, grave caps, gazing on the grand man,
>   All alike adore me.

As the King entered the Abbey, shortly before eleven o'clock, the choir, at his own suggestion, sang the "Hallelujah Chorus." But the singing and the firing of the guns outside were all completely drowned by the shouts of enthusiasm from every corner of the building. The heat in the Abbey was extreme, and it was feared that the King, encumbered with his robes, would faint, but he managed to go through with the ceremony, which lasted until nearly four o'clock. After the actual crowning the enthusiasm of the spectators broke out again, ladies' handkerchiefs, knights' caps, and peers' coronets were all waved in the air amidst thunderings of "God Bless the King." It was said, though it was obviously untrue, that during the Communion Service the King repeatedly kissed a ring (given to him by Lady Conyngham) which he wore on his left hand. If the King was kissing any ring, it was unquestionably the Coronation ring, which had just been placed on his finger. On the return journey to Westminster Hall he wore robes of purple velvet, the crown on his head, and carried the orb and sceptre in his hand.

After resting a few minutes, which allowed time for the peeresses and privileged spectators to take their seats, the King took his place at the dais in preparation for the banquet. The peers were seated at the tables, which ran lengthways down the Hall. The first course was then served by a procession which entered through the Gothic arch at the north end of the Hall. After clerks of the kitchen and serjeants came the Lord High Constable (the Duke of Wellington), the Lord High Steward (the Marquess of Anglesey), and the Deputy Earl-Marshal (Lord Howard of Effingham) in their peers' robes, mounted on horses, caparisoned with plumes and feathers. Behind them came the Gentlemen Pensioners with the dishes of meat. After the course had been served, the three peers backed from the Royal presence down the whole length of the Hall—a particularly commendable performance for Lord Anglesey, who had left one of his legs on the field of Waterloo. The spectacle was perhaps slightly marred. by the vigour with which Lord Howard swore at his horse, as his language was clearly heard all over the Hall.

While the King was eating his dinner the ceremony of the Challenge took place. The hereditary office of King's Champion had descended to the Reverend John Dymoke, rector of Scrivelsby in Lincolnshire, who rightly decided that his appearance on horseback in shining armour hardly became his calling, and he accordingly deputed his son, not then quite twenty-one, to act for him. The youthful champion, in full armour with a plumed helmet, carrying the gauntlet, and riding a white charger (borrowed from Astley's circus), won universal admiration as he capered through the Gothic arch. He was supported by the Duke of Wellington and Lord Howard, also on horseback. The gauntlet was flung down three times, the last one at the foot of the dais, when the King drank to the champion out of a gold cup. The three horsemen then backed from the Hall. Hood addressed a poem to Dymoke, congratulating him on his brilliant appearance, and containing the verse:

> How delightful to sit by your beans and peas
> With a goblet of gooseberry gallantly clutch'd
> And chat of the blood that had delug'd the Pleas
> And drench'd the King's Bench—if the glove
> had been touched.

After this ceremony the King's health was drunk with three times three, i.e. nine rounds of cheering, and he replied in a voice which could be heard by all the company, "The King thanks the peers for drinking his health and does them the honour of drinking their health and that of his good people." He shortly afterwards withdrew and drove back in a closed carriage to Carlton House.

By this time the peers were thoroughly hungry, having eaten nothing since the early morning, and settled down to do justice to 160 tureens of soup (80 of turtle, 40 of rice, 40 of vermicelli), 160 dishes of fish (80 of turbot, 40 of trout, 40 of salmon), 160 hot joints (80 of venison, 40 of roast beef with three barons, 40 of mutton and veal), 160 dishes of vegetables (potatoes, peas, and cauliflowers), 480 sauce boats (240 of lobster, 120 of butter, 120 of mint), 80 dishes of braised ham, 80 savoury pies, 80 dishes of daubed geese (two on each dish), 80 dishes of savoury cakes, 80 pieces of braised beef, 80 dishes of braised capons, 1,190 side dishes, 320 dishes of mounted pastry, 320 dishes of small pastry, 400 dishes of jellies and creams, 160 dishes of shell-fish (80 of lobster and 80 of crayfish), 160 dishes of cold roast fowl, 80 dishes of cold house lamb. As the peeresses in the galleries had had nothing to eat, efforts were made to convey some of the cold food to them, and one nobleman was observed tying up a cold chicken in his handkerchief and throwing it to his son. The day ended with a fête in Hyde Park, with fireworks and balloons.

The Coronation of George IV, like the Gothic revival and Sir Walter Scott's novels, was symptomatic of the enthusiasm for the Middle Ages which began with the nineteenth century. It is easy enough to ridicule the fancy dresses of the privy councillors, the trappings of the horses of the great officers of state, and the armour of the Champion as only another effort to conjure up that imaginary world of jousts and tourneys where every knight was "bolde" and every lady "fayre." They may not have been in accordance with the tastes of our own generation, accustomed to a nobility recruited from commercial and irreligious sources, but they did constitute the most spectacular and effective display of the vested interests of Great Britain which has ever been staged, and brought home to the observers the full dignity of the kingly office.

It was a striking triumph for the King's personality that only eight months after the rejoicings in connexion with the dropping of the Bill against the Queen he should have carried through a ceremony of that kind amid scenes of the greatest enthusiasm, for, as Sir Walter Scott said, "never monarch received a more general welcome from his subjects." What no doubt pleased him more than anything was that it marked the final overthrow of the Queen. Having unsuccessfully claimed a right to be crowned with the King, she foolishly decided to present herself at the Abbey. At 5.30 she drove down from Cambridge House in Piccadilly,[1] in which she was then living, in an open carriage, accompanied by Lord and Lady Hood, and demanded admittance at each of the doors of the Abbey in turn. The doorkeepers explained that they had orders to admit no one but ticket-holders, and it seems clear that the authorities had decided to admit her (as a spectator) if she showed a ticket. She could, of course, have easily secured a ticket (Lord Hood, as a peer, had five); her only object was to parade herself before the crowds and to rouse the enthusiasm and cheers which she regarded as her due. Instead of that sweet music, she was assailed with cries of "Shame! Shame!" "Go! Go!" and "Go to Como." The jeers were renewed when she used

[1] Now the Naval and Military Club.

strong language, and she sadly drove back to Piccadilly, surrounded by a seedy mob of her supporters.

It is curious that if the Coronation marked the setting of the Queen's popularity, it also marked the dawning intelligence of an even more formidable enemy to the King. Thackeray, in *The Roundabout Papers* ("On a Peal of Bells"), writes, "I am reminded somehow of a July day, a garden and a great clanging of bells years and years ago, on the very day when George IV was crowned. I remember a little boy lying in that garden reading his first novel. It was called *The Scottish Chiefs*." How unfortunate that he ever deserted the realms of fiction, so entrancingly opened for him by Miss Porter's novel, for the tricky paths of historical fact, that, instead of drawing on his imagination to produce *The Four Georges*, he had not bequeathed to us instead a novel "sweet and delicious as the raspberry open-tarts of budding boyhood."

III

The King had determined to inaugurate his reign by visits to Ireland, Hanover, and Scotland, and as soon as the Coronation was over preparations were put in train for him to go to Ireland— a visit which was made peculiarly congenial by the fact that Lord and Lady Conyngham lived there. He set out from Carlton House on July 31st, and travelled to Portsmouth, where he embarked on the royal yacht, the *Royal George*, and leisurely cruised round the coast to Holyhead.

The yacht anchored off Holyhead on Monday, August 6th, where the King received a message to say that the Queen had been taken dangerously ill with inflammation of the bowels. The King was daily expected to make his state entry into Dublin, and he was therefore placed in a very difficult situation, particularly as his Ministers left him completely in the dark as to how he should act. He decided meanwhile to land in Wales, and stay quietly with Lord Anglesey at Plâs Newydd until there was further news. On Wednesday, August 8th, he returned to the yacht, where he met the Home Secretary, Lord Sidmouth, who was in charge of the preparations in Ireland, and who had crossed over to find out why the King had not come. They arranged between them that, if the next day's report was favourable, the King should proceed and make the state entry as soon as possible.

The following day's report was far from reassuring, and the King, with the approval of the Foreign Secretary, Lord Castlereagh, who had arrived that morning, agreed to go over to Ireland and land privately as soon as possible, and wait in retirement until the Queen had either died or recovered.

The weather was too boisterous for an immediate start, and, as they were still without news on Thursday evening, Lord Londonderry decided to open a letter which had arrived for Lord Sidmouth, who had returned to Ireland on the Wednesday. This letter was from Hobhouse,[1] and announced that the Queen was "suddenly much worse." Lord Londonderry read it out loud to the King, but suddenly stopped, with a look of horror, when he came to a sentence beginning, "The Duke of York . . ." "Come, come," said the King, "you must go on with it." The sentence was, "The Duke of York is in despair at an event which so much diminishes his chance of the Crown." The King was fortunately amused. The following day was still too rough for the crossing, and in the evening the news came that the Queen had died on Tuesday night. In Croker's happy phrase, the King was affected, but not afflicted, though he was heard throughout the greater part of the night pacing up and down his cabin, no doubt reflecting on all the misery and unhappiness since that April day twenty-six years earlier when his wife had landed at Greenwich.

The following day was somewhat less stormy, and the King decided to cross in the *Lightning* steamboat, hoping to make an unexpected, and therefore more private, landing. But in fact a considerable crowd collected at Howth, anticipating that with the better weather he would arrive. As soon as the boat stopped by the landing-stage the familiar figure of the King, with a black band on his left arm, was observed on deck. He was at once loudly cheered, and in reply he solemnly waved his seal-skin travelling cap above his head. On landing he got at once into his carriage and drove to Viceregal Lodge, attended by a considerable, and increasing, escort of Irish gentry on horseback. They followed him to the door of Viceregal Lodge, and, when he got out of his carriage, he turned to them and said: "I may not be able to express my feelings as I wish. I have travelled far. I have made a rough sea voyage—besides which particular circumstances have occurred, known to you all, of which it is better at present not to

[1] Probably Sir Benjamin Hobhouse, M.P., father of John Cam Hobhouse.

speak. Upon these subjects I leave it to delicate and generous hearts to appreciate my feelings. . . . Rank, station, honour are nothing; but to feel that I live in the hearts of my Irish subjects is to me the most exalted happiness. I must now once more thank you for your kindness and bid you farewell. Go and do by me as I shall do by you—drink my health in a bumper. I shall drink all yours—in a bumper of Irish whiskey punch." It was this gracious, almost brilliant, impromptu speech which paved the King's way to the hearts of the Irish, though stern critics might think that such a very recent widower should not have been talking quite so much about that beaker of whiskey. The King remained in complete retirement until after the Queen's funeral, and as he could have hardly been expected to remain tossing at anchor in Holyhead harbour indefinitely it is difficult not to agree with his own words to Knighton that "every regard to decency and decorum" was paid.

The scenes that characterised the Queen's death in London were the most disgraceful, the most degrading to conventional decency, and the most discreditable to Government of all the turbulent incidents connected with her name. She, poor woman, played her part with dignity and fortitude, and at the end she said, "I am going to die, Mr. Brougham; but it does not signify. . . . I tell you I shall die, but I don't mind it." History does not record whether those who had advised her so foolishly, so recklessly, and so selfishly felt any qualms of conscience as they watched her dying penniless and powerless. We only know that her death gave Creevey "an infernal lump in my throat," and that Denman, that master of meaningless and unfortunate verbiage, exclaimed that "no death could be more amiable." She had in her will[1] expressed a desire to be buried in Brunswick, and Lord Liverpool arranged that the coffin should be embarked at Harwich and that the funeral procession, in order to avoid the City and the possibility of a popular demonstration, should go along the new road from Paddington to Islington, and so to the

[1] By her will she bequeathed everything to William Austin. She had nothing but debts to leave, and he was maintained by the income of a trust executed in her lifetime. Austin spent many years in an asylum in Milan: he was brought to a private asylum in Chelsea in 1845, where he was described as "so lost and imbecile in mind that he requires the attention paid to a child. He occasionally appears cheerful and attempts to sing, but never enters into conversation." He died in 1849.

Colchester and Harwich road. The funeral procession set out from Brandenburgh House on August 14th, and the mob treated the *cortège* as though it had been a popular election candidate, hustling it in triumph through the streets of the City in defiance of the orders of the Government and the drawn swords of the military.

Partisan writers[1] have glibly and eagerly assumed that the King was responsible for the refusal to allow the funeral procession to pass through the City, though a moment's reflection as to the state of communications in the early nineteenth century should have shown them the impossibility of this. The King only heard the news of the Queen's death late on August 10th. The following day Lord Castlereagh wrote to Lord Liverpool to say that the King wished the funeral to go the whole way from Hammersmith by water. This cannot have reached the Prime Minister until Sunday night (August 12th) or Monday morning, and it was impossible to make the arrangements in time. The decision to divert the procession from the City was Lord Liverpool's alone, and the blame for taking a decision which he was incapable of enforcing must be his and his alone. Indeed the Cabinet in general, and Lord Liverpool in particular, were in a singularly drowsy condition. It is almost incredible that Lord Liverpool should not have troubled to write to the King at all, and that he was left without any advice from London as to his behaviour in Ireland in face of the very difficult situation created by the Queen's death. The King was so angry with the Prime Minister that he said to Croker, "I will not go on with him any longer."

On August 15th, the day after the Queen's funeral, the King held a private levee, at which he appeared in deep mourning. Two days later he made his state entry into Dublin. He wore the uniform of a Field Marshal and a mourning crape on his left arm: in his hat was a great octagon rosette of full-grown shamrocks. He was followed by a train of at least one hundred carriages, and was everywhere received with the greatest enthusiasm, the people shouting, as the Irish did not know how to cheer. He stood up in his carriage, repeatedly bowing, pointing to the shamrock in his hat and then placing his right hand over his heart. He was heard to say, "They are a fine, a noble people."

After the usual round of reviews, drawing-rooms, levees, dinners, he drove out, on August 24th, to stay with Lord and

[1] Notably His Honour Sir Edward Parry.

Lady Conyngham at Slane Castle, which is twenty-two miles north-west of Dublin. Slane Castle is one of the fairly early examples of the Gothic revival, having been altered by James Wyatt at the end of the eighteenth century. It is built on the edge of a hill, the ground falling sharply away from it down to the Boyne, which runs for two miles through the Castle grounds. The King thoroughly enjoyed his visit, particularly as there was practically no one invited to meet him apart from members of the Conyngham family, and he jokingly said that he would remain where he was and send the Lord Lieutenant of Ireland to rule England. After a stay of a few days—which included a visit to the Curragh races, where the King had a rather embarrassing attack of what one of Creevey's female correspondents called "merry-go-whimbles"—he embarked on September 3rd. On the shore Mr. Daniel O'Connell presented him with a laurel crown, and no doubt the spontaneous and general welcome given to him by the Irish of all classes was attributable partly to the belief that he would grant at any rate some electoral rights to the Roman Catholics. As night fell, the royal yacht stood out from Dunleary harbour (renamed Kingstown in honour of George IV), and the King sat on a sofa on deck while the strains of his band playing St. Patrick's Day and Garryowen were carried across the water to those on shore.

As the King reclined on his sofa he may justifiably have felt pleased with himself. The first English sovereign to visit Ireland in time of peace since Richard II, and not like King Richard a young romantic figure, but as Byron crudely put it, "in the promise and bloom of threescore," he had by his graciousness, his kindliness, and his charm of manner completely captured the hearts of the nation. *The Times* hoped that the Irish had recovered "from the excess of their late intoxication," but it takes more than this to explain away what was for the King a great personal triumph.

Unfortunately the success of the visit was slightly marred by the return journey. For many days the weather had been exceedingly rough, and Croker, who crossed some days before the King, tried the experiment of sitting in his travelling carriage on deck, as he thought the springs counteracted the motion of the sea. For two days the King remained in the *Royal George* off Dunleary, waiting for a favourable wind, and when at last the wind changed they ran into the most violent storm: it took them forty-eight hours to toss across the Irish Sea, and the royal yacht was separated from the accompanying squadron. They arrived at Milford Haven on September 9th, and the following day the King wrote to Sir William Knighton:

"Royal George Yacht.

Most even of our crew and company were deadly sick, but the very worst of all was my poor self; and I am now for the first time, since we are again at anchor in smooth water, risen from my bed, and not without considerable exertion and inconvenience to myself. I have suffered so much solely for the purpose of writing to you; for I too gratefully feel the warmth of your affectionate heart towards me at all times, not only not to neglect you, but to prove to you that you are always present to my mind. . . ."

Even at Milford Haven their misfortunes were by no means over. They were 270 miles from London, the roads through South Wales were then very rough, and the accommodation for travellers was primitive and for kings fantastic. They could have expected no comforts until they reached Gloucester. Although, as the King wrote, "I am so completely shattered and torn to pieces by the effects and sickness of an eight and forty hours tempest," he gallantly decided to brave the sea again and to sail round Land's End to Portsmouth. Two days later he wrote again to Knighton: ". . . There is no time for a florid description. We sailed again yesterday morning between four and five o'clock, with a most promising breeze in our favour to make the Land's End. About two or three in the evening [? afternoon] the wind shifted immediately in our teeth; a violent hurricane and tempest suddenly arose; the most dreadful possible of nights and of scenes ensued, the sea breaking everywhere over the ship. We lost the tiller, and the vessel was for some minutes down on her beam-ends; and nothing, I believe, but the undaunted presence of mind, perseverance, experience, and courage of Paget[1] preserved us from a watery grave. The oldest and most experienced of our sailors were petrified and paralysed; you may judge somewhat, then, of what was the state of most of the passengers; every one almost

---

[1] Captain of the Royal yacht.

flew up in their shirts upon deck in terrors that are not to be described." The King himself showed rather surprising coolness, and it was observed that his gratitude to the Almighty for his deliverance was truly edifying.

He finally reached Carlton House on September 16th, almost a fortnight after leaving Ireland. On September 24th he set out for Hanover, although, as he said, he was not well and he was tired of his journey before he had begun it, though this may have been explained by the fact that he could not take Lady Conyngham with him. He refused to sail from Dover, because of the way in which the inhabitants had cheered the Queen on her landing in the previous year: as he explained to Lord Liverpool, "It is the King's fixed determination to show as often as the occasion may occur, the thorough disgust he feels at the unpardonable conduct of such part of his subjects as reside within the town of Dover." He accordingly drove down to Ramsgate, and stayed the night at Cliff House, which belonged to Sir William Curtis. "The fat knight," as Curtis was called, was a Tory of ludicrous but persistent oratorical achievement, and of enormous wealth derived from a sea-biscuit manufactory at Wapping. He was a coarse, blunt, outspoken, rather common man, whose society soothed and amused, but can hardly have fascinated, the King. Sir William was immensely powerful and popular in Ramsgate, and the whole town turned out to give the King a tumultuous welcome.

He sailed from Ramsgate in the royal yacht and spent the first night of his life, abroad, at Calais. Living in Calais in honourable bankruptcy was Beau Brummell, not yet reduced to those phantom parties where in his dingy lodgings he went through the ceremony of receiving the tremendous guests who years before had gladly accepted his hospitality, and there was much speculation as to whether the King would show any acknowledgment of his former friend, but he is believed to have said, as he drove out of the town the next morning, "I leave Calais and have not seen Brummell." From Calais he drove on to Laeken, the royal palace near Brussels, where he stayed with the King and Queen of the Netherlands. It was a slightly embarrassing visit, as the Prince of Orange was there, who had been engaged to the Princess Charlotte but had since married a Grand Duchess of Russia. This lady, in order to impress the King, was glittering with diamonds, but his only comment to her on this rather vulgar display was, *"Madame, vous êtes très brillante."* However he was exceedingly agreeable, and the guests at dinner were surprised to see the King and Queen of the Netherlands convulsed with helpless laughter: it turned out that King George was giving a brilliant imitation of the King's father, the drunken old Stadtholder of Holland, whom he had known in his young days at Carlton House.

On September 29th he left Brussels to visit the battlefield of Waterloo. Sir William Knighton, who was in charge of all the arrangements, insisted on his attending divine service at eight o'clock before he started. On the battlefield the King met the Duke of Wellington, and in pouring rain they examined the various positions of the armies: the King showed the greatest interest in everything, notably in the burial place of Lord Anglesey's leg. He gave orders that a tree which stood in the middle of the battlefield, and which was rather damaged by gunfire, should be cut down, and that a chair should be carved out of it and inscribed *GEORGIO AUGUSTO EUROPÆ LIBERATORI*, and placed in Carlton House. A distinguished writer[1] has drawn a contrast between what he styles "the florid, still handsome, but bloated and diseased voluptuary, and the lean keen-eyed soldier-statesman." But physical contrasts, even when they are accurately drawn, are seldom important: the real contrast is between the Duke gravely expounding the precise positions of the two armies —the point where the stubborn English resistance turned the fortunes of the day, and the exact line along which the Old Guard advanced—and the King really much more interested in poking about for Lord Anglesey's leg, and phrasing a suitable inscription for his chair. Naturally there is no dispute as to which was, in the Victorian phrase, "the nobler character," but few could fail to see that there was something whimsically attractive and essentially human in the trivial interests of the King, so infinitely preferable to the ridiculous sententiousness of Sir William Knighton, who said, "The blades of grass on which we tread might be a part of some warrior's frame."

From Waterloo the King proceeded to Hanover. Everywhere in the kingdom he was received with the greatest enthusiasm, as was perhaps natural from the Hanoverians, who were a devotedly loyal people and had not seen their sovereign since George II

[1] Sir Herbert Maxwell.

visited them some sixty years before. The King was overwhelmed with his reception when he made his state entry on horseback into the city of Hanover. He had originally intended to go on to Vienna to visit the Emperor, and then to Paris to visit Louis XVIII, but the lateness of the season decided him to return direct to England. However the Emperor sent Metternich—then in the heyday of his power—to convey his greetings to the King, and the latter delicately kissed Metternich and in a complimentary speech compared him to Minos, Cato, Cæsar, Gustavus Adolphus, Pitt, and Wellington.

As it turned out, it was just as well that the King had decided to return, because just when he would have been starting for Vienna he was seized with "a severe fit of the gout," brought on by spraining his knee when he got on horseback for the state entry. However "the dearest King," as Knighton calls him, was sufficiently recovered to start for England on October 30th. At Göttingen the King drove in under a triumphal arch, and a train of young women in white, carrying festoons of flowers, presented him with a poem borne on a scarlet cushion. There was a tournament and a long address from the University authorities, who conferred a doctorate of medicine on Knighton. Travelling rapidly, the King arrived at Carlton House on November 8th.

George IV's tour of his kingdoms was completed by his visit to Edinburgh in the summer of 1822. He left London on August 10th, driving to Greenwich in "a plain green carriage and four," and carefully avoiding the City to mark his disapproval of the citizens' behaviour during the troubles with the Queen. Wearing a plain blue surtout and foraging cap, he embarked at Greenwich, and his appearance was the signal for volleys of cheering from the crowds lining both banks and from the occupants of many small boats on the river. The *Royal George* was attached by hawser to the *Comet* steam packet. Attended by the Lord Mayor's state barge, similarly attached to another steam packet, the procession of boats moved slowly down the Thames to the accompaniment of much cheering, gun-firing, and playing of the National Anthem. The Lord Mayor's barge parted from the King at Sheerness, and on August 11th the *Royal George*, still drawn by the *Comet*, proceeded up the coast. As it passed Scarborough the Mayor and Corporation, in their robes, put off in a boat with a loyal address, but the *Comet* was going along in such fine style that all they could do was to hand up the address on the end of a long stick. On August 14th, in torrential rain, the royal squadron anchored off Leith.

The morning had been fine, and steamboats set out with parties of ladies and gentlemen to greet the King. One of these boats contained that loyal and faithful subject, Mr. Creevey, who joined with his fellow-passengers in singing God Save the King, though whether he sang "Confound their knavish tricks" with full voice and swelling heart, history does not record. The rain decided the King to postpone his landing until the following day, and it was during this interval that Sir Walter Scott came on board. The King himself brought Sir Walter a glass of cherry brandy,[1] and, after drinking the King's health, Sir Walter bore off the glass in triumph, but when he got home the unexpected arrival of George Crabbe—the poetical rector of Trowbridge—made him forget the glass and he sat on it. Crabbe's visit was not an outstanding success, because the following morning Scott discovered him talking in polished and animated French to a group of Highland chieftains whom he had mistaken for foreigners.

On August 15th the King was rowed to the landing-place in the royal barge. He was dressed in full admiral's uniform, with a gold-laced hat in which were the Cross of St. Andrew and a large thistle. He then drove in state to Holyroodhouse, and was received with wild enthusiasm by a crowd which Knighton estimated at a million. The King repeated again and again the rather surprising judgment, "They are a nation of gentlemen."

He stayed during the whole visit outside Edinburgh, at Dalkeith Palace, with the young Duke of Buccleuch, then aged sixteen. The King brought his own cooks with him, and did what he could to put his youthful host at ease, even to seeing that he did not have too much to drink, for when the Duke was offered a glass of liqueur, the King said, "No! No! It is too strong for his grace to drink."

On the 19th the King held a levee at Holyroodhouse. He wore full Highland uniform, with the Stuart tartan, and was said to have "quite a martial air." This dress caused a certain amount of amusement, and inspired the verse:

[1] Not whiskey, as is commonly stated (vide Sir W. Knighton's Memoirs).

With his tartan plaid and kelt so wide,
The ladies blush who stand beside;
And as he bows, behind each fan,
Exclaim—O gallant Highlandman.[1]

But an unfortunate circumstance almost reduced the levee to a farce. For several days before the King's visit Sir William Curtis had been in Edinburgh supervising the arrangements, and the inhabitants had begun to grow accustomed to his bulky figure parading the streets in frock-coat, white trousers, and foraging cap. Seized by a loyal but unfortunate impulse, he decided to appear at the levee in the Stuart tartan—to which the long residence of his forbears in the commercial quarters of London certainly did not entitle him—and every one felt his portly appearance to be a hideous caricature of the King. Sir Walter Scott described it as "a portentous apparition." But the King could not for long be angry with Sir William, who was obviously thoroughly jolly, enjoying himself, and laughing heartily. The levee was also rendered somewhat remarkable by some of the Scotsmen who, on being told to kiss hands, bowed and kissed their own hands to the King.

There were drawing-rooms and many other functions attended by the King, but the most memorable was the state drive along the royal mile from Holyroodhouse to Edinburgh Castle. Troops were stationed on the ground in front of the Castle and lined the walls. When the King arrived, he climbed up to the highest battery and appeared alone, the Royal Standard flapping above him in the wind. His appearance was the signal for a great roar from the crowd, which completely drowned the massed bands, playing the National Anthem, and the firing of the guns. It was pouring with rain, and the smoke from the guns periodically hid the King from view, but he could be clearly seen waving his hat in answer to the acclamation of the crowd below.

At the end of the visit he dined with the Lord Provost and Corporation of the City. In reply to the toast of his health, he said, "I am quite unable to express my sense of the gratitude which I owe to the people of this country; but I beg to assure them that I shall ever remember as one of the proudest moments

---

[1] In fact, there would have been no ladies at the levee and, according to Sir David Wilkie, the King wore flesh-coloured pantaloons under his kilt.

of my life the day I came among them, and the gratifying reception which they gave me. I return you, my Lord Provost, my lords and gentlemen, my warmest thanks for your attention this day; and I can assure you with truth, with earnestness and sincerity that I shall never forget your dutiful attention to me on my visit to Scotland, and particularly the pleasure I have derived from dining in your hall this day." Just before he left the dinner, he rose and said, "I have one more toast to give, in which I trust you will join me, and it is—Health to the Chieftains and Clans, and God Almighty bless the Land of Cakes. Drink this three times three, gentlemen."

It is, of course, easy to ridicule the King's visit to Edinburgh, and to echo with approval Byron's verse:

> *Teach them the decencies of good threescore;*
> *Cure them of tours, hussar and highland dresses;*
> *Tell them that youth once gone returns no more,*
> *That hired huzzas redeem no land's distresses;*
> *Tell them Sir William Curtis is a bore,*
> *Too dull even for the dullest of excesses—*
> *The witless Falstaff of a hoary Hall,*
> *A fool whose bells have ceased to ring at all.*[1]

Sir Walter Scott, in a letter to the King's private secretary, alluded to one fact which undoubtedly impressed the Scots. Instead of the monster described in the newspaper and portrayed in countless caricatures "their delight was extreme at seeing a portly handsome man looking and moving every inch a king." Certainly it would be a mistake to allow the droll and unfortunate incidents of the King's visit to engross our attention to the exclusion of its importance. The ceremonial, arranged by Sir Walter Scott, is still followed with surprisingly few alterations on the occasion of the sovereign's visit to Edinburgh, and it marks an interest in the historic past and a dawning of national pride which were to be such definite characteristics of nineteenth-century Britain. George IV was the first King to visit Scotland since Charles II, and at the age of sixty he carried out an exhausting programme with a zest which surprised his *entourage*, and a charm which delighted the populace. And it says much for his personality that in Edinburgh, among whose citizens, renowned for their

[1] *Don Juan.*

hardiness and tenacity of life, there were some who recalled seventy-five years earlier when the palace of Holyroodhouse was brilliantly lighted and filled with men and women met to honour a Stuart Prince, and many who from childhood had been steeped in the bitterness and animosities of those times, he should have been received as though all memory of the past had been obliterated.

IV

Although the King had promised both the Irish and the Scots that he would return to their countries, his visit to Edinburgh marks the end of that long series of state functions for which the beginning of the Regency, the triumphs against Napoleon, and his accession to the throne had provided the excuse. After 1822 he lived more and more in retirement though in the summer he used to come up to London for a few weeks at the end of June, and every season he gave a juvenile ball, in the early years of his reign at Carlton House, where the little guests sat down to dinner in the Gothic Conservatory, and towards the end of his reign in St. James's Palace. At these functions he moved about among his guests with great affability and obvious enjoyment. He occasionally gave a grand ball for members of the nobility, and it was on one of these occasions that Lord Charles Russell, who, at the age of eighteen, had just been commissioned in the Blues, had forgotten to put on his aiguillette. As he passed the King, who was sitting on a sofa because of a mild attack of gout, and whose attention to the details of military dress was notorious, he was horrified to hear him call out in a high voice, "Good evening sir, I suppose that you are the regimental doctor."

But apart from these functions, and from twice driving in state to open Parliament, he was no more seen in public, gave up yachting at Cowes, and spent the greater part of the year in complete seclusion at the Royal Lodge. Even his visits to Brighton grew less and less frequent, and he last stayed there at the beginning of 1827. The Pavilion had been finally finished in 1822, after forty years of adding, altering, and embellishing, but its owner found that its situation surrounded by a growing town made privacy, even in the grounds, impossible, and prevented him from having any fresh air, as he could only take exercise in the riding school. Writers have tried to suggest that Lady Conyngham had taken a dislike to the place (certainly her homely ways and pietistic views hardly fitted in to the surroundings or suited her to appreciate them), but there is no doubt that the real reason why he ceased to go there was the lack of privacy. It is true that William IV spent a great deal of time at the Pavilion, but it has to be remembered that there was nothing that curious monarch enjoyed more than a staring, tittering crowd: Queen Victoria was eventually compelled to sell it, because she found its publicity quite intolerable.

It has long been accepted that the chief reason for the King's withdrawal into privacy was his fear of ridicule on account of his size, but, as his fatness had been a national joke for at least fifteen years, it seems a trifle obscure why he was supposed to have suddenly desired to hide it. Lord Folkestone's statement to Creevey, that "Prinny has let loose his belly which now reaches his knees," has, through its brilliant coarseness, stamped itself on our minds, though a little reflection might have prompted us to ask how Lord Folkestone, a radical member of Parliament, acquired this intimate detail of the dressing-room which must have alarmed even the most lethargic medical man and would have entitled the King to go on tour with General Tom Thumb and the Siamese twins. The truth of the matter is that the King was always portly, but never became immense nor unwieldy; his withdrawal into privacy was the result of less spectacular causes.

In the autumn of 1822 he was seized with a severe attack of gout, complained of much "flying gout," and could only walk with great difficulty, and after that he was never really well, and there are constant references in the memoirs of the period to his lameness, to the fact that he looked ill, or that he looked well, "but was glittering with incessant perspiration." These "accessions of gout," as they were called, enfeebled and depressed him, as the following letter from him to Sir William Knighton shows:

"Royal Lodge,
June 18th, 1827.

. . . As to myself, I am pretty well bodily; but I have little or no use of my poor limbs, for I can neither walk up nor down stairs, and am obliged to be carried, and in general to be wheeled about everywhere; for my powers of walking, and even of crawling about with crutches, or with the aid of a strong stick are not in the smallest respect improved since you last saw me,—at the same time that my knees, legs, ankles and feet swell more formidably and terribly than ever. This, I am sure you will agree with me, ought now to be seriously attended to without delay by some plan devised and steadily acted upon, in order to stop the further progress, and to remedy it effectually and finally; for there is no question it is an increasing and progressive evil (at least so I fear) unless steps be found, and that speedily too, of averting it.

You must now have had enough of my epistolary quality; I shall therefore, dear friend, hasten to a conclusion with the assurance that I am always your sincere and affectionate friend,

G. R."

It should not, however, be imagined that, because the King's life was bounded by Windsor Great Park, he had lost his knowledge of the art of existence. In 1823 the Royal Lodge was repaired by Wyatt (afterwards Wyattville), but as has been said before no adequate account of the building survives. William IV and Queen Adelaide had little sympathy with the tastes or habits of their predecessor on the throne. Once, when King William was shown a picture which had been greatly admired by George IV, he remarked, "Ay, it seems pretty—I daresay it is—my brother was very fond of this sort of nicknackery. Damned expensive taste though," and he allowed Queen Adelaide, in a fit of vandalistic piety, to pull down the greater part of the Royal Lodge, which she imagined to have been the scene of terrible wickedness between the King and Lady Conyngham. Only one room, the drawing-room, of the original building now survives, but we know from Greville that it was "a delightful place to live in. . . . Nothing can exceed the luxury of the internal arrangements." Greville criticised the rooms for being too low, but the King always liked to live in low rooms, as is obvious from the Pavilion and from what we know of Carlton House. Princess Lieven described it as at once "royal and rustic, on the outside the simplicity of the cottage, within the rarest requirements of comfort, elegance and magnificence," and she went on to say that its chief charm lay in its situation, surrounded by superb trees and with magnificent views stretching up to the Castle in the distance; and that it was *"une charmante béatitude."* The King himself loved it, and referred to his delight when "I inhale the pure air of this delightful spot." His family thought it damp and unhealthy in the winter.

Under the King's directions, the Park land between the Royal Lodge and Virginia Water had been laid out in a number of secluded drives, and he very much altered and improved Virginia Water itself. This had originally been created by the Duke of Cumberland ("the Butcher"), who was ranger of Windsor Park and had lived in Cumberland Lodge, he it was who was responsible for the Chinese Temple on the island. George IV added a fishing temple and a "ruined temple," which was built from several antique columns and remains of classical architecture which had for a long time stood neglected in the courtyard of the British Museum.

In the winter afternoons the King invariably took "the exercise of the phaeton," taking Lady Conyngham through the drives he had had made in the Park, from which strangers were rigorously excluded. In summer the programme was slightly varied, and he drove in his pony phaeton after luncheon to Virginia Water, members of the household following in landaus. As the King arrived at the landing-place, his private band would strike up God Save the King from a boat on the lake, and the company embarked on a barge, from which they fished while the band played, keeping to windward to add to the effect of the music. In fine weather the King's party dined in tents, put up at the water's edge at a cost of over £3,000.

Only guests of especial distinction, like the Duke of Wellington, or the King's most intimate friends, like Prince and Princess Lieven, ever stayed at the Royal Lodge; ordinary guests, Ministers, and members of the Royal Family stayed at Cumberland Lodge, about a quarter of a mile away, driving across to the Royal Lodge for dinner, which was always chosen by the King himself. Quite the best account of the King's life at this period is from the pen of Queen Victoria, written in the early 'seventies. In 1826 she went down with her mother to stay at Cumberland Lodge with her aunt, the Duchess of Gloucester. "When we arrived at the Royal Lodge the King took me by the hand saying 'Give me your little paw.' He was large and gouty but with a wonderful dignity and charm of manner. He wore the wig which was so much worn in those days. Then he said he would give me something for me to wear, and that was his picture set in diamonds, which was worn by the Princesses as an order to a blue ribbon on the left shoulder. I was very proud of this,—and Lady Conyngham pinned it on my shoulder."[1] Members of the Conyngham family then took the little Princess for a drive in one of the pony phaetons drawn by four grey ponies, and showed her the King's menagerie at Sandpit Gate, where he kept wapitis, gazelles, and chamois. The Queen goes on to say, "Then we went (I think the next day) to Virginia Water and met the King in his phaeton in which he was driving the Duchess of Gloucester —and he said 'Pop her in' and I was lifted in and placed between him and Aunt Gloucester who held me round the waist. (Mamma was much frightened) I was great pleased." The King drove her to Virginia Water, and took her on board with him to fish. In the evening the little Princess was allowed to go across to the Royal Lodge to listen to the band which was playing in the conservatory, lit up by coloured lamps. Afterwards, when she was asked what she had enjoyed most, she said, "When I was taken in the phaeton with my uncle and Aunt Mary." Long, long afterwards, when the passage of years had somewhat dimmed her pleasure at her uncle's kindness, she said of George IV to a friend, "He asked me to kiss him, and it was too disgusting because his face was covered in grease paint," though whether the Queen was equally shocked by her other uncle, the virtuous Leopold, who even on his deathbed was rouged and raddled to the eyes, history does not relate.

The only break in the King's life at Windsor was during Ascot week, when he drove to the course in semi-state, sitting generally with the Duke of Wellington in the first carriage. In 1826 Creevey, who was at Ascot for the races, describes how "Prinny came as before, bowling along the course in his carriage and four . . . he played off his nods and winks and kissing his hand, just as he did to all of you 20 years ago on the Brighton racecourse."

This retired life did nothing to diminish the King's interest in literature and painting. He read all Sir Walter Scott's novels as they came out, and most of his reading was done in bed in the early morning. After Napoleon's death, when the library which

[1] In the miniature of the Queen, by Plant, at Buckingham Palace, she is wearing the King's picture.

had been sent out to him was returned, the King asked his librarian to go through all the books and show him any which Napoleon had marked. He and his librarian came to the conclusion that Ossian was his favourite author, and they found in the book that he had drawn a comparison between himself and Alexander the Great.[1] The King continued to spend large sums on the collection of pictures, still buying principally through the third Lord Hertford—though no longer on such intimate terms with him. In 1826 he lent his pictures at Carlton House to the Galleries of the British Institution for Promoting the Fine Arts in the United Kingdom, and he said of his collection, "I have not formed it for my own pleasure alone, but to gratify the public taste." In 1825 it was very nearly destroyed when a fire broke out at Carlton House when the King was in residence. The King was moved to one end of the building, and Sir William Knighton showed much efficiency and gallantry in fighting the flames, but four pictures of the Royal Family were destroyed.

The year 1823 was marked by two actions of the King which have never been adequately recognised, and which have put the world of scholarship permanently in his debt. At the beginning of the year, he gave to the nation the magnificent library formed by his father, and he wrote to Lord Liverpool:

> "Pavilion, Brighton.
> *January* 15, 1823.
>
> DEAR LORD LIVERPOOL,
> The King, my late revered and excellent Father, having formed, during a long series of years, a most valuable and extensive Library, I have resolved to present this collection to the British Nation.
>
> Whilst I have the satisfaction by this means of advancing the literature of my country, I also feel that I am paying a just tribute to the memory of a parent, whose life was adorned with every public and private virtue. . . .
> Believe me, with great regard,
>
> Your sincere friend
> G. R."

---

[1] According to Lord Rosebery, *Napoleon: The Last Phase*, these books were sold in London by order of the Government.

Many who visit the British Museum, and all who use the Library there, have recognised the importance and value of the King's Library.[1]

In the same year there came into the market a splendid collection of pictures formed by Mr. Julius Angerstein, a wealthy merchant of Russian origin. The King, who had long been personally familiar with the collection, and who had always regretted that there was no permanent exhibition in London either of foreign or English pictures, urged Lord Liverpool to buy them for the nation. The Cabinet agreed to act on the King's advice, and bought the pictures for just over £50,000. This collection, which was for a few years exhibited in Pall Mall, formed the nucleus for the National Gallery, and it is therefore peculiarly fitting, though it may be feared that it is too seldom observed, that visitors enter the Gallery through the columns which once graced the front of Carlton House.

A new development in the King's character, the result of his withdrawal from the world, was a most edifying attention to religious matters, well summed up in W. M. Praed's verse on him:

> And drinking homilies and gin,
> And chewing pork and adulation,
> And looking backwards upon sin
> And looking forwards to salvation.

George IV was a severe critic of sermons, disliking moral lectures, but thoroughly enjoying "doctrinal explanations." He told Lord Liverpool that preachers at his private chapel at Brighton must be men to whom he could listen with "pleasure and satisfaction," and who showed great activity "at the bedsides of the sick and dying." Certainly the influence of his chaplain, Mr. Sumner, over him was wholly admirable. He persuaded the King to have family prayers for the members of the household at the Royal Lodge, and to take Communion with the members of his household instead of, as previously, alone. The King generally attended Communion, fasting, at ten o'clock, but on one occasion he wished to have the Service at nine and sent a message by a

[1] The exact circumstances of this gift are discussed in *The Quarterly Review* for Dec. 1850, p. 143. This account should be corrected by *Notes and Queries* for July 1851, p. 69.

servant to Sumner to be ready at that hour. Unluckily the servant forgot to deliver the message, and the King, boiling with pre-breakfast anger, had to wait an hour. When Sumner arrived he saw that the King was not "in charity with all men," and thus in no state to receive the Communion, and he said that he would retire while the King thought the matter over and recovered his temper. The King subsequently thanked Sumner for the way in which he had handled the whole matter.

Although, in his own words, he was "too far advanced in life not to give subjects of this description the most serious and attentive consideration," and although he was doubtless sincerely penitent for many of his past sins and follies, it cannot be said that his conduct became permeated with Christian principles, or that there was any diminution of the selfishness which was so great a blot on his character. Princess Lieven, who knew him at the end of his life as well as anyone except members of the Conyngham family, has written a shrewd analysis of his character. "Unquestionably he had some wit and great penetration; he quickly summed up persons and things; he was educated and had much tact, easy, animated and varied conversation, not at all pedantic. He adorned the subjects he touched, he knew how to listen, he was very polished. For my part I had never known a person like him, who was also affectionate, sympathetic and *galant*. But he was full of vanity and could be flattered at will. Weary of all the joys of life, having only taste, not one true sentiment, he was hardly susceptible to attachment and never, I believe, sincerely inspired anyone with it. . . . No one trusted him."

It is curious that although he was thoroughly comfortable at the Royal Lodge, and lived there, as was observed in a contemporary publication, "as snugly as a bug in a rug," he was engrossed till the end of his life with building operations on a far grander scale than anything which the Pavilion or Carlton House could show. At the beginning of his reign he had made certain small alterations and improvements at Windsor Castle which were finished in the autumn of 1823, and on October 3rd he went to live there, driving in state with a sovereign's escort of Life Guards from the Royal Lodge to the Castle. The good people of Windsor celebrated the event with a banquet in the High Street for the poor—fireworks, illuminations, and roast oxen—and the healths of the King and the members of his household were drunk with musical honours. Lord Conyngham's health was drunk to the accompaniment of "Now the Bright Morning Star, Day's Harbinger, comes dancing from the East," and the toast of Sir William Knighton, baronet, was greeted with "The Wind that blows, the Ship that goes, the Girl that loves a Sailor." Despite these saturnalia the Castle with its rotten floors, damp walls and leaky roofs was still quite unsuitable to be the home of any elderly, gouty gentleman, let alone a King with a highly developed sense of dignity and personal comfort. George III had done a good deal towards restoring it after a prolonged period of neglect; sufficient at any rate to enable him with his family to move in in 1805 after inhabiting Queen's Lodge for a quarter of a century. Such further work as he had in mind had been suspended when he finally went mad in 1811.

George IV at once decided that the Castle should be made both dignified and habitable, and Parliament, at the beginning of 1824, sanctioned an expenditure of £300,000 on a thorough restoration. Jeffry Wyatt's plans were chosen in preference to those of Nash and Smirke. A number of small houses, which had sprung up in the grounds since the sixteenth century, were pulled down, the approach to the Long Walk was opened up, new gateways, battlements, and towers were added, and the Round Tower itself was raised more than 30 feet. The inside was entirely altered so as to make way for a series of state apartments —the grandest of which was the Waterloo Chamber, in which were hung the pictures of all the Allied sovereigns and generals. The work was more or less finished in 1828, when the King was able to live in the Castle, and it remains substantially unaltered, apart from certain additions of William IV. At the death of George IV it was found that more than double the sum originally voted by Parliament had been spent. Part of this increase is explained by the very large purchases of furniture for the Castle which the King made in Paris through the third Lord Hertford.

A contemporary wit wrote:

> *Let George, whose restlessness leaves nothing quiet,*
> *Change if he must the good old name of Wyatt;*
> *But let us hope that their united skill*
> *Will not make Windsor Castle Wyattville.*

There are those who are inclined to regret Wyattville's work at Windsor; at the same time an essentially Gothic structure demands Gothic treatment rather than the Renaissance veneer which Wren had so curiously put upon it in the 17th century. Wyattville has met many harsh critics in our age; but it must in justice be admitted that the appearance of the Castle as he left it, from whichever point of the compass it is seen, deserves the admiration which it evokes. There can be few buildings more widely known throughour the world; none, largely thanks to George IV and his architect, more fitted to house an ancient monarchy.

The King also found that there was no place in London adequate for a British sovereign. Carlton House, as a result of the hundreds of thousands of pounds he had spent on it, had become a spectacular, though thoroughly comfortable, gentleman's residence, but its small, low rooms made it quite unsuitable for large state functions. It might have been possible to have made this the sovereign's home and to have held state functions at St. James's Palace, but such an arrangement savoured of frugality, which made no appeal to the King. Buckingham House had been Queen Charlotte's private house, and, as it stood, was quite unsuited for the official headquarters of the sovereign. The fact was that since Whitehall, the Stuart palace in London, had been burned down at the end of the seventeenth century, the Kings of England had had no adequate palace in the heart of London. Hampton Court, in those days of leisurely transport, was too far from the centre for the transaction of political business and for Courts and Drawing-Rooms; and Kensington Palace too was little less rural. George IV accordingly decided that, as both St. James's Palace and Carlton House were too much hemmed in by buildings to be enlarged, he would transform Buckingham House into a palace, worthy of the British monarchy and worthy of the capital city. He decided that Carlton House should be pulled down, and that the furniture and pictures should be moved to the new palace. Private houses, to be known as Carlton House Terrace, were to be built on the site of Carlton House and its gardens to compensate by their rent for some part of the fortune that had been lavished on the site.

The King can have hardly failed to reflect that Windsor Castle, Buckingham Palace, the Pavilion, and the Royal Lodge, with their furniture and pictures, would one day all go to that small niece whom he had driven to Virginia Water while "Aunt Gloucester" clasped her round the waist, but he can never have guessed that she, with her dumpy figure and dowdy clothes, would give to the British monarchy a splendour and significance which all the triumphs of 1814 and 1815 had failed to give it, and to house which all the magnificence of Windsor Castle or Buckingham Palace seemed merely adequate and fitting.

V

The politics of George IV's reign were not the conventional struggle between Whigs and Tories, because the Whigs, by espousing the Queen's cause, had personally antagonised the King, and it was therefore most unlikely that in his lifetime they could expect to form a Government. The real struggle was between the two sections of the Tory Party, between the extreme Toryism of Castlereagh, Sidmouth, and Eldon and what may be called the Liberal Toryism of Canning.

When George IV came to the throne it was more than seven years since Lord Liverpool had formed the existing Government on an extreme Tory basis, with Lord Sidmouth as Home Secretary, Lord Castlereagh as Foreign Secretary and Lord Eldon as Lord Chancellor: Canning, at the Board of Control, provided a less reactionary element. This administration, in the middle of the financial confusion and trade depression following the war, provided an essential stability for bankers and those engaged in trade, but it pursued a policy which to the eager reformers of the day seemed humdrum and uninspiring: it dealt with ferocious severity with any symptoms of popular disapproval or discontent, which brought down upon the heads of its members the savage vituperation of Liberal poets like Byron and Shelley and the lesser fry of intellectuals who followed them. Lord Liverpool is one of those statesmen who failed to impress their personality on the public, and he figures in the pages of history as the most insipid of English Prime Ministers. As is now generally recognised he was in fact a talented and industrious head of a Cabinet, most of whose members exceeded him in the extent of their Toryism, but only two of whom (Castlereagh and Canning) excelled him in ability.

On political issues—except when these trenched on personal

feelings, as in the case of Queen Caroline—the relations between George IV and Liverpool were tolerably good. Friction between the two was derived from personal matters, especially those connected with patronage. Few Prime Ministers can have received a more peremptory letter from their sovereign than did Liverpool on the question of admitting Knighton to the Privy Council in July, 1823: "the thing is so proper and so just that I wish to have no conversation on the subject; as my first Minister, I wish to do nothing but what is in unison with your feelings, as far as I can; nevertheless, there are occasions on which I must use my own judgment." Liverpool, with little tact, held out against the appointment, which gave rise to great stuffiness and surliness on the part of the King. A much more serious conflict had arisen between them on a not dissimilar subject two years before which rankled deeply with the King for many months. This arose over Mr. Sumner—then a curate of thirty, and subsequently Bishop of Winchester—who had been tutor to Lady Conyngham's elder sons, Lord Mount Charles and Lord Francis Conyngham. In 1820 Lord Mount Charles introduced Mr. Sumner to the King at the Pavilion, and it was obvious that the King had taken a great fancy to the curate, as he sat talking to him for three hours after dinner. In the spring of 1821 a canonry at Windsor fell vacant, and the King immediately offered it to Mr. Sumner. Lord Liverpool refused to sanction this appointment, and a stern correspondence passed between the King and his Prime Minister. As the King had already promised the canonry to Mr. Sumner, it was, as he pointed out to the Prime Minister, a question "whether the *King's word* is to be held *sacred* or to be of no *avail*"; to which Liverpool replied, "It must be a sufficient answer on such an occasion that the appointment has been obstructed in a quarter which cannot by the laws of the country be passed by." Liverpool remained quite firm, and threatened to resign if the King persisted in the appointment.

The King was obliged to give way, but it cannot be felt that Mr. Sumner was the loser. He was immediately appointed a Domestic Chaplain, with £300 a year and a capital house at Windsor opposite the Park gates; he was also made the King's librarian, and within five years he was successively appointed Vicar of Abingdon, Canon of Worcester, Canon of Canterbury, Bishop of Llandaff and Dean of St. Paul's, and Bishop of Winchester.[1] But, although the King was thus able to show the diversity of his ecclesiastical patronage, he never forgave Lord Liverpool for thwarting him over the canonry of Windsor, as is quite clear from a letter written by Lord Mount Charles to Sumner: ". . . it is true that you will not be canon at Windsor this time, but as the King most kindly quoted at dinner when he saw my agony:

Nil desperandum Teucro duce, et auspice Teucro.

You cannot conceive what he suffered on the occasion. He is, without exception, the best hearted man that ever breathed. . . . His feelings have been mortally wounded. He never will forget it." It is clear that, before the King left for Hanover, in 1821, he again seriously thought of dismissing Liverpool, but on his return saner counsels prevailed.

Liverpool's greatness lay in the fact that, although his personal sympathies were with the right-wing Tories, he always struggled to see that the left wing were generously represented in the Cabinet. From 1816 Canning was in the Cabinet, at the Board of Control, but he resigned in November 1820, because he strongly disapproved of the Government's proceeding against the Queen, and the resignation was accepted by the King with the rather cold phrase, "The King feels, as he should do, the loss of a servant whose great talents rendered him so very useful to the Government and the country."

The removal of Canning substantially increased the balance in favour of the extreme Tories, and as soon as the Queen's case was forgotten Liverpool was pressing the King to re-admit Canning to the Cabinet. The opportunity was offered by the retirement of Lord Sidmouth, whose political career should long before have been terminated by incompetence, but was now drawing to a stately close through increasing years. The King, who felt the circumstances of Canning's resignation as a personal insult, and who was nervous of his political views, absolutely refused to hear of his reappointment and undertook to facilitate his appointment as Governor-General of India in order to get him out of the country. Liverpool had, therefore, to agree to Peel's appointment

[1] It should not be imagined that Sumner was an unworthy object of ecclesiastical preferment. He was a member of a family distinguished in service to the Church through many generations, and he made an admirable bishop.

as Home Secretary in succession to Sidmouth, while he was able to give a more Liberal air to his Cabinet by admitting some of the followers of Grenville who still called themselves Whigs. "These ticklish cattle," as Castlereagh grandly described them, were full of honour and high principles, but were only too eager to barter both for high office. Tories who had borne the heat and burden of the day, and saw their rewards going to these converted Whigs, sadly echoed Lord Holland's phrase, "All articles are now to be had at low prices, except Grenvilles."

In the summer of 1822 there was a change in the King's immediate *entourage* which adversely affected Lord Liverpool. Sir Benjamin Bloomfield, who had been the King's private secretary and Keeper of the Privy Purse since the latter years of the Regency, was dismissed. The reason seems to have been partly that he was not good at managing the King's income, but chiefly that when he was in Ireland preparing for the King's visit he went to the theatre, and, when God save the King was played, was "kind enough"—in Creevey's words—"to step to the front of the box he was in, and to express by his bows and gestures his deep sense of gratitude for this distinction." The King never forgave his presumption, but apart from this there seemed to be signs that Bloomfield was getting rather past his services, because he soon joined the Methodist Church, and his modest Christian neighbours in Portman Square were embarrassed to see a large white placard constantly hanging outside Bloomfield's door, with the words on it: "At Prayer." A further cause was the embarrassment and painful distress suffered by the King through Bloomfield's "unhappy, uncertain and oppressive temper." These are the King's own words which he wished repeated to Bloomfield. The King made him a peer as a reward for his services, and when he died the Methodists published a tract called, *A Coronet Laid at the Feet of Jesus.* Sir William Knighton was immediately appointed as Bloomfield's successor, and he managed the King's finances with firmness and skill. The following letter written by the King after a tiff with Knighton about expenditure, shows the power of Knighton and the King's affection for him.

"You may easily imagine, warm and sincere as my affections are towards you, I have had but little rest since we separated last night. The feeling that I may possibly and unfortunately, in a hurried moment, when my mind and heart were torn in fifty different ways from fifty different causes, have let an unjust or a hasty expression escape me to any one, but most especially to you, whom I so *truly love,* and who are so *invaluable* to me as my *friend,* is to *me* a sensation *much too painful* to be *endured*: therefore let me *implore* you to come to me, *be it but for a moment,* the *very first thing* you do this morning: for I shall hate myself until I have the opportunity of expressing *personally* to you those pure and genuine feelings of affection which will never cease to live in *my heart* so long as that heart itself continues to beat. I am much too unhappy to say more, but that I am ever your affte friend.

G. R.

C.H. W^{dy.} M^{g.} eight o'clock *July* 11*th* 1822."

The dismissal of Bloomfield, who had been particularly favourable to Lord Liverpool, was a serious blow for the Prime Minister, because the King was now entirely swayed by the advice of Knighton and the Conynghams, none of whom had strong political allegiances, but all of whom were influenced by a desire for peace and to take the line of least resistance. Their peace was unfortunately of short duration.

On August 9th, 1822, the King had had an interview with Castlereagh who had recently succeeded to the peerage as Lord Londonderry, and was so shocked with his appearance and manner that he sent for Liverpool and told him "that Londonderry's mind was gone." Three days later, in spite of every precaution on the part of the doctors, Londonderry cut his throat, as Croker says, "with anatomical accuracy." The political consequences of this were not immediately felt, as the King was on the high seas, *en route* for Scotland. His personal enjoyment of this visit was entirely spoiled by the news of Lord Londonderry's death which he heard when he was anchored off Leith, and he wrote at once to Lord Liverpool.

"Private.

'Royal George Yacht,'
Leith Roads,
August 15 1822.

DEAR LORD LIVERPOOL,

I cannot express the painful grief which I feel at your melancholy communication; melancholy indeed both for myself and others who knew the inestimable value of this superior and excellent person.

The ways of Providence are so inscrutable to us poor blind creatures that, on occasions of this description, the agony of one's mind is lost in amazement. You, my lord, will not be surprised that I should feel this. I think you have judged rightly in not coming, and I quite approve that no arrangements should be thought of till my return to Town.

Your sincere friend,

GEORGE R.

PS. I write one word more, to desire that you will favour no intentions respecting the blue ribbon."

It was quite obvious to everyone except the King and the extreme Tories that there was only one person to fill the vacancy in the Cabinet and that was Canning, who was on the point of leaving England to take up the Governor-Generalship of India, and the King wrote from Edinburgh to Lord Liverpool that he was on no account to impede the arrangements respecting India, which were "final and unalterable." It was preposterously foolish that Canning's brilliant gifts of statesmansip and oratory should have been exported to India "like the skates and warming pans to Buenos Ayres" but the King returned to London at the beginning of September determined to fight to the last against Canning's inclusion in the Cabinet, and nervously enquired whether Liverpool was in a good temper—in Croker's words, "amost as a boy after a holiday asked in what temper Dr. Busby may be." After an interview with Lord Liverpool, the King wrote to Wellington. "If I could get over that which is so *intimately connected* with *my private honour,* all might be well, but how, my friend, is that to be effected?"

The Duke replied with a long memorandum stressing the importance of Canning's talents as strengthening the administration, and adding, "The honour of your Majesty consists in acts of mercy and grace," and advising that he should forgive Canning for the good of the country.

The day after receiving this memorandum from the Duke, the King wrote to Lord Liverpool withdrawing all his opposition. ". . . you will see that I have sacrificed my private feelings, as you and other members of the Cabinet have represented to me that it is what you consider to be for the good of the public service. I have, on every occasion, as in this instance, shown my regard and sincerity towards my Government, and I therefore look with confidence to a similar return. This is the greatest sacrifice of my opinions and feelings that I have ever made in my life." To Lord Eldon he wrote that he had made "the greatest personal sacrifice that a Sovereign ever made to a subject, or indeed, taking *all the circumstances* that man ever made to man." This was an allusion to Canning's supposed liaison with the Queen. And to Wellington he wrote, "Thus ends the last calamity: my reliance is on you, my friend, be watchful therefore. God bless you."

It was possible for George IV, embarrassed by the manifestations of old age, to hide himself from the gaze of his people in the seclusion of the Royal Lodge, but while health and strength remained he could not cut himself off from their concerns. Politics in the 1820's were quiet but treacherous, flowing swiftly and evenly, with the roar of the weir clearly to be heard in the distance. People realised that the smooth progress of Lord Liverpool's Government must be upset when approach to the Roman Catholic question became imminent and inevitable. It is of course unnecessary to explain that George IV was no politician: he ascended the throne with three political principles: to keep his throne, to enjoy freedom from political worries, and to have plenty of public money for his schemes of rebuilding. But, although he was not a politician, he was quite as conscious as those who were of the danger ahead, and more alarmed than they because he had no clear idea of how to negotiate it.

With some show of consistency, he could claim that he had always been against Roman Catholic emancipation, and could point to his conduct at the time of the Ministry of All the Talents.[1] Once the Coronation was over, and he had taken the oath, his opposition to emancipation became even stronger, and he could write to Peel, "The sentiments of the King upon Catholic Emancipation are those of his revered and excellent father." It is, of course, easy for those who have not had to burden their consciences with the tremendous oath which the laws of England imposed on her sovereigns to ridicule the importance which George III and George IV attached to it.

[1] See p. 69.

Each had sworn before God and in the presence of their people to "maintain . . . the Protestant Reformed Religion established by law . . . and maintain and preserve inviolably the settlement of the United Church of England and Ireland, and the doctrine, worship, discipline and government thereof. . . ." In the Church of England there was no archiepiscopal dispensation to soothe the conscience of the King if political necessity obliged him to violate that oath. Before his Coronation he had consulted with Lord Londonderry as to the possibility of modifying the oath, but, when he was assured that it was impossible, he said, "Remember, once I take that oath, I am for ever a Protestant King, a Protestant upholder, a Protestant adherent."

The King's objections to Canning's inclusion in the Government in 1822 were based on his conduct during the troubles with the Queen, but they were strengthened by misgivings about his Liberal opinions, and particularly by the fact that Canning, since 1812, had been an open supporter of the Catholic claims. The King showed at once that, although he was obliged to admit Canning to the Cabinet, he was not obliged to admit him to his confidence. The Royal Lodge, with only the tops of its chimneys visible to the public, became the scene of a royal display of dabbling in foreign politics reminiscent of the days of Charles II and the Treaty of Dover. George IV, as King of Hanover, was in a position to correspond with foreign Ministers and foreign sovereigns independently of his British Ministers, and he frequently invited down to the Royal Lodge the Russian Ambassador and his wife, Prince and Princess Lieven, the Austrian Ambassador, Prince Esterhazy, and the French Ambassador, Prince Jules de Polignac. These representatives of the Holy Alliance, that guild of reactionary sovereigns formed to stamp out all revolutionary and novel doctrines in Europe, most improperly joined by a member of the Cabinet, Wellington, did their utmost to encourage the King's absolutist views and his intrigues against Canning's foreign policy.

In 1823 the French Bourbon King, Louis XVIII, was preparing an invasion of Spain to suppress a revolutionary movement which had broken out against his Spanish Bourbon cousin, Ferdinand VII. The official British policy was to attempt to dissuade the French Government from this very dangerous step, and certainly to give no countenance to it. There is, however, clear evidence that George IV privately sent a message to Louis XVIII wishing him every success in the projected invasion. News of this began to be suspected, and *The Times* bluntly declared that the King must be mad, while the *Sunday Times* spoke more delicately of "mental afflictions" and "hereditary disorders." The King, nothing daunted, at a ball at Carlton House said to a member of the French Embassy, "Don't be carried away by our system of Government which is said to be so reasonable. If there are advantages there are inconveniences, and I have never forgotten what a witty King once said of it to me. 'Your English Government,' he assured me, 'is only good to protect rascals and intimidate honest men.' " Then turning to Canning, who had had to listen to this outburst, he said, "What do you think of that, Mr. Canning? Is there not a great fund of truth in it?" As Canning did not reply, the King went on, "We are still alone in our kind of Government, and for the good of the world we ought not to desire our institutions for any other people. What is almost good with us would not be so with others. Every land has not the same fruits above, or minerals below, its surface. It is thus with nations, with their manners and with their character." A wise, cosmopolitan view (made wiser by the century of European history which has passed), but hardly likely to commend itself to the Foreign Minister who was the originator of England's nineteenth-century foreign policy of forcing Europe to be free.

Throughout 1824, strengthened by the advice and insinuations of his foreign advisers and Wellington, the King struggled manfully against the recognition by England of the South American republics which had revolted from Spain. Sir William Knighton sped across Europe on confidential agencies to Spain, Italy, Paris, and Vienna. (His published letters descriptive of these tours are unfortunately only filled with pious references to the Almighty and descriptions of beautiful flowers.) But at the end of 1824 Wellington was obliged to advise the King that public opinion was so strongly in favour of recognising the South American republics that he must give way. The King saw that he must submit, though he did so with an ill grace, writing in the course of a long memorandum to the Cabinet that "if the present line of policy is to be *further* pursued, the King will feel himself justified in taking such measures as the Government will be least prepared to expect." But from that moment his relations with Canning completely changed.

In April 1825 Knighton called to enquire after Canning's gout, and stayed for a two-hour confidential discussion, which was really an overture from the King, and Knighton admitted that the "continental gossipings" at the Royal Lodge were at an end. In the November of that year the King received the Minister of one of the new republics (Columbia) with great grace and charm, adding, at the end of the interview, "Peace, peace by all means, and above all things. We have had 30 years of convulsions —let us all now conspire to keep the peace."

The truth of the matter was that, as Canning's foreign policy began to unfold itself, the King realised that the prestige of Britain abroad had been enormously enhanced. Instead of lumbering along in the train of the Holy Alliance, the King had been placed by Canning at the head of Europe. All his life the King had been accustomed to the society of intelligent men, and there was something far more congenial, far more reminiscent of Fox, in the wit and charm of Canning than in the rigid views of Wellington, the old womanish fears of Eldon, or the solid sense of Peel. With all the whims, prejudices, oddities, and super-ficialities which went to make up George IV's political outlook, it is surprising that he forgave Canning and admirable that he took him into his confidence. Stapleton, who was Canning's secretary and very largely reflected Canning's opinion, said that after the King gave Canning his confidence till the day of Canning's death "nothing could surpass the good faith and kindness which the King manifested in the whole of his conduct towards him."[1] On his side Canning was a far better courtier than his predecessor had been. His letters to the King often began "Mr. Canning presents his humble and affectionate duty to His Majesty." King George IV, himself, in a memorandum for the Cabinet stated that "one of the many agreeable qualities Mr.

[1] I have, of course, relied principally on Professor Temperley's *Foreign Policy of Canning* for these details, though I think he is insufficiently appreciative of the King's later behaviour to Canning, and it suggests too great a reliance on the gossip writers of the period when he attributes the change in the King's attitude largely to Canning's appointment of Lord Francis Conyngham as Under Secretary for Foreign Affairs, and to Canning's skill in keeping Lord Ponsonby (formerly Lady Conyngham's lover) out of the country. Canning himself, and his friends, were always loud in their praises of the King's conduct.

Canning possessed as the King's First Minister was—that Mr. Canning never kept anything back from the King. There were no minor secrets."

It is obvious that the nice balance between the two wings of the Tory Party in the Cabinet depended on Lord Liverpool. On February 18th, 1827, he was discovered in his library, speechless from the effects of an apopletic seizure. Immediately the Government and the Tory Party fell into hopeless confusion. By the middle of March it was clear that Lord Liverpool would never recover, and immediate action was forced on the King.

To contemporaries it appeared that there were only two possible successors to the Prime Minister: Canning or some dummy who without Lord Liverpool's ability would bridge the gap between the two sections of the Cabinet. It was not believed that Wellington desired the office for himself, and Peel was thought to be too inexperienced. At the end of March the King, who was fortunately in particularly good health and spirits, sent for Peel, Wellington, and Canning to stay with him at the Royal Lodge. The morning after their arrival the King was closeted with Wellington. Princess Lieven, who was also of the party, described how Canning's face grew longer and longer, particularly when luncheon came and the King was making himself peculiarly agreeable to Wellington. After luncheon the King began to arrange the order in which they should drive out in the little pony-drawn chaises which held two people, and in which he used to drive about the Park. It was known that he always drove Lady Conyngham, and he arranged for everyone except Canning, who was ready to explode, while the King was obviously thoroughly enjoying the situation. He suddenly squeezed Canning by the arm, and said, "I want to talk with you. I shan't go out." At this interview the King fully explained his attitude to Canning on the Catholic question, and Canning advised him to form an exclusively Protestant Government but the King said, "I cannot part with you." And Canning's terms were that, if he was not to be Prime Minister, he should have the substantive power (i.e. leadership of the House of Commons) with a dummy Prime Minister in the House of Lords.

It seems that the King thought—or most probably persuaded himself to think—that Canning had agreed to shelve the Catholic question but it is most unlikely that Canning, who had supported Catholic emancipation since 1812, gave any such pledge. The King told Peel that if he would serve under Canning he would guarantee that the Catholic question would not be raised— an assurance which was constitutionally highly improper and had apparently no foundation in fact. But the King was ready for any little embellishment of truth which might lead to peace and quiet, till a totally unexpected development removed peace and quiet to very remote regions.

It became apparent that the Duke of Wellington had decided that he himself would like to be Prime Minister—a decision which lost him his popularity in his lifetime and has baffled and embarrassed even his most devoted posthumous admirers. It was quite obvious that Canning could not be expected to serve under the leader of the right-wing Tories and the consistent opponent of his foreign policy. At the beginning of April the King came up to London, and prepared to deal with this very difficult situation. On April 6th he wrote to Knighton, ". . . I am jaded and quite worn out, and writing from my bed, where I have laid down for a little rest. . . . Little or no advance, I regret to say, has as yet been made, amidst perhaps almost unravelable perplexities." Four days later he entrusted Canning with the formation of a Government, but none of the right-wing Tories would consent to serve under Canning. It is doubtful if the King ever forgave Peel and Wellington for resigning, and for obliging Canning to fill his Cabinet with Whigs and ex-Whigs. The most childish thing of all was Wellington's resignation of the command of the Army, in which he had succeeded the Duke of York only a few weeks before, which was certainly not a political appointment as it came straight from the Crown. The King made his annoyance plain by the terms in which he accepted the resignation:

"The King assures the Duke of Wellington that the King receives the Duke's resignation of the offices of Commander-in-Chief and Master-General of the Ordnance with the same sentiments of deep regret with which the Duke of Wellington states himself to offer it.

The King abstains from any further expression of his feelings.

G. R."

Privately he said, "I shall keep the command of the Army in my own hands until my friend Arthur recovers his temper."

The horror of the Tories, accustomed as always to the maximum of party advantage from any political disturbance, was unbounded at finding Canning and a Whiggish Government in office, and seven of their leading men squeezed out. A lethargic Tory duke, swollen with rotten boroughs, toiled down to Windsor to lecture the King, but he was blandly met with an invitation to a little fishing at Virginia Water in the summer, and the King diverted the conversation to a discussion of the merits of certain tailors. And to Lord Londonderry[1] who went on a similar mission the King said, "To those persons who pressed Mr. Canning upon me against my will[2]—to those friends who now leave me in the lurch—may all the mischief and perplexity which I felt be ascribed." At the same time he was anxious to make it plain that his views on the Catholic question were unaltered, and when Lord Mansfield, in the House of Lords, alleged that his opinion had changed he sent for the Archbishop of Canterbury and told him to go and tell Lord Mansfield he was a liar, adding, "Tell him he lies, and kick his behind in my name."

Some of the difficulty in which he found himself is illustrated by his relations with the Duke of Wellington. In the summer he expressed to Wellington's brother some surprise that the Duke had never been near him, although he had been in the neighbourhood of Windsor. The Duke accordingly rode over to the Royal Lodge, and at the end of the visit the King wrote to Canning:

"DEAR MR. CANNING,

I delay not a moment in acquainting you with a circumstance that has just occurred very unexpectedly to me—a visit from the Duke of Wellington. I can only attribute this visit to its being the anniversary of my coronation. Our interview was not long, and our conversation for the most part was on general topics. Of course it was impossible here and there, occasionally, not to have some reference to matters which have recently occurred. I found the Duke extremely temperate, but I could easily perceive, from little expressions which now and then dropped, that the most assiduous pains had been taken, and are still actively employed to give the strongest jaundiced complexion to the past, as well as the present state of things,

---

[1] 3rd Marquess, brother of the statesman.   [2] In 1822.

and to keep up if not to widen as much as malice and wickedness can contrive it, the breach which exists between him and my Government. I sincerely hope that you are rapidly recovering from the odious lumbago.

> Believe me always,
>
> Your sincere friend,
>
> G. R.

Royal Lodge
Thursday, *July* 19 Half-past two P.M. 1827."

Considering that the King had expressed surprise at not having seen Wellington, this letter was slightly deceptive, but the incident, which was widely canvassed in the Press and among politicians of the day, is surely only a proof that the King, while remaining loyal to his Prime Minister, was anxious not to be completely alienated from Wellington.

Unfortunately "the odious lumbago" turned out to be something far worse, and on August 8th Canning was dead, saying before his death, "This may be hard upon me, but it is still harder upon the King." Canning's death placed the King in a position of great difficulty, because, if the Government was to continue, it was essential to have at its head someone of outstanding ability in order to keep together the discordant Whig and Tory elements in the Cabinet. Being still irritated with the Tories as a result of their desertion of Canning, the King was anxious for the present arrangement to continue, and he decided to send for Mr. Robinson, recently created Lord Goderich, to form an administration. "Prosperity Robinson," as Cobbett called him, or, "Goody Goderich," as he was more generally called, was charming, industrious, and honourable, but his almost fabulous weakness of character made him quite unsuitable for high office. Even in the task of forming his Government he showed alarming signs of vacillation. He and the King agreed that Herries, a Tory, but a financier of unquestioned ability, should be Chancellor of the Exchequer. Whig supporters of the Government wished Palmerston to be appointed, and bullied the Prime Minister until he wobbled and asked Herries to accept some other but less important office. The King, who was reluctant to increase the Whig strength of the Government, sent for Herries to the Royal Lodge, and tried to drop the seals of the

Chancellor of the Exchequer into his hands, Herries loyally striving to avoid this embarrassing gift. Finally the King sent for the leading Whig members of the Government and insisted on Herries being appointed.

Whig writers, principally relying on the biased and erratic memory of Lord Palmerston, have succeeded in presenting Herries to posterity as a royal minion who, in return for office, was to pander to the King's passion for building. In fact the King thought Herries had been abominably treated (which he had) and he was also influenced by the fear of the Tories being inadequately represented in the Cabinet. When he sent for the leading Whigs, he explained that the whole difficulty had arisen through a series of blunders which, he added, "were neither yours nor mine." The unhappy Goderich blithely proceeded from blunder to blunder, and in December, only four months after accepting office, he resigned and then quickly withdrew his resignation. The King took no immediate action, characteristically saying that he did not see why he should be the only gentleman in his kingdom not to be allowed to eat his Christmas dinner in peace; but in January 1828 fresh dissensions broke out in the Cabinet, and this time Goderich offered his resignation with a burst of weeping. The King accepted the resignation and offered him a pocket handkerchief.

The King had then only two alternatives—to form either an exclusively Whig Government, or else an exclusively Tory one—and he decided on what was to him the lesser evil by standing for Wellington and the Tories. At first everything seemed to show that the new Government was in high favour with the King. He received Wellington in bed, groaning under a severe attack of gout, but he sat up and proceeded to give a series of brilliant imitations of his late Ministers. But he had in fact never forgiven the Tories for their behaviour during Canning's premiership: in particular he had never forgotten Wellington's giving up the command of the Army and he had also conceived a strong dislike for Peel, whom he regarded as a pompous bore and whose bowing he took peculiar pleasure in mimicking. In a confidential letter to his secretary about his new Government the King said "these are strange times. . . . We have very queer and odd people to deal with." The King had really thoroughly enjoyed the weak Governments of Canning and Goderich, because their weakness had enabled him to exercise considerable patronage and to enjoy a feeling of power which he had never known under Lord Liverpool's Government. He treated Wellington's Government with the fractious petulance of a child returning to its nurse after the glorious liberty of a few hours with its parents. Afterwards Wellington admitted that he would never have accepted office if he had realised the King's attitude, and said that he would thereby have avoided "loads of misery." But the Tories had only themselves to thank for antagonising the King, and we can certainly echo Croker's comment on their behaviour in April 1827, which was the cause of all the trouble, "What fools, fools, fools, our Tory friends have been."

As the year 1828 advanced it became obvious that the storm, which for thirty years public men had dreaded or hoped for, must break. The election at Clare in July, when O'Connell, although a Roman Catholic and therefore barred from sitting in the House of Commons, had been triumphantly elected in preference to a popular landlord, decided both Peel and Wellington and the majority of intelligent observers that Catholic emancipation could no longer be resisted, and that the time had come to grant members of that faith equal political rights with Protestants. Unfortunately the King was not to be found in the ranks of these intelligent observers, and Wellington had the greatest difficulty in managing him. He insisted on the recall of the Lord Lieutenant, Lord Anglesey (in the whereabouts of whose leg he had shown such great curiosity on the field of Waterloo), who was favourable to concessions, and he described Lord Anglesey's letter to Wellington justifying his conduct as "a proud and pompous *farrago* of the most *outré* bombast." But in January 1829 he agreed to the consideration of the question by the Cabinet, though he made it clear that he reserved the right to reject any Relief Bill which they might succeed in carrying through Parliament.

During the next two months the King's behaviour was contemptible but understandable. He was, as has been explained and as is generally agreed, sincerely opposed to emancipation, but, instead of having a straightforward tussle with his Ministers, he characteristically preferred to thwart and harass them in every way he could. In explanation and in partial extenuation of the King's conduct it must be remembered that the old prejudices against Roman Catholics still permeated English life, and that it was certainly only a minority which favoured emancipation. As the strength of these obscurantists views became apparent, the King's behaviour to his Ministers grew shiftier and his efforts to squash the Bill grew bolder. Two events in particular encouraged him.

The first was the defeat of Peel for Oxford University. On changing his opinions he decided to give his constituents the chance of endorsing his view, by resigning and offering himself for re-election. As the election drew near, the streets of Oxford were black with clerical cloth, each reverend gentleman loud in abuse of those who dared to support Peel and pulling hideous faces at any of their number who were known to favour tolerance to their fellow-Christians. They were largely responsible for Peel's defeat, and they went whooping back to their country rectories spreading their militant Protestant views with far more zest than they had hitherto shown in the discharge of their normal and pacific duties.

The second event which encouraged the King was the return from the Continent of his brother the Duke of Cumberland. This Prince had all the prejudices of his family on the Catholic question, reinforced by a pronounced ability and an alarmingly sarcastic tongue. His influence over George IV had always been extraordinary. At the beginning of 1829 Wellington persuaded the King to send Knighton abroad to prevent the Duke from coming to England. Knighton was despatched post-haste, and had only time to write to his wife, "Take care of your health. If you should feel a weight on your head, unusual sleepiness, a tight feeling about the throat, or a queer odd sickness about the stomach apply half a dozen (not more) of leeches to the temple." In spite of these great exertions he was too late to intercept the Duke, who arrived in London on Valentine's Day. For the next fortnight the Duke was constantly with the King, reminding him of their sainted father's attitude to the Roman Catholic question, reminding him of the Coronation oath, pointing to the strength of the opponents of the Bill, emphasising the importance of the prejudiced utterances of bishops and elderly peers till the King was worked up to a frenzy of irritation and embarrassment. At last, on March 3rd, two days before the Bill was to be introduced in the Commons, he sent for Wellington, Peel, and Lyndhurst to see him at Windsor. He spoke to them for nearly six hours, fortifying himself with repeated sips of brandy and water. Threats to retire to Hanover, tears, and even kisses, were all tried to shake the Ministers' attachment to the Bill, but all in vain, and the King boldly dismissed them from office. He was found after the interview by Lady Conyngham and Knighton lying on a sofa, utterly exhausted. They pointed out to him that the opponents of the Bill lacked the strength in the House of Commons to form a Government, and that there was no alternative to Wellington. Accordingly that evening he wrote to Wellington:

"*4th March,* 1829.

My dear Friend,

As I find the country would be left without an administration, I have decided to yield my opinion to *that* which is considered by the Cabinet to be for the immediate interests of the country. Under these circumstances you have my consent to proceed as you propose with the measure. God knows what pain it causes me to write these words.

G. R."

After much whimpering, many protestations, and constant invocation of the Almighty's name, he gave his consent to the Bill on April 10th.

It has for long been a commonplace observation in history books and lives of Wellington that no one but the Duke could have induced the King to agree to Catholic emancipation. The truth of this is exceedingly doubtful. In 1827 the Tories had left him in the lurch simply because Canning was favourable to emancipation; he could hardly have been expected to be very impressed by any arguments which these same Tories adduced in favour of the measure a short eighteen months after their desertion. It is surely obvious that the King's mental distress over appointing Canning Prime Minister rose from his feeling that emancipation under his premiership would be a *fait accompli*. It is idle to speculate, but reasonable to suggest, that the King would have swallowed the dreaded dose with far better grace had it been administered by one like Canning who genuinely believed in its efficacy rather than by Wellington who simply advocated it because he knew of no alternative.

No one in their senses could deny that George IV must have been an exceedingly trying master to serve, for as the Duke of Wellington expressed it "When one goes to Windsor no person can answer for the hour of return." And this was made perhaps the more trying by the fact that he could be extraordinarily gracious and charming to his Ministers, as is shown by the following letter to Mr. Huskisson, written in September 1827:

"The King is very desirous not to interrupt Mr. Huskisson's short relaxation from the labours of Office, which is so necessary to the re-establishment of his Health, and which the King feels is so very important, both for his own, as well as for the service, and best interests of the Country at this very critical moment—The King therefore prefers communicating his wishes to Mr. Huskisson through the medium of the Pen, to the putting Mr. Huskisson to all the trouble of a Journey to the Royal Lodge. . . ."

But particularly at the end of his life he seems to have taken a special delight in mocking the rather solemn personalities of Wellington and Peel. The stories he used to tell the Duke of how he won the battle of Salamanca by a clever use of German cavalry "when things were looking very black indeed," and of similar triumphs at Waterloo, have been seized on as an example of his having inherited his father's madness. A joke which reaches us at third hand, and which depends for its humour entirely on the way in which it was originally told, loses much of its original character, particularly when it takes its final form from the merrily scorbutic pen of Mr. Creevey. It is quite obvious that the King enjoyed watching the effect of these fantastic stories on the Duke, and to suggest that he came to believe them himself is ridiculous.[1]

The King enjoyed tempering business with humour, and a meeting of the Council at Windsor was once interrupted while he had a whispered discussion with Greville as to the merits of a horse called Cadland and a mare called Bess of Bedlam, and then he called across to the solemn figure of the Duke, "A little bit of

[1] There was a very sensible letter published in *The Times* of August 26th, 1933, from Mr. Richard Edgcumbe, whose father accompanied George IV over the battlefield of Waterloo, to which I would refer the reader who may still think that these stories prove that George IV was mad.

Newmarket." Another example of his humour was his pencilled comment on the order awarding the G.C.B. to Admiral Codrington, who had destroyed the Turkish fleet at Navarino although we were at peace with Turkey, "I send him the ribbon but he deserves the rope."

He was of course a constant anxiety to his Ministers through his endeavours to influence appointments and to exercise patronage on behalf of his friends. This was not always discreditable as, for example, his efforts on behalf of the famous Irish actor O'Keefe, who in his old age was destitute. "A little charitable impulse induces me to desire you to enquire into the distressed circumstances of poor old O'Keefe, now ninety years of age[1] and stone blind, whom I knew a little of formerly, having occasionally met him at parties of my juvenile recreation and hilarity. . . ." A creditable proof of his good nature, though not without its embarrassment to his Ministers, was his exertions on behalf of condemned persons. There are many letters from the King to Peel in which he insists on exercising the prerogative of mercy, "a word more consoling to the King's mind than words can express." It was in connexion with a condemned criminal that he sent in the middle of the night for Peel, who was staying at the Pavilion, and begged to be allowed to pardon the man. At the end of the interview, having obtained his way, he kissed Peel, and, suddenly observing the rather indifferent dressing-gown the statesman was wearing, said, "Peel, where did you get your dressing-gown? I'll show you what a dressing-gown ought to be," and he insisted on Peel trying on one of his own.

But no one could accuse George IV of being a politician: no one would be so foolish as even to suggest that he understood politics. He was intellectually far more gifted than the great majority of English sovereigns, but he was one of the very few to whom it is possible to attribute no political objects except the avoidance of trouble and the indulgence of their own whims and fancies. His political horizon was bounded by personalities and prejudices. It was not that he was indifferent to the fate of his country or to the happiness of his people, for, as the artist Haydon said of him, he was "as thoroughbred an Englishman as ever existed in the country. He admired her sports, gloried in her prejudices, had confidence in her bottom and spirit." But the

[1] He was eighty.

England he understood was the England of his youth—broad
acres, spreading oaks, paternal landlords, four-in-hands, pugilists,
a little cock-fighting, strong, deferential workmen, with here
and there a town where the quality might dance, chatter, and go
to the play; but the England which had developed in his lifetime, "with the breath of the manufacturing town, which made
a cloudy day and a red gloom by night on the horizon, diffusing
itself over all the surrounding country, filling the air with eager
unrest,"[1] was unknown to the King, and the misery and aspira-
tions of those who worked there were unappreciated by him. It
was these rapidly changing conditions, for which rapid reforms
were necessary, which made politics unintelligible to him, and it
was his indifference to them which explained, and almost
justified, his unpopularity.

VI

Yet as this gifted, wayward personality drifted towards the
grave, few could escape some feelings of pity for him. Like all
who surrounded themselves with favourites rather than friends,
he was encompassed by feuds, jealousy and backbiting. Lady
Conyngham was frequently a disturbing element, fractious and
discontented if she did not have her own way and too plainly
trying to manage the King. She and Knighton were apt to
squabble, upsetting the peace of the King's domestic background.
In the King's letters to Knighton there are constant veiled allusions
to these breaches in his domestic peace, and it is probable that the
following extract refers to these *scompiglios* in the household: "I
cannot likewise disguise from you that I have also had different
causes of the most poignant and distressing nature to tear my
poor feelings almost to shreds and to drive me for a time almost
distracted." He goes on to refer to "that host of vipers and
hornets which seem in particular at this moment to have con-
gregated itself together and purposely, to sting me personally."
In one of the few letters of Lady Conyngham which have survived,
that humdrum personality alludes to the "ups and downs" which
go on as usual. George IV had sufficient knowledge of the world
(of which he once pertinently observed: "so long as it lasts, and
is a world, it will continue to talk") to know that through all the

[1] George Eliot, *Felix Holt the Radical.*

blankets of flattery by which he was surrounded, the flatterers behind his back were whispering and mocking. Even Knighton, who certainly served the King with true fidelity, put down in his diary that all the actions of royalty have their origins in selfishness —"the love of self is always predominant." The sense that his own domestic circle was not wholeheartedly loyal to him perhaps explains why the King gave his confidence in the closing months of his life to his valets and to his sister, the Duchess of Gloucester. His own family stuck to him with affection which was constant and uncritical and was well expressed by the Duke of Cumberland, who wrote to Knighton when he heard of the King's illness, "Christ what a loss to us all."

In the autumn of 1828 those in attendance on the King were alarmed by his serious illness. It originated with an attack of gout so severe that Knighton wrote to Wellington, "If His Majesty's Kingdom depended upon it, His Majesty can not hold a pen in his right hand. The hand is full of gouty inflammation and as large as two hands." This attack was accompanied with inflammation of the lungs and by a disorder in the bladder which greatly frightened the King. From now onwards his letters to Knighton are filled with such phrases as "In much pain, dear friend." He sufficiently recovered in December to make his state entry into Windsor Castle, which was then habitable, and to receive there with the greatest affability and attention the young Queen Maria II of Portugal, aged ten, who had been driven out of her kingdom. And in the summer he was able to come up to London and to give his annual juvenile ball, which was attended by Queen Maria and Princess Victoria, and also to attend the Jockey Club dinner, but he was observed to speak little and to appear in pain. A few days after this dinner he received Madame du Cayla, who had been mistress of Louis XVIII, and she was astonished with his good looks, particularly his *"belles jambes et sa perruque bien arrangée."* It was, however, clear that he was fast breaking up, as he had got into the habit of taking heavy doses of laudanum to relieve the pain in his bladder. In the autumn he began to grow blind in one eye, and he was obliged to sign all documents by means of a stamp. He starts one of his letters to Knighton "Though blind as a beetle." He could only walk with the aid of crutches and had to be carried out of his carriage when he drove up to London, and he had a solid gate, instead of a railed one, placed at the garden entrance to St. James's Palace so that people should not see him being carried.

At Windsor the greater part of his time was spent in bed. He was called between six and seven in the morning, read books and all the newspapers, possibly transacted a little business, and then dozed. He would then get up about six o'clock in the evening and go down to dinner with Lady Conyngham. Apart from that meal his feeding was quite capricious, and he would call at any hour of the day for "chicken and a goblet of soda water." He slept badly at night and constantly rang his bell, demanding to know the time or to have a glass of water brought to him. Sir Walter Scott went to see him at the end of 1829 and found him sitting up in bed wearing a white cotton nightcap and a rather dirty flannel jacket. He was sipping chocolate, while Chantrey sat on one side of the bed discussing the statues for the Castle: a doctor was on the other side of the bed talking about the giraffes in the King's menagerie, and the Duke of Cumberland and a tailor also stood by the bed discussing new uniforms for the Guards. A servant came in and announced the Prime Minister; the King got out of bed, put on a gorgeous blue silk *douillette* and a black velvet cap with a gold tassel, and hobbled into the next room to receive him in the character of George IV. Greville sums up his existence by saying that "a more despicable scene cannot be exhibited than that which our Court presents"; and it must have been intolerable for those who had business to transact with him, as he was quite capable of arranging to see a Minister and then taking a heavy dose of laudanum, which made the audience impossible.

The summer of 1829 was spent at the Royal Lodge, but in December he moved into Windsor Castle, while a new dining-room was being built at the Royal Lodge. In the spring of 1830 he seemed to improve, and drove out in his pony chaise to see the alterations at the Royal Lodge. In April, when he was getting into his chaise he was attacked with difficulty of breathing and demanded cherry brandy, saying after he had drunk it, "I am very nervous but very brave." Knighton and all his doctors were summoned, and it was found that his heart was affected and it was felt unlikely that he would live much longer. Knighton thought the royal heart "much loaded with fat and that His Majesty's death will be sudden." He was extremely irritable with Knighton who thought that his health was governed by drink. The doctors however comforted themselves with the reflection that "we have a Herculean constitution to deal with." Bulletins were issued at the end of April, and informed opinion drew the conclusion that "it must end in water." It did. By the middle of May the Duchess of Gloucester said that he had become enormous, "like a feather bed." It was decided that he must be tapped, and the soles of his feet were punctured to draw off the water, an operation from which he suffered the greatest discomfort and pain.

However, he immediately began to improve, and he himself began to think that he might recover, and spoke of moving to the Royal Lodge in August and then going down to Brighton. He even discussed the possibility of a journey to Aix-la-Chapelle, and was able to take a little exercise in the gallery in a wheeled chair. But at the end of May he became worse again, discussed his funeral procession to St. George's, and said to Peel, "Ah the poor Cottage, I shall never see it again." It was forcibly brought home to him that he was dying. Sir William Knighton, uninvited, placed a large quarto Bible by his bedside, and sent for the Bishop of Chichester, with whom the King had two satisfactory conversations. The Bishop knelt down by the King, and said the prayer for his recovery which was to be read in all churches; at the end of it, the King said, "Amen, Amen, Amen," and added, "It is in very good taste." As late as June 9th he sat up laughing and joking with Knighton with all his old brilliance, but for the last week of his life he hardly spoke. His heart prevented him from lying down, so that he slept in an easy chair, his head in his hands, which rested on a table. There seemed no reason to suppose that death was imminent, but in the early morning of June 26th he burst a blood vessel in his stomach and died, clasping his physician's hand, saying, "My boy, this is death."

As the news that the King was dead sped through the Castle, it reached the person whom it principally affected. For weeks, ever since the King had first been ill, Lady Conyngham had been torn between anxiety on his account and determination to acquire a variety of valuable mementos of her august lover. As was said at the time—

First she packed and then she prayed
And then she packed again.

It would doubtless be an affectation to say that she was broken-hearted, but she can scarcely have helped genuinely mourning one round whose life her own had revolved for a decade. Her mind must have travelled back beyond the immediate crotchets of illness and old age to the brilliant days at the beginning of the reign when she and the King were at Brighton, and he had murmured those gratifying words, "Everything to show that you are mistress here"; or to that splendid week when she had entertained the King at Slane. With these memories she was to linger on to the very heart of the Victorian age, dying in 1861, at her house Bifrons, between Tunbridge Wells and Canterbury, an imposing, pious, exemplary widow of ninety-one, but possibly eyed slightly askance by her fellow-dowagers in those eminently respectable towns as they thought, in the depths of their mahogany cosiness, of the Royal Lodge and the Pavilion.

Nor can the news have been received without emotion when it reached Temple Newsam, where Lady Hertford was spending the last years of her life in widowed retirement. As she passed through the small sitting-room on the ground floor, decorated entirely in the Chinese style, the walls hung with hand-painted Chinese paper given to her by the late King, she must have been reminded of all the splendours of the Regency, of great, fashionable parties in Manchester Square, with the Prince as the centre of attraction, of long quiet days at Ragley or at Sudbourne, with the Prince discussing pictures with Lord Yarmouth.

When the news reached London and the great city prepared to lower its blinds and its flags, and its citizens began to look out their black, there was at least one house where grief was genuine and appropriate. Mrs. Fitzherbert, whose miniature was still hanging round the dead King's neck, had come up from Brighton to her house in Tilney Street to be within reach of Windsor in case he should send for her. She had written an affectionate letter to him, but it reached him when he was far too ill for so agitating an interview and far too weak to struggle against Sir William Knighton's opposition to it. Although Mrs. Fitzherbert's mind, after the King's death, was much occupied with anxiety about her annuity and the problem of whether she should put her servants into black, she must often have thought of her long reign as Queen of Brighton, of those days when she and the Prince were ridiculously poor but as "happy as crickets," and of nearly half a century earlier when the Prince, in hopeless love, was prostrate before her.

Among his surviving brothers and sisters who, with the exception of the Duke of Sussex, had looked up to him and loved him since he was a handsome, self-willed youth at Buckingham House, his loss was acutely felt, though it may be questioned whether they would all have subscribed to the sentiments of their sister, the Princess Elizabeth, who, when she heard of his death, wrote, "I humbly blessed God that he was, dear Angel! at peace, and prepared to appear before his Maker, through that Saviour who pleaded for him at the throne of Grace; and in heaven will all his noble and generous deeds be registered; and who ever did more?"

To the Whigs, who had long regarded him as an obstacle to reforms, his death was the signal for rejoicing and for raking up all the old gibes and scandals. W. M. Praed wrote:

> *The ladies say who laid him out,*
> *And earned thereby the usual pensions,*
> *They never wreathed a shroud about*
> *A corpse of more genteel dimensions.*

The Times, although it appeared in the most decorous of black edges, called him "that Leviathan of that *haut ton*" and spat out from its leading article the questions, "What eye has wept for him? What heart has heaved one throb of unmercenary sorrow?" It also published an article with all the details of the way in which Edward III's mistress, Alice Perrers, had robbed him on his deathbed, and added a footnote, "Such was the conduct of a royal concubine in *those* ages. The above extracts are purely historical: the reader will make his comments."

Yet, in spite of these efforts to whip up popular feeling against the dead King, it was clear that by the majority of his subjects he was forgotten. Lord Broughton, who was in London on the morning that the news became known, wrote, "I saw nothing like grief or joy—only a bustle in the streets."

LIST OF AUTHORITIES

GENERALLY

George IV. Percy Fitzgerald. 1881.
Dictionary of National Biography.
Cambridge Modern History.
The Political History of England.
The Times.
The Complete Peerage. Edited by Vicary Gibbs and others. 1910 *et seq.*
Reports of the Historical Manuscripts Commission.
The Annual Register.
Hansard's Parliamentary Debates.
Buckingham Palace. H. Clifford Smith. 1931.
Memoirs of the Court of England 1811–1820. The Duke of Buckingham and Chandos. 1856.
Memoirs of the Court of George IV. The Duke of Buckingham and Chandos. 1859.
The Croker Papers. Edited by L. J. Jennings. 1884.
The Creevey Papers. Edited by Sir H. Maxwell. 1904.
Life and Times of Creevey. Edited by John Gore. 1933.
The Greville Memoirs. Edited by Henry Reeve. 1874.
Moore's Memoirs. Edited by Lord John Russell. 1853–1856.
Lord Byron's Poems.
The Four Georges. Thackeray.
The Regent and his Daughter. Dormer Creston. 1932.
George IV. Shane Leslie. 1926.
The First Gentleman. Miss Grace Thompson. 1931.
The First Gentleman of Europe. Lewis Melville. 1906.
Historical Account of George IV. 1830.
Memoirs of George IV. Huish. 1831.
Mrs. Fitzherbert and George IV. W. H. Wilkins. 1905.
Queen Caroline. Sir Edward Parry. 1930.
George IV. H. E. Lloyd. 1830.
Personal History of George IV. Croly. 1841.

BOOK I

Memoirs of H.R.H. the Prince of Wales. 3 vols. 1808.
Memoirs of Mary Robinson. Edited by J. F. Molloy. 1894.
The Letters of George III. Edited by Sir John Fortescue. 1927 *et seq.*
The Devonshire House Circle. Hugh Stokes. 1917.
Mrs. Papendiek's Journal. Edited by Mrs. Broughton. 1887.
Life and Letters of Lady Sarah Lennox. Edited by the Countess of Ilchester. 1901.
Old and New London. Thornbury. 1873–1878.
Abbeys and Castles of England. John Timbs. 1870.
Fox. Hammond. 1903.

Wraxall's Memoirs. 1884.

The Temple Bar Magazine. Vol. 56, p. 513.

History of the Westminster Election, Lovers of Truth and Justice. 1784.

Memorials and Correspondence of Charles James Fox. Edited by Lord John Russell. 1853.

Memoirs of the Whig Party. Lord Holland. 1852–1854.

The Jerningham Letters. 1896.

Royal Residence. Pyne. 1819.

Letters of George III and George IV in the Public Record Office.

Diaries and Correspondence of the Earl of Malmesbury. 1844.

Letters of Horace Walpole. Edited by Toynbee. 1903.

Life of Pitt. Stanhope. 1861.

Sheridan. Walter Sichel. 1909.

Life and Letters of Sir Gilbert Elliot. 1874.

"The Tour of York." A Circumstantial Account. 1789.

The Harcourt Papers. Privately printed. 1880–1905.

Memoirs of the House of Orleans. W. Cooke Taylor. 1849.

The Humours of Brighthelmston. J. West. 1788.

Genius Genuine. Samuel Chifney. 1804.

British Turf. Rice. 1879.

Architecture of Robert and James Adam. A. T. Bolton. 1922.

Rodney Stone. Conan Doyle.

Illustrations to the Brighton Pavilion. E. W. Brayley. 1838.

Anthem for the Marriage of the Prince of Wales. Manuscript at the British Museum.

Chatham Papers at the Public Record Office.

Memoirs of the Comtesse de Boigne. 1907.

Beau Brummell. Captain Jesse. 1844.

Correspondence of Lord Granville Leveson-Gower. Edited by Lady Granville. 1916.

The Brighton Pavilion and its Royal Associations. J. G. Bishop. 1876.

Coast of Sussex. J. D. Parry. 1833.

Plans of Carlton House at the British Museum.

Political Memorandum of the 5th Duke of Leeds. Edited by O. Browning. 1884.

Letters of Mary Hamilton. E. G. and F. Anson. 1925.

Diaries of a Duchess. James Greig. 1926.

Madame d'Arblay's Diary. Edited by Austin Dobson. 1904–1906.

BOOK II

Spencer Perceval. Sir Spencer Walpole. 1874.

The Bath Archives. Lady Jackson. 1873.

Life of Robert Coates. J. R. and H. H. Robinson. 1891.

Reminiscences. Captain Gronow. 1889.

The Paget Brothers. Lord Hylton. 1918.

Diary and Correspondence of Lord Colchester. 1861.

Diaries and Correspondence of George Rose. 1860.

Life of B. R. Haydon. T. Taylor. 1853.

Memoirs of the Whig Party. Lord Holland. 1852–1854.

LIST OF AUTHORITIES

The Taylor Papers. Arranged by Ernest Taylor. 1913.
Correspondence of Lord Granville Leveson-Gower. Edited by Lady Granville. 1916.
Autobiography. Miss Cornelia Knight. 1861.
Diary Illustrative of the Times of George IV. Lady Charlotte Bury. 1908.
The Return of Louis XVIII. G. Stenger. 1909.
Beauties of England and Wales. J. N. Brewer. 1818.
The Regent and the King. Peter Pindar. 1814.
William of Germany. Archibald Forbes. 1888.
Account of the Visit of His Royal Highness the Prince Regent to the University of Oxford. 1815.
Letters of the 1st Earl of Malmesbury. Edited by the third Earl. 1870.
Life of Sir Samuel Romilly. 1840.
Scenes of Russian Court Life. Edited by the Grand Duke Nicholas. 1917.
Repository of Arts. Ackermann. 1814.
Lamb's Poems.
Diary of Crabb Robinson. 1869.
The History of The Times, the Thunderer in the Making. 1935.
Memoirs of R. P. Ward. Edited by the Hon. E. Phipps. 1850.
Letters of Sir Walter Scott. Edited by H. J. C. Grierson. 1932 *et seq.*
Life and Administration of Lord Liverpool. C. D. Yonge. 1868.
Memoirs of Queen Caroline. J. Nightingale. 1820.
Diaries of a Lady of Quality. Edited by A. Hayward. 1864.
Harcourt Papers. Privately printed. 1880–1905.
Illustrations of the Brighton Pavilion. Brayley. 1838.
Brighton As It Is. 1828.
Extracts of Miss Berry's Journals and Correspondence. 1865.
Life of William Wilberforce by His Sons. 1838.
Sheridan. Thomas Moore. 2nd Edition. 1825.
Life of Walter Scott. Lockhart. 1837.
Memoir of Jane Austen. J. E. Austen Leigh. 1870.
History of Windsor Armoury. Sir Guy Laking. 1904.
Furniture of Windsor Castle. Sir Guy Laking. 1905.
Gold and Silver Plate of Windsor Castle. E. Alfred Jones. 1911.
Royal Collection of Paintings at Windsor Castle. Sir Lionel Cust. 1905.
Wellesley MSS. at the British Museum.
Tierney. H. K. Olphin. 1934.
The Farington Diary. 1922 *et seq.*
The Royal Brood. Peter Pindar. 1813.
The Royal Pavilion. Henry D. Roberts. 1934.
Art in England (1800–1820). T. Whitley. 1928.
Memoirs of Sir Philip Francis. J. Parkes. 1867.
Memoirs and Correspondence of Francis Horner. 1853.
Memoirs of Dr. Burney. Arranged by Madame d'Arblay. 1832.
Social Hours with Celebrities. Mrs. Pitt Byrne. 1898.
Rossini. Francis Toye. 1934.
Diary of Benjamin Newton. 1933.
Wine and Food. October, 1934.

BOOK III

Royal Windsor Guide. 1831.

Letters of Princess Lieven during her Residence in London 1812–1834. L. G. Robinson. 1902.

Correspondence of Princess Lieven and Earl Grey. G. Le Strange. 1890–1891.

Sir Astley Cooper. B. B. Cooper. 1843.

Journal of Mary Frampton. Edited by H. G. Mundy. 1885.

Windsor Old and New. T. E. Harwood. 1929.

The Barnard Letters. Edited by Anthony Powell. 1928.

Memoirs of C. M. Young. J. C. Young. 1871.

Sir Robert Peel. C. S. Parker. 1891.

Despatches of the Duke of Wellington (1819–1832). Edited by his son. 1867.

Memoirs of Caroline Bauer. 1885.

Memoirs of the Comtesse de Boigne. Charles Nicoulland. 1907.

A Queen of Indiscretions. By Clerici. 1907.

Lord Liverpool. C. D. Yonge. 1868.

Lord Castlereagh's Memoirs and Correspondence. Edited by Lord Londonderry. 1848–1853.

Diary Illustrative of the times of George IV. Lady Charlotte Bury.

The Jerningham Letters. E. Castle. 1896.

Rogers and His Contemporaries. P. W. Clayden. 1889.

A Coronet laid at the Feet of Jesus. Rev. G. Scott. 1856.

Diary of Lord Colchester. 1861.

Foreign Policy of Castlereagh. Webster. 1925.

Memoirs of Sir William Knighton. 1838.

Hood's Poems.

Leigh Hunt's Poems.

History of the Coronation of George IV. R. Huish.

Life of B. R. Haydon. T. Taylor. 1853.

Roundabout Papers. W. M. Thackeray.

Ireland Fifty Years Ago. S. H. Burke. 1885.

Impartial Narration of those Momentous Events which have taken place in this Country, 1816–1823. 1823.

Life of Lord Sidmouth. Pellow. 1847.

Life of Beau Brummell. Jesse. 1844.

Gentleman's Magazine. 1821–1822.

Blackwood's Magazine. 1822.

Description of the Landing of His Gracious Majesty George IV on the Pier of Leith 15th August, 1822.

Life of Walter Scott. Lockhart. 1837.

Life of Sir David Wilkie. Allan Cunningham. 1843.

Canning's Foreign Policy. Harold Temperley. 1925.

Life of Sumner, Bishop of Winchester. G. H. Sumner. 1876.

Lady Shelley's Diary. Edited by Richard Edgecumbe. 1912.

Collections and Recollections. G. W. E. Russell. 1898.

Illustrations of Windsor Castle. Sir J. Wyattville. 1841.

Diary of Princess Lieven. Edited by Harold Temperley. 1925.

Life of Lord Eldon. Edited by H. Twiss. 1844.
Sèvres Porcelain of Buckingham Palace and Windsor Castle. Sir Guy Laking. 1907.
Journal of Thomas Raikes. 1856.
Recollections of a Long Life. Lord Broughton. 1909.
Political and Occasional Poems of W. M. Praed. Sir G. Young. 1888.
History of the Dress of the British Soldier. Laurd. 1852.
Correspondence of Joseph Jekyll. 1894.
Royal Yachts. Paymaster Commander Gavin. 1932.
Life and Memoirs of Theodore Hook. R. H. D. Barham. 1849.
George Canning and His Friends. Bagot. 1909.
The Mirror of Literature. 1830.
Diary of Philip von Neumann. Edited by B. Chancellor. 1928.
Diary of Lord Ellenborough. 1881.
Private Letter Books of Sir Walter Scott. Partington. 1930.
Life of J. C. Herries. By E. Herries. 1880.
The Letters of Queen Victoria. Edited by A. C. Benson and Viscount Esher. 1907.

INDEX

INDEX